NEWBORN & MATERNITY PHOTOGRAPHY

An Hachette UK Company
www.hachette.co.uk

First published in the UK in 2024 by ILEX,
an imprint of Octopus Publishing Group Ltd
Octopus Publishing Group
Carmelite House
50 Victoria Embankment
London, EC4Y 0DZ
www.octopusbooks.co.uk
www.octopusbooksusa.com

Distributed in the US by Hachette Book Group
1290 Avenue of the Americas, 4th & 5th Floors
New York, NY 10104

Distributed in Canada by Canadian Manda Group
664 Annette St, Toronto, Ontario, Canada M6S2C8

Design and layout copyright
© Octopus Publishing Group 2024
Text and illustrations copyright © Kristina Mack 2024

Publisher: Alison Starling
Commissioning Editor: Richard Collins
Managing Editor: Rachel Silverlight
Editorial Assistant: Stephanie Selçuk-Frank
Art Director: Ben Gardiner
Design: Leonardo Collina
Production Controllers: Lucy Carter and Nic Jones

ISBN 978-1-78157-946-6

A CIP catalogue record for this book
is available from the British Library

Printed and bound in China

10 9 8 7 6 5 4 3 2 1

Kristina Mack

NEWBORN & MATERNITY PHOTOGRAPHY

Learn the Skills & Build a Business

ilex

CONTENTS

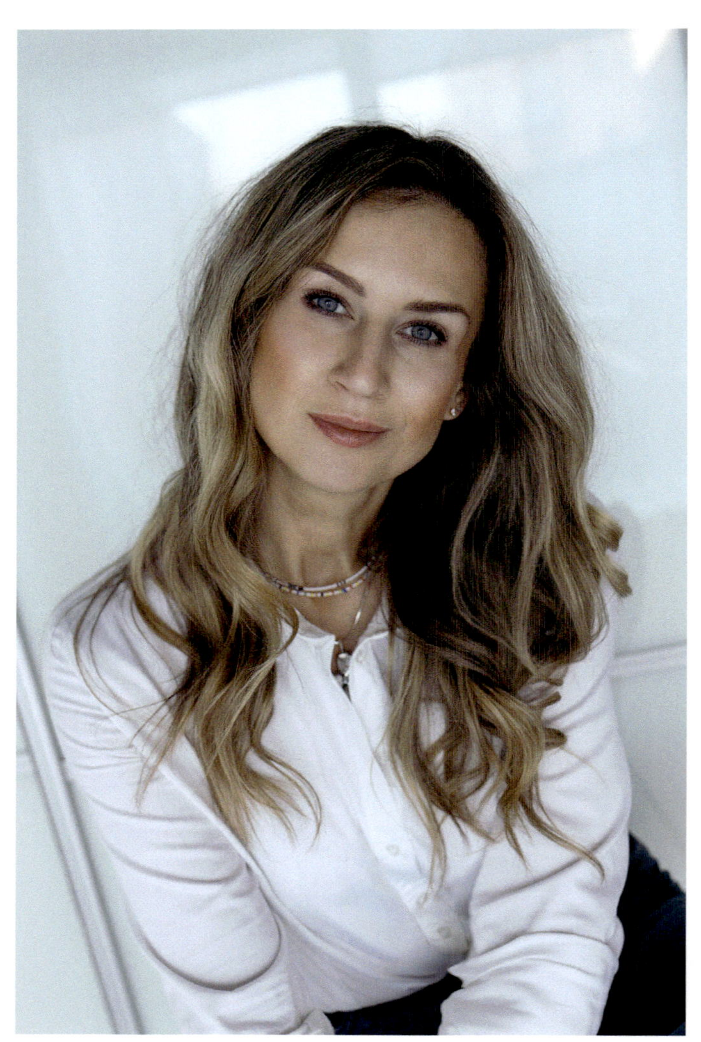

INTRODUCTION

If you had told me that I would be a baby photographer 20 years ago, I would have laughed and said that you'd lost your mind. In fact, at the very beginning of my photography career, one of my uncles asked if I'd take a few pictures of his baby. 'Are you serious?' I replied. This sounded so absurd that 20-plus years later, I still remember it.

I was young, wild and ready for adventure. Growing up in one of the Soviet countries, all I wanted to do was travel, something my parents could never do. I wanted to see the world and photograph it all. Different countries, landscapes, architecture and cultures fascinated me.

After I met my husband and fell in love, I settled in the UK. This was when, instead of being self-taught, I decided it was time to study photography. I wanted to venture into commercial and fashion photography. I was slowly heading there, but the universe had a different plan: my maternal instincts kicked in! Everywhere I looked, I saw babies, and I started to imagine how I would photograph my baby one day. Without realizing it, I began cutting out images from magazines and creating mood boards. While falling pregnant wasn't as easy as I thought it would be, I had many friends around me who were having babies and were happy for me to photograph their precious bundles of joy.

I still enjoyed commercial and fashion photography, but baby photography was slowly taking over. Seamlessly, I was becoming a newborn baby photographer without me even realizing it.

The beginning of motherhood is full of sleepless nights, uncertainty, worry and the constant urge to check if your baby is still breathing. You question every step you make and every thought that comes into your head. Although you are forever worrying and struggling, you are full of happiness and unimaginable love.

When I finally fell pregnant, a melange of anxiety and bliss took my breath away. The miraculous life growing inside me was changing my body, and I developed a lot more respect for the female body. This was the beginning of the most fantastic experience of my life. All of a sudden, motherhood and baby photography gained a new meaning: I wanted to photograph the feeling new parents feel when holding the most beautiful baby they have ever seen.

I craved to capture that vulnerability and unimaginable beauty of the changing female body, the new human being and the tender love that the baby brings.

I have been blessed with two beautiful children. Being a full-time mum with very little help was hard. It wasn't just the lack of sleep and constant running around; I also felt that I was losing myself. I was clinging to my photography as the only chance to feed my creativity and do something to feed my soul.

While documenting my kids' lives, I was still not allowing myself to look at this photographic niche as worthy of my time and attention. However, I started photographing other people's newborn babies more and more, and soon realized that it might be an excellent little side job while I look after my own babies. By April 2007, I had registered as a newborn photographer and started charging for my work.

This little adventure fit perfectly around my family life and seemed like a brilliant solution. It not only allowed me to be a full-time mum but also generated a little pocket money. I photographed at weekends when my husband was home with the kids, and edited images when the kids went to bed. Although I started to make money, I was still treating my maternity and newborn photography venture as a passion project and a temporary adventure rather than a tangible business.

It took me a few years to realize that this adventure had potential. I was earning a reasonable wage from a side hustle that I wasn't giving much thought to. My first tax bill changed my outlook, and I took maternity and newborn photography seriously for the first time. I was not only trying to perfect my work but also starting to learn about the business side of things.

I've written this book to share my journey and knowledge with you, not just the creative side but also the business side of this specialized photographic niche.

I want to teach you the craft of maternity and newborn photography and to motivate you to challenge your creative self. I want to inspire you not just to learn how to capture motherhood and the sweetest beginning of a newborn life, but also how to build and grow a profitable business that supports your family and allows you to live the life you always dreamed of.

Photography is an art, and there are many different ways to photograph the same subject. I want you to find your own style, and I want to share my love for creating timeless, simple, beautiful images.

Starting with a simple workflow for maternity sessions, we will move onto basic newborn posing and learn how to move babies from pose to pose, keeping them calm and hopefully asleep while doing so. Remember that love that I was talking about earlier, the feelings that I so love to capture? I will share how to photograph newborns with parents and siblings and create everlasting memories for those families.

I will also take you through my post-processing workflow and show you how I apply simple editing techniques in Adobe Camera Raw and Adobe Photoshop.

Business is an art in itself. Many photographers find it hard to sell their work, and photography often remains a hobby or a side hustle rather than a profitable business. I genuinely love the business aspect almost as much as I love the photography side.

I made it happen, and I hope to inspire you so you can do it too.

Always keep an open mind – whether you are a new mum and want to learn how to photograph your own baby, a new photographer or have been in business for a while – you never know where life and knowledge will take you.

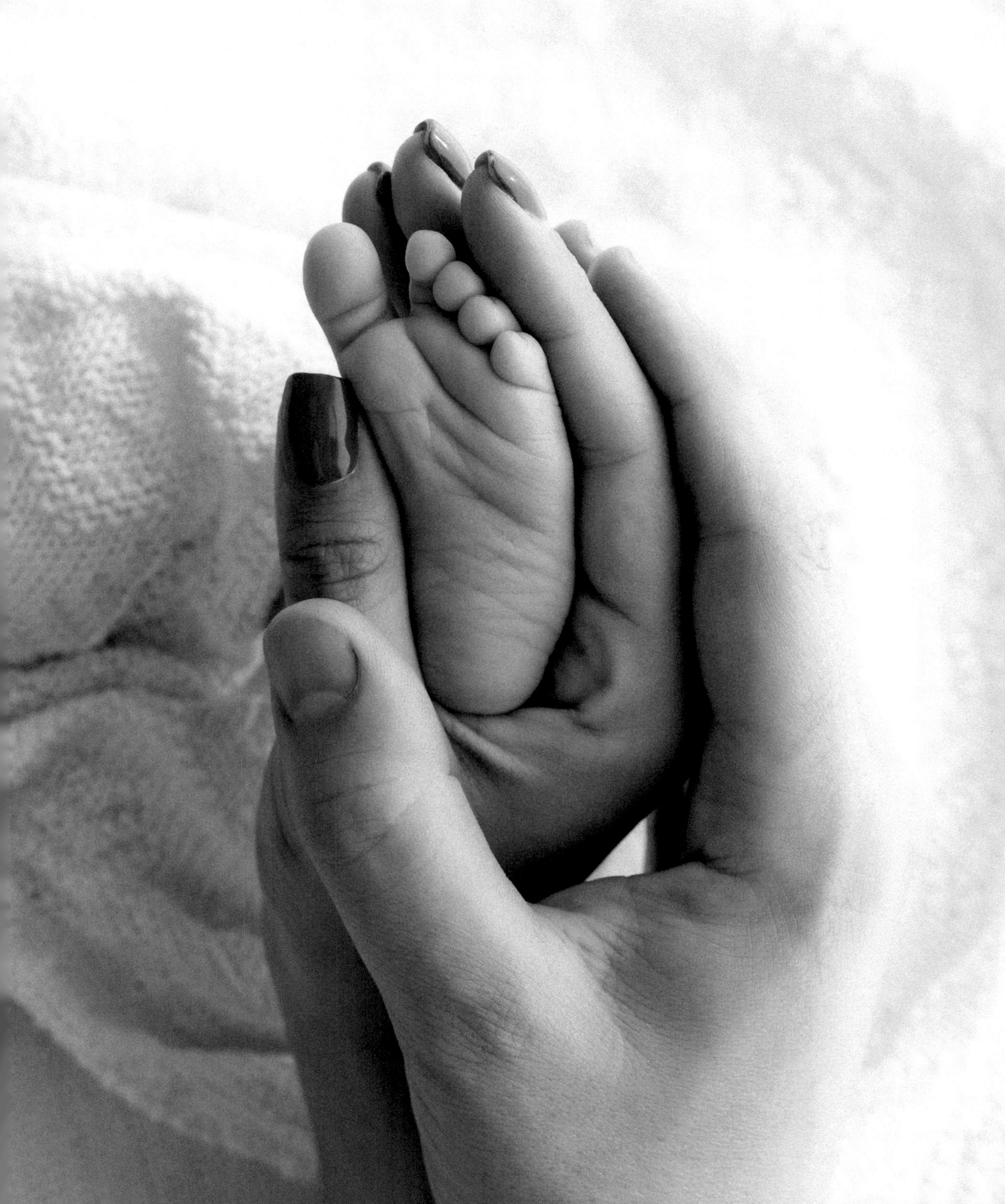

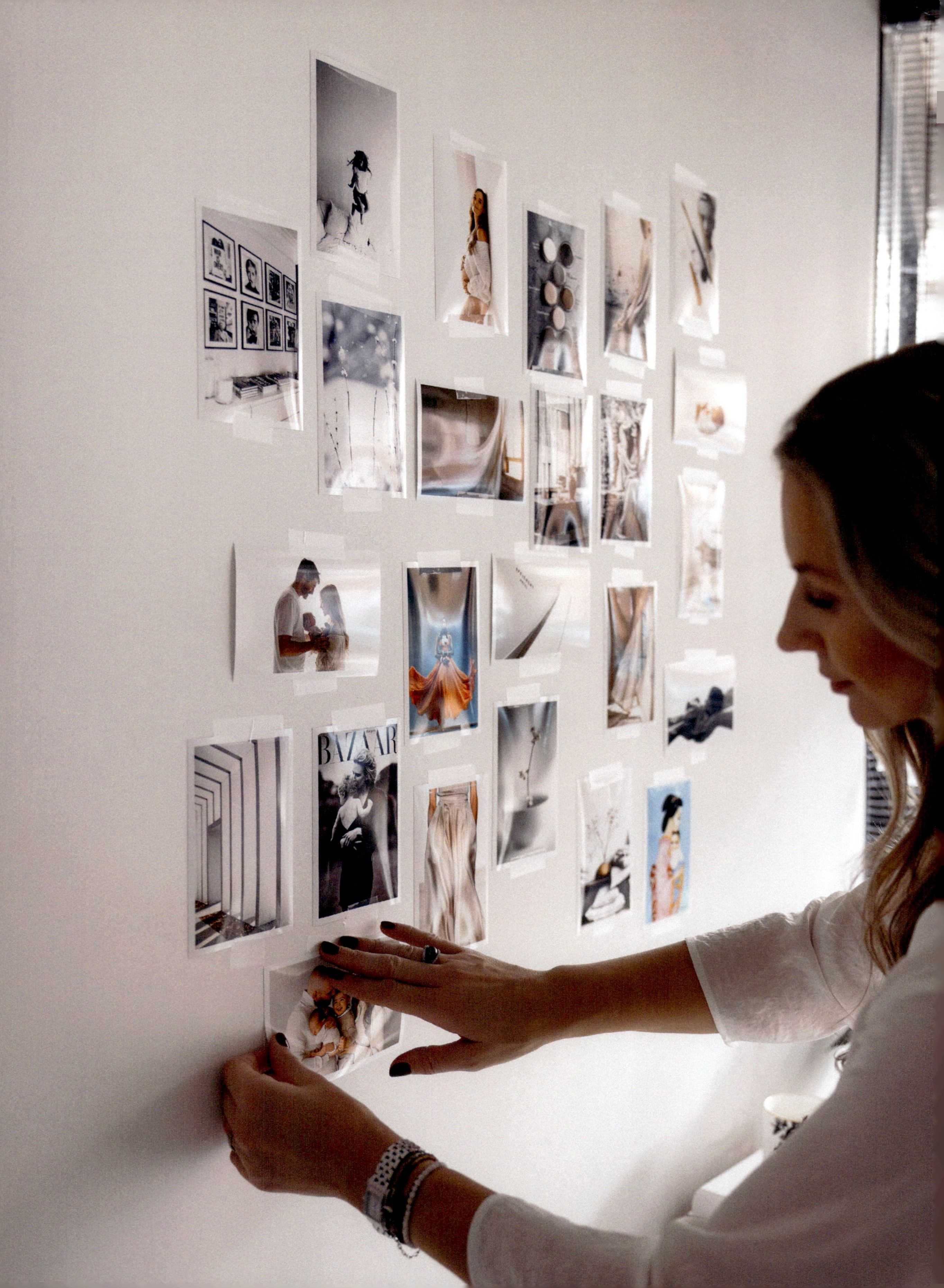

GETTING STARTED

Getting started as a maternity and newborn photographer can be overwhelming. Newcomers often don't realize just how much there is to think about, from basic things like gear, lighting, props, camera settings, correct environment and posing to more complex elements like managing clients, and most importantly, making sure your clients are happy.

In this book, I will simplify and share the lessons I've learned over more than 15 years as a professional maternity and newborn photographer.

I should stress that before you embark on working with pregnant mums and newborns, you must have a general understanding of photography and know how to use your camera. This book will not explain the exposure triangle or other technical aspects of photography, however, it will equip you with the specific building blocks needed to be a successful maternity and newborn photographer if you put in the hard work.

Whether you are just starting out or have been trying to master the craft for a couple of years, understand that the more you learn and the more you practise, the better you will become. Yes, it might be more challenging than it looks from a distance, but I am here to guide you.

CAMERAS, ACCESSORIES & SETTINGS

Whether you plan to venture into maternity and newborn photography or any other genre, you will need the right camera, lenses and settings.

Camera

I cringe every time someone says, 'Your camera takes great pictures' or 'Your images are amazing, what camera and/or lens do you use?'. I often hear photographers blaming their equipment for their inability to create beautiful work. While gear is important, it is also important to remember that it is not the camera that takes a picture, it is you.

I receive questions all the time about equipment. What camera would I recommend? What is the best lens? There is no correct answer.

I recommend a full-frame mirrorless camera. However, you can only buy what you can afford, so do not let gear stop you from being creative.

An interchangeable-lens full-frame mirrorless camera will allow you to create high-quality images. They are usually lightweight and easy to use. However, a digital single-lens reflex (DSLR) camera is excellent too. Most important is that the camera allows you to shoot in full manual mode, so you can select ISO, aperture and shutter speed.

What is the difference between a full-frame and a crop sensor? A full-frame camera is more expensive, but gives you the same image sensor size as 35mm film. A cropped-sensor camera will crop the edges of a frame. Most professional photographers use full-frame cameras, but if you are working to a tight budget, a cropped-sensor camera is absolutely fine to start with.

Currently, I work with a Canon EOS R5 and a trio of Canon lenses. Why Canon? Simply because the first DSLR camera my dad bought me was a Canon, so that's where I started my digital photography journey, and I never swapped. There is a variety of brands that make professional cameras, so research what is available and what you should invest in.

One factor to consider, especially if you plan to use natural and available light, is how noisy images are when shot at high ISOs. I often use a high ISO, and while I'm comfortable with a little bit of noise, too much noise can spoil an image.

It is natural to believe that once you have a particular lens or a specific camera body, you will become a certain type of photographer, but while it is easier to work with better equipment, never forget that you are creating the images.

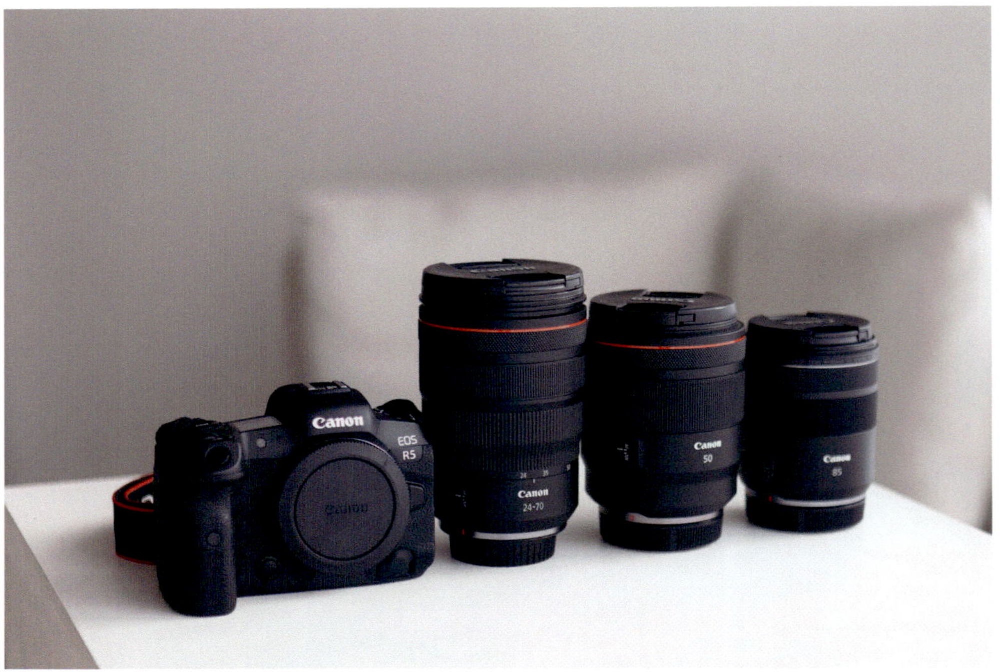

Lenses

Currently, I shoot with three lenses.

85mm f/2 Macro – I use it for all the detail shots.

50mm f/1.2 – I take 99 percent of my newborn images with it.

24–70mm f/2.8 – I use it for maternity sessions, older baby sessions, indoor and outdoor family sessions, and newborns with siblings or parents.

Similar to cameras, there are so many 'ifs' when it comes to choosing the right lens. If I could only own one, it would definitely be a 24–70mm. I also absolutely love my 50mm – it has a fixed focal length and is perfect for newborn photography, but if your working space is small and you're not able to get closer to and further away from your subject, it will limit you. Also, if you are a little shorter in terms of height and you want to photograph a newborn baby from above, you would either have to stand on a step (which I would never recommend) or settle for less-than-perfect compositions. A 50mm prime is a fantastic lens, but it's not a versatile one.

Zoom lenses vs. prime lenses

Zoom lenses have a variable focal length, which allows you to zoom in and out to determine how big or small the subject appears in the frame without having to move your feet. Prime lenses have a fixed focal length – for example, 50mm – which means you will need to physically get closer or move further away from your subject to change the composition.

The best option for maternity and newborn photography is to have both a zoom and a prime lens. A zoom is the most flexible, so if you can only afford one lens, start with a zoom – you will be able to adjust your focal length as needed without having to think about it much.

One thing I recommend paying attention to is the aperture or f-stop. A lens with a wider aperture (lower f-number on the lens) allows for more light and faster shutter speeds but will be more expensive. Most entry-level lenses have a widest aperture of f/4 or f/5.6, which is not ideal, especially for natural-light photography. You will have to compensate for this by using a higher ISO or slower shutter speed.

My settings

When talking about settings, it is essential to consider the environment and conditions. Most of the time I use natural light, therefore my settings vary a lot depending on the available light.

In general, my f-stop is kept at f/2.8 for baby images and f/3.5–5.6 for family and maternity images. I love the look of an image with a shallow depth of field, and an aperture of f/2.8 is the best one for me to keep enough of the subject in focus while also creating a soft background.

For maternity and family portraits, I prefer to have a little more of the image in focus, and I find that an aperture of f/4 is usually sufficient for getting everyone in focus. I keep my shutter speed set to at least 1/200sec to avoid camera shake. Most of the time, my ISO is set to either 640 or 400. However, I do crank it up to 1600 if need be.

For maternity, sibling and family portraits, I start with an ISO of 640 and an aperture of f/3.5, and set my shutter speed accordingly. If light levels are high, I lower my ISO to 400 and increase my f-stop and shutter speed. If light levels are low, I set my f-stop to f/2.8, my shutter speed to 1/200sec and my ISO accordingly.

For a newborn session, I start with an ISO of 640 and an aperture of f/2.8 and set my shutter speed accordingly. If conditions are bright, I lower my ISO to 400, keep my f-stop at f/2.8 and increase my shutter speed.

It might sound complicated, but this is where an understanding of how aperture, shutter speed and ISO work together is essential. To master the craft of photography, you must start with the basics.

Many factors contribute to great photography, but none are more important than light. I am sure you've heard sayings like 'photography is a language of light' and 'photography is painting with light' and so on. This is because light is the most powerful tool we have at our disposal.

Learning how to use light properly will have a huge impact on the quality of your images. You can have a perfectly posed and composed subject, but if the light is poor, the image won't look right. You might not know exactly what is wrong with it, but you will know it lacks something.

A perfectly lit and exposed portrait will not only be pleasing to the eye and full of detail, but post-processing will become much simpler once proper lighting is achieved.

It's easy to assume that the best images are taken in environments with the most light, but this couldn't be further from the truth. Too much light can create 'flat' or contrasty images, with harsh highlights and strong shadows.

I'm all about light and airy set-ups and large light sources. When photographing mothers-to-be and newborn babies, I usually use gentle, even light, which allows me to create soft shadows. However, there are times when I do use stronger, more dramatic light, for instance when I want to create silhouettes, dark backgrounds or low-key portraits.

Whether you are an on-location photographer or have your own space, you should always start with the light. Once you master this, you will be able to create whatever mood and atmosphere you desire.

TYPES OF LIGHT

1. **Natural or available light** – For indoor maternity and newborn photography, this would be a window light. Natural daylight can be unpredictable. However, it doesn't require any investment or take up space.

2. **Strobe/flash** – The term 'strobe' refers to lighting units that use a burst of light to illuminate the subject. A strobe light emits a short, powerful burst of light when triggered. You can fully control the light intensity, position and shape.

3. **Continuous light** – A cross between available light and flash. You will need some kind of device, but you can see where your shadows fall as well as the intensity of your light.

Whichever light source you choose to work with, you must understand how to control the light to produce beautiful images.

Long ago, at the beginning of my professional career, I often used a single strobe with a giant softbox. But while you can make artificial light look the same as or similar to window light, I now use natural light to photograph my newborns almost exclusively. Artificial light didn't allow me to shoot with the freedom I wanted. Plus, my first two studios were tiny, and studio flash with a giant softbox took up too much space. So, I started shooting with more and more natural light, and eventually it took over completely. My tiny studio felt so much larger, and my style of photography and compositions evolved. I've never regretted becoming a natural-light photographer.

Natural light can, however, be extremely unpredictable. There are many aspects to it, and no two windows will produce the same light. Factors such as window size, its height from the floor, its direction (north-facing, south-facing etc.), the time of day or year, your subject's distance from the window and what is immediately outside reflecting in, all influence the quality of light.

If you are an on-location photographer and want to work with natural light, you must be able to recognize and find good light. Before setting up for your shoot, you can either walk through the client's home to find an ideal light source or you can ask your client to send you some images or videos of their home in advance of the shoot. Don't forget to ask what direction the windows are facing. Most of the time, clients will think that the brightest window is the best, but remember, the ideal light is a soft light.

If you have a studio, either at home or in a commercial space, you will quickly learn to use and control the available light that you have.

There are several key considerations when evaluating possible shooting areas. The first is the size of your window. Optimally, this should be floor-to-ceiling or low to the ground. Don't worry if the window is higher – you can still use it, but setting up for a newborn will be slightly different. I will cover this in the next chapter.

The second key consideration will be the type of light. There are two main types: indirect and direct. Indirect light is any kind of light that isn't a result of direct sunlight. Such light can be produced by a window facing away from the sun or light created on a cloudy day. Direct light is harsh sunlight shining through the window. It is not very flattering and can be very hard to work with, especially when photographing newborn babies. Harsh light also enhances texture, which is not something we want when we are trying to minimize imperfections in the skin. If possible, choose a window that is east-, north- or west-facing, as this will provide you with an indirect light source that is already reasonably soft.

To create perfect light, you will need to use some kind of diffuser. These are used in the photography world to diffuse or spread light that is hitting a subject. The type and thickness of the diffuser will depend on where in the world you live, the direction your windows are facing, the time of year and the time of day. You can use sheer curtains, opaque polyester fabric, nylon diffuser panels, a white shower curtain or even a white bed sheet, depending on how soft or harsh the light pouring through your window is. Your window will become a giant softbox and will create a flattering light.

My studio window is southwest-facing, therefore I use white sheer curtains and thick white roller blinds to diffuse harsher light. I typically shoot most of my sessions in the morning. However, there are days when I photograph all day. I have beautiful soft light in my studio in the morning, which I further diffuse with a sheer curtain. If I photograph in the afternoon on a sunny day, I will use both my thick white roller blinds and sheer curtains to ensure the light remains soft enough.

The human eye needs shadows to see the depth, form and shape that bring subjects to life. If you have multiple windows or a skylight in the room where you plan to photograph, there will be too much light coming from too many different directions, the shadows will disappear, and you will have a flat light. As a result your subject will lose depth.

Most of the time, I only use one light source, with a few rare exceptions. I strive to see a bit of shadow to contour my subject, especially pregnant women's bellies and newborn babies.

If you photograph in your own space, you can use blackout blinds to cover windows you are not using. Covering windows with thick black fabric, black foam board or anything that stops light from coming through a window will help to avoid flat lighting where multiple light sources exist.

It doesn't matter where in the world you live, there will always be rainy and cloudy days. On overcast days, clouds will act as giant diffusers, producing a moodier quality of light. It's worth noting that while it is easy to diffuse harsh light, it's impossible to add natural light. In this situation, you have two options: you can either use artificial light or adjust your camera settings, depending on how dark it is. Open your lens wide and increase the ISO. Modern digital cameras are great at handling higher ISOs. However, if you use an older digital camera, you might have more noise in your images than you would like.

TIP

During the darker winter months, I often have my aperture set to f/2.5, my shutter speed set to 1/160sec and my ISO as high as 1600.

While the exposure and white balance of images taken with artificial light are easily set, determining the exposure and white balance using window light is an entirely different experience. A single cloud could pass over and your settings will need to be adjusted. You must always be aware of light levels, so pay attention to your camera's light meter. I watch the light move as a session progresses, and I adjust my camera settings accordingly. It is not unusual for me to start with one lot of settings for a newborn session (1/200sec, f/2.8, ISO 640) and end up with something quite different (1/1000sec, f/2.8, ISO 400).

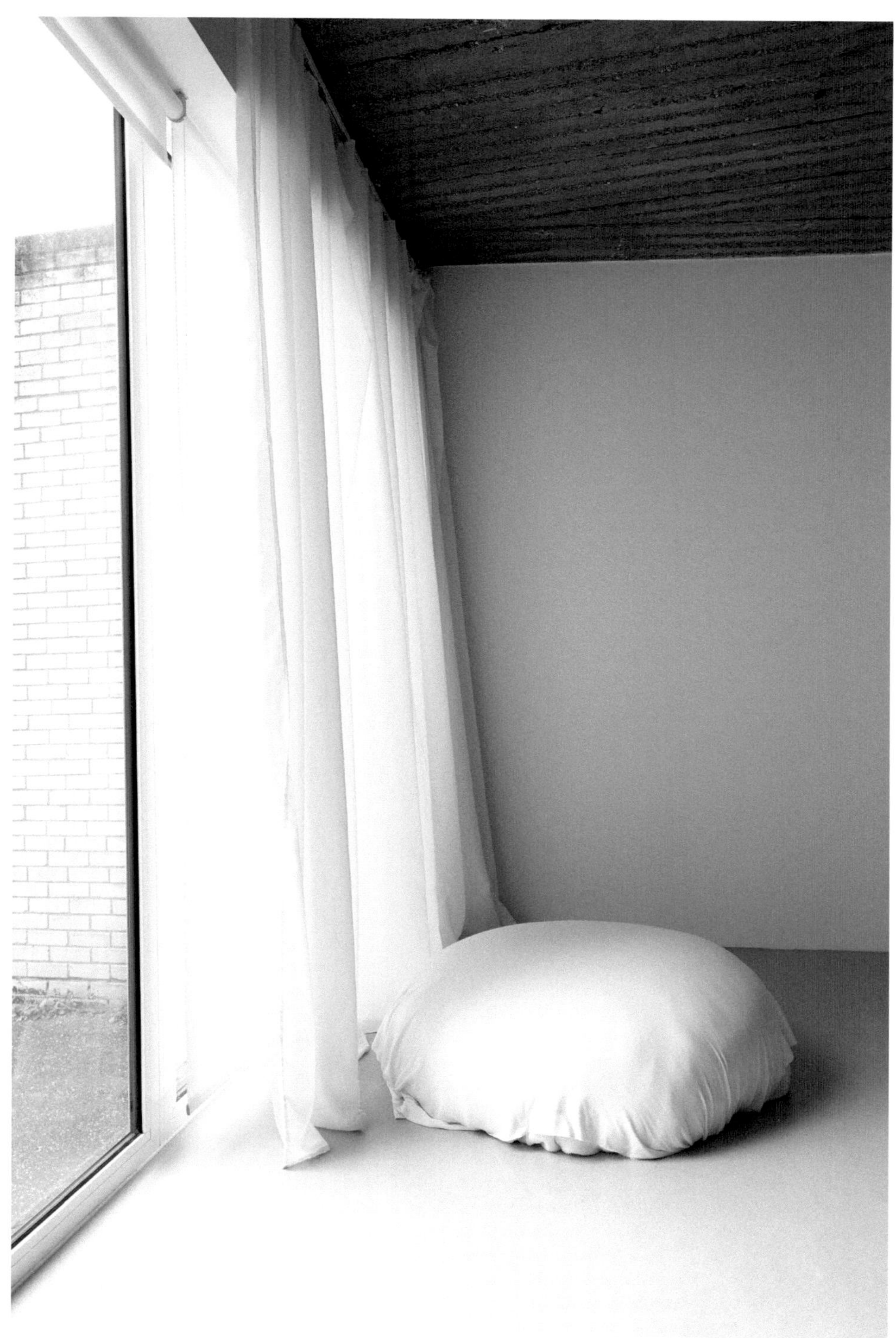

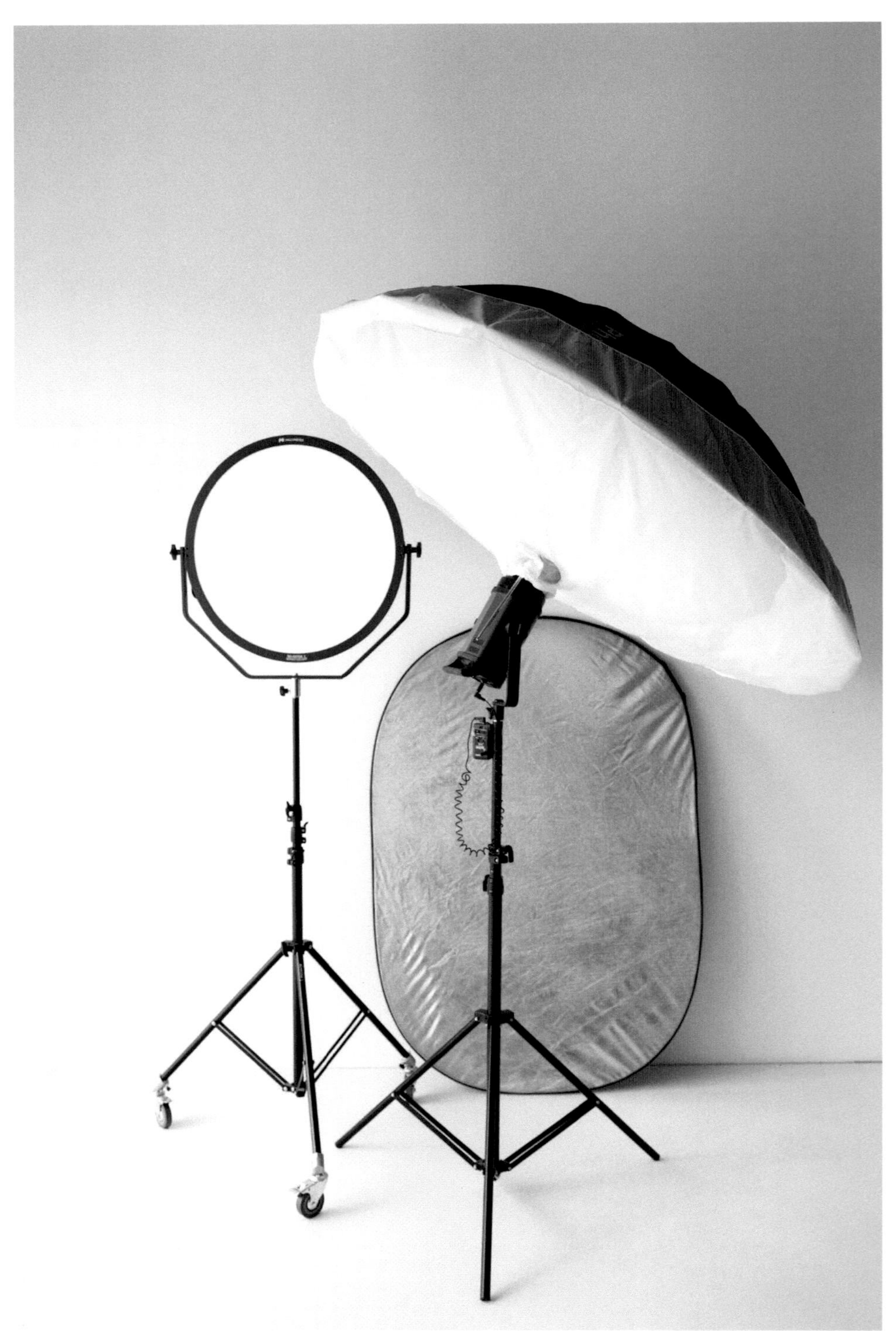

There are many reasons why you might choose to use artificial light instead of natural light: changing weather conditions, the size and height of the window, more consistent results and so less work in post-production. Consider investing in lighting equipment if you have insufficient light or prefer not having to deal with permanently changing daylight.

On-camera flash isn't suitable for newborn photography. If you are trying to create a more stylized 'fashion' look, it might work for a maternity session. However, it is not something I would ever recommend.

Flash and continuous lights are the two other options to consider when natural light is unavailable. Some photographers prefer continuous light, as it is always on, and it is easier to see the direction of the light. Others prefer strobe/flash, which fires as you click the camera.

Strobe/flash

There is a wide range of options for studio strobe/flash. For newborn babies, small family groups and simple maternity images, you will need a strobe paired with a large 170cm (5.6ft) umbrella or softbox. It doesn't matter which one you choose, as size is the most important consideration. A larger light source will provide a soft, flattering light. Most photographers use either reflective or shoot-through umbrellas.

WHAT TO PAY ATTENTION TO WHEN BUYING LIGHTS

1. **Choose a monolight.** The lamp and power supply are contained within the same unit. Another option is strobe pack systems, often used in commercial studios. The bulb and power generator are two units, and the controls are on the power pack. Monolights are the most common form of lighting used by studio portrait photographers.

2. **Choose a light with a modelling lamp.** The modelling lamp will help you see where the light will fall and set the position and angle of the flash and its modifier.

3. **Probably most important is strobe power, the range of output brightness, from maximum to minimum.** For newborn photography, you will need a lower output than for family and maternity photography. If the minimum flash output is too strong, you will overexpose your images.

Lights can be very expensive, so start with what you have or what you can afford – you can always upgrade in the future.

Continuous light

A continuous light is simply a light source that stays on constantly. It is mostly used in video production, but is also a very popular light choice, especially for newborn photography.

It comes in many shapes and sizes. You can have a traditional monolight-style continuous light, portable LED panel lights, or custom-made LED 'studio windows'.

The type you choose will depend on your style, budget and space. If you have a small space and want to achieve a natural-light effect, a wall with LED panel lights covered with a sheer curtain will create a fake window. If you mainly shoot at clients' homes, a flat LED panel light might be the most portable option.

When choosing a continuous light, colour temperature is a key consideration – daylight is the best colour temperature option. Another key consideration is power range, as with strobe lights.

Light is light

Some photographers are scared to use flash or artificial light; others find using daylight daunting. Some think it is too complicated to set a flash up and learn how to use it; others believe daylight is too unpredictable and unreliable. It doesn't matter what you use; the most important thing is how you use it. In the end, light is light, and you simply need to learn how to use it.

LIGHTING: PROS & CONS

There's no straightforward answer to which light is better, as it depends on several factors. Let's discuss the advantages and disadvantages of all three light types.

Natural/available light:

- One of the most significant advantages of available (daylight/window) light is the fact that it's natural and usually looks right visually. Badly used artificial light will cause many more problems than poorly used natural light.
- You get what you see.
- Daylight is the most readily available light.
- It's free.
- It doesn't take up space.
- It's inconsistent. You will have to keep adjusting camera settings, and it might take slightly longer to adjust the white balance in post-production.
- It's unreliable. Depending on where in the world you live, you might have really dark days and you simply won't have enough daylight.

Strobe/flash light:

- It's consistent. You set your flash and camera once, and you can replicate the same lighting set-up in every session. The same applies to post-production.
- It's not weather dependent. You have ultimate control of your light.
- It can take up a lot of space.
- You need to be careful not to trip over cords and the strobe itself, unless you use a tracking system (where the tracks are mounted to a ceiling and 'scissors' allow you to pull the lights into place).
- It can be very expensive.
- There is an ongoing debate about whether flash is suitable for newborn babies's eyes. You will find that some parents will only want their baby photographed in natural light.

Continuous light:

- It has the best of both – natural and strobe light.
- You get what you see.
- It's consistent and not weather dependent.
- Usually, it is less expensive than a strobe.
- It produces a lot more heat and noise.
- It consumes more power than flash.
- It has a shorter lifespan.

White balance, in simple terms, is the colour of the light. Different times of the day, weather conditions and various light sources all have different colour temperatures. An overcast day and a dramatic sunset are perfect examples: a room on a cloudy day will most likely have a cold, blueish shade, while the same room in the evening when the sun is going down will look warm and orangey. Our brain compensates for different colour temperatures. However, cameras aren't as clever as our brain, and they don't automatically compensate for different colour temperatures. All light has a temperature, measured in units of Kelvin (K). Candlelight produces a different colour temperature than fluorescent light.

Most cameras allow you to manually set or adjust the white balance. Typical settings include auto white balance (AWB), sun, shade, tungsten, fluorescent, flash and custom Kelvin value.

When using AWB, the camera automatically searches for a mid-tone grey hue to determine the correct white balance. Sometimes, it will guess correctly; other times, it won't.

There are many ways to set your white balance, so experiment and find what suits you best.

Some photographers leave their settings on auto and correct the colour temperature in post-production. However, I would highly recommend you customize your white balance, and you can use a grey card or other specialist device to do so.

I've experimented with various grey cards, ExpoDisc and colour temperature charts, but I was never happy with the results. After playing around with custom Kelvin settings, I now always set my white balance manually. In the mornings, the light in my studio is cold and blue, so I usually start with my Kelvin set to 6500 and adjust from there. If images still look blue, I increase the number; if they look orange, I lower it. My colour temperature settings also depend on the colour of the baby – if a baby's skin is very red, I try to find a setting where the skin and the background look good. Different camera brands will produce different colour temperature results, so experiment with your camera and test the variations.

If you are starting out and get anxious about camera settings, stick to AWB and correct white balance in post-production. Also, if you are working with natural light, you might have a bright but cloudy day, where the sun comes out and hides behind a cloud every few seconds. In a situation like this, the light will be faster than you, so make sure you expose correctly and worry about the white balance later.

ESSENTIAL EQUIPMENT

The things you will need:
- Camera
- Lenses
- Lighting (natural, strobes or continuous)
- A background or a plain wall to use as a backdrop
- Fast memory cards
- An extra battery
- Computer and software for post-production
- A sheer curtain to diffuse the light

If you are using artificial light, you will need:
- Spare bulbs for your studio lights
- A spare battery for your trigger
- Stands for your lights
- Sandbags to weigh down stands
- Light modifier (softbox or umbrella)
- A sync cord in case the trigger/receiver fails

I started doing maternity sessions outdoors and travelling to people's homes for newborn sessions. When I shot my first newborn session, I had nothing but my camera and had to improvise with whatever the client had. After every session, I learned something and slowly started investing in blankets, baskets and accessories. My first home studio was also very basic. Now, many home studios are fully equipped with everything that one can possibly need, and apart from being in a residential building, they are not very different to retail/commercial spaces.

Although I started as an on-location photographer, I soon stopped going to clients' homes and converted a spare bedroom into a home studio. This was a huge turning point in my newborn photography career. I never knew what was waiting for me at clients' homes. British homes, especially in London, are often small and dark, and I always struggled to find enough space or the right light. Also, I never felt completely comfortable because I was in someone else's space, and I didn't feel in charge. I would be stressed before every session, worrying about getting there on time, finding a space to park, carrying all my equipment inside, the time it would take to set up, remembering to pack everything up and so on.

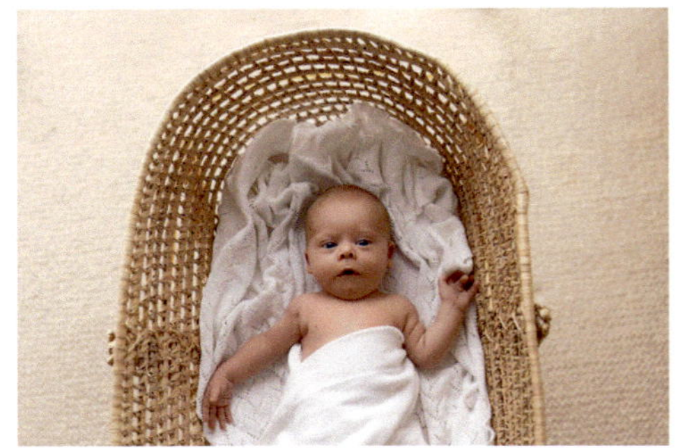

After converting a spare room into a studio, I realized how great having my own space is. I didn't have to spend time travelling, my equipment was always there, I knew my light and I even had backdrops. I had everything at my disposal. I would prepare for a shoot the night before and relax. Although the room was small, it was plenty big enough for maternity sessions and I didn't need to rely on the weather for my outdoor sessions.

As time passed, my kids and my business grew, and I've now outgrown my home studio. Although it was my home, I always tried to keep it as professional as possible – it is not easy to keep a house full of children clean and presentable. Having clients in the house started to affect everyone's lives, and I knew it was time to take the next step and move to a commercial space. I started out travelling to my clients with only my camera and now have a beautiful commercial studio in a town centre. It doesn't matter where you start – you can make it work.

Although I have a studio now, I still go to clients' homes occasionally. Never for a maternity session, but sometimes for a newborn session.

Some people love the convenience of not going anywhere, while others love leaving home and not worrying about it. If I shoot at a client's home, I always explain that I don't bring backdrops, and the shoot is slightly more of a lifestyle session than a studio session where I shoot against a white wall. Their home becomes my backdrop, although I still bring a beanbag and blankets.

I carefully plan home sessions to ensure they go smoothly, and I am not stressed trying to find the best light or a big enough space. I always ask clients to send a video or some pictures of a room they think we could use, and I ask what direction the windows face. If the light in that room isn't great, I ask them to send me pictures or a video of another room. On most occasions, I will use either a lounge or a bedroom.

I often have to move furniture around, and if I'm photographing in a bedroom, I always ask clients to ensure the bed sheets are white.

I always ask my clients to feed their baby just before a session. I get there 20–15 minutes before starting time to set up, wind the baby and have a friendly chat with my clients.

Before every home session, I ask what images my clients like most, so I know their expectations and can pack accordingly.

I often bring an assistant with me for home sessions. She helps to set up quickly and tidy up and load the car; she is there if I need someone to keep an eye on the baby, pass me something or provide support. I always leave the space as I found it and always tidy up after myself.

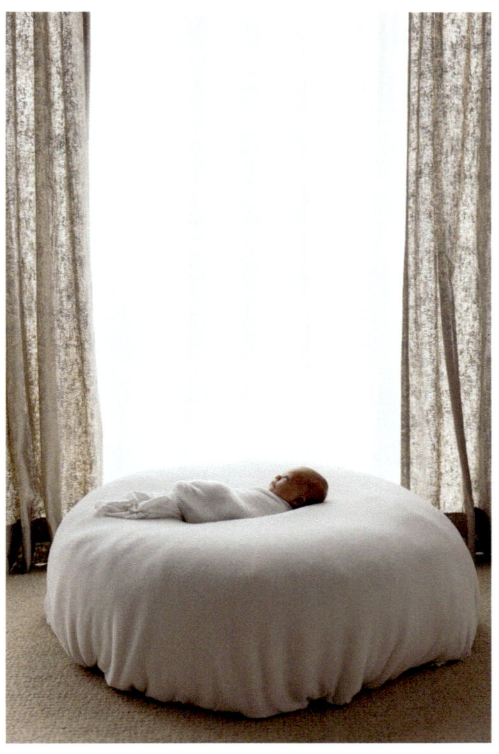

The client's living room had floor-to-ceiling windows, which was the perfect place to set up.

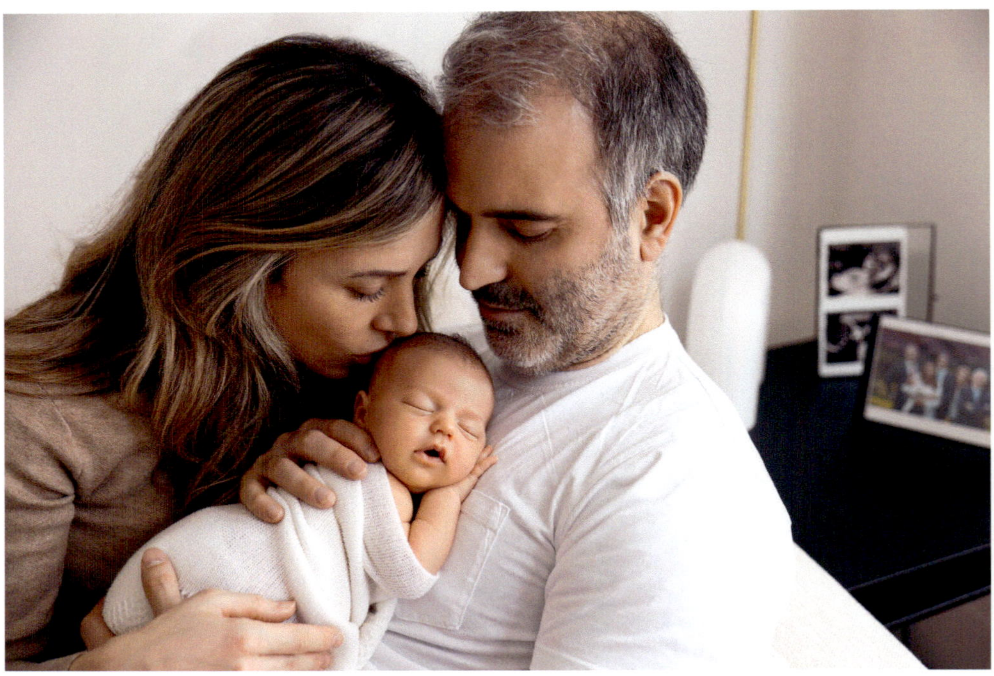

Remember, you must create a fantastic experience for your clients, whether photographing them in their homes or your studio. To make sure that a home session goes smoothly:

1. Ask for reference pictures of their home in advance and plan the space you will be shooting in well before the session.

2. Bring sheer curtains or opaque polyester fabric to defuse the light and black sheets to block the light if need be.

3. Ensure you know where to park and if it is free or paid parking.

4. Always ask clients about the images they like most so you can bring what you need.

5. Plan for accidents. Bring spare blankets and accessories in case they get soiled.

6. Plan the session timings with your clients and discuss feeding and shooting times.

7. Bring your own water and supplies so you don't need to ask for anything, including baby wipes and bin bags. Tidy up after yourself and take your rubbish with you.

8. Ask if they would prefer you to remove your shoes. And don't forget clean socks.

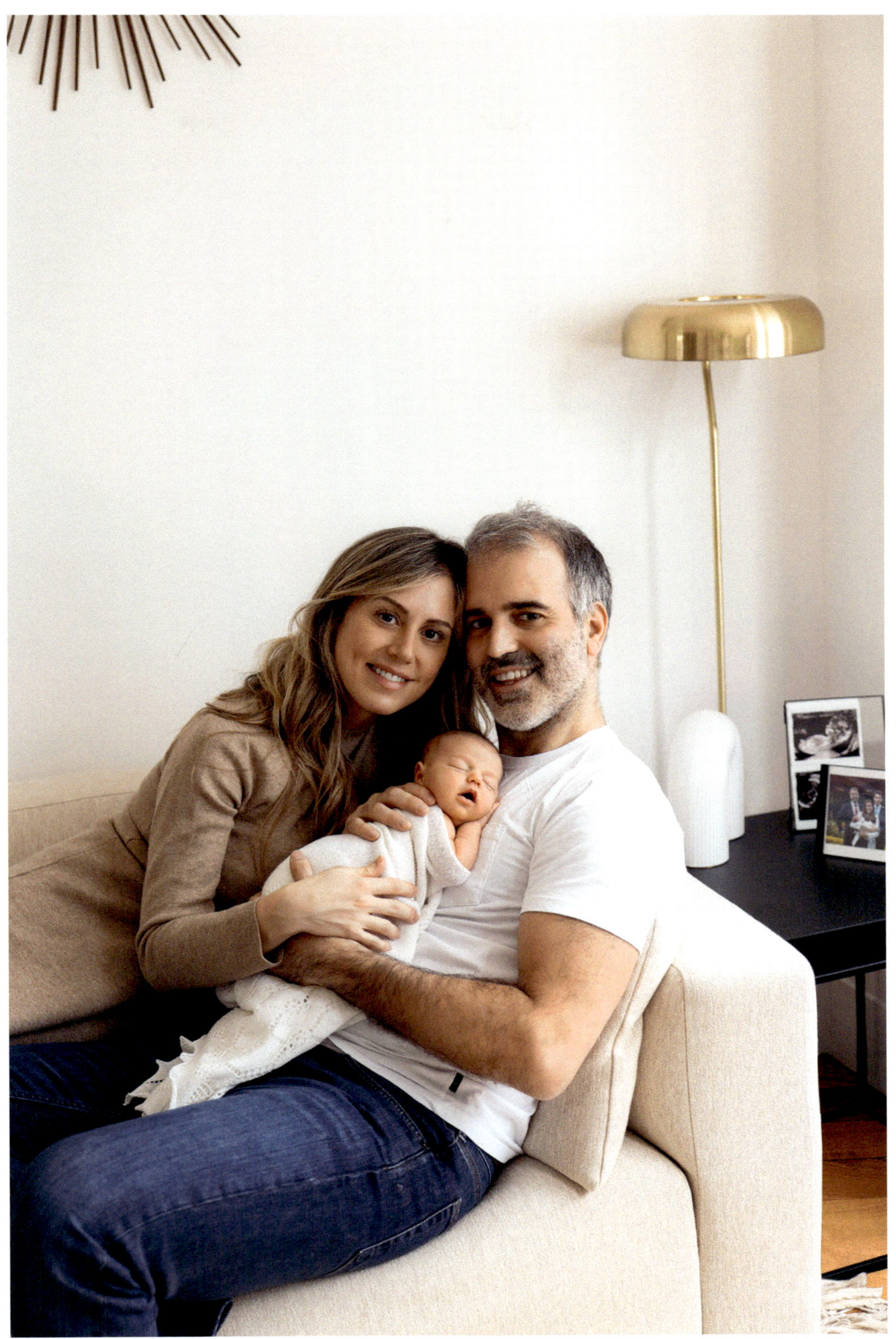

HOME STUDIO

Home studios are very popular among maternity and newborn photographers. They allow you to create a cosy 'home away from home' environment and for you to have all your equipment in one place. The light and space will be familiar, allowing for more consistent results. Being in your own space will also make you feel much more relaxed and bring more cohesiveness to your work.

Having a dedicated space in your home means you don't have to set your equipment up every time you have a session planned. If you don't have a dedicated space, make sure to keep things organized. Clients will form their own opinion of you based on how your house looks, so it is essential to keep your home studio looking immaculate and therefore professional.

The biggest challenge with working from home is making sure it is clean at all times. Don't forget the smell too! When I worked from home, no one was allowed to cook anything until all my clients had left to ensure the house smelled nice.

Another thing to consider when working from home is pets. If you have cats or dogs, you need to be aware of clients who may suffer from pet-related allergies or simply be scared of animals. Also, not everyone wants to sit on a sofa where a cat or dog sat a few moments ago.

There are a lot of challenges when it comes to working from a home studio, not least making sure your space is clean, presentable and as professional as possible. Many clients will prefer this set-up because they can get out of their own house for a while and won't have to worry about cleaning up.

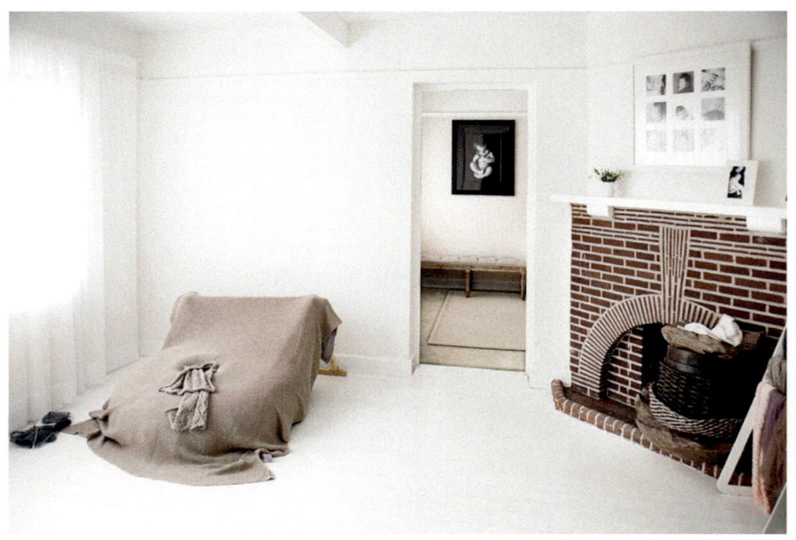

My home studio, ten years or so ago.

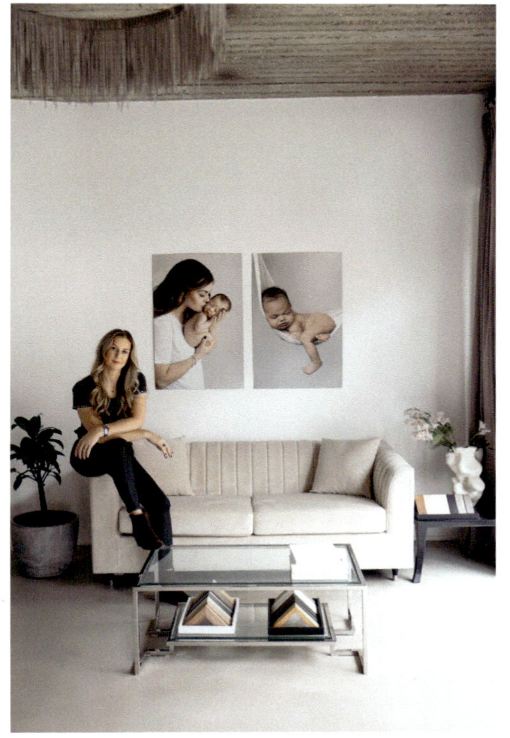

As I mentioned earlier, I currently have a beautiful commercial studio and I absolutely love it. I love going to work and coming back home. I love how I can separate my private life from work and how I don't need to worry about kids' shoes left in the middle of my hallway.

Both my clients and I love coming here; the space feels professional and is always clean and ready. My studio is designed with mothers-to-be and newborns in mind. It is big, spacious and has beautiful natural light.

The biggest downside of a commercial space is that it requires investment and often long-term commitment. It is worth considering renting a beautiful office or smaller retail space with a shorter lease.

Although most people will automatically treat you a bit differently when you have a commercial studio space, it is not worth risking everything and going into debt for it. You will know when the time comes and your business is ready.

'You will know when the time comes and your business is ready.'

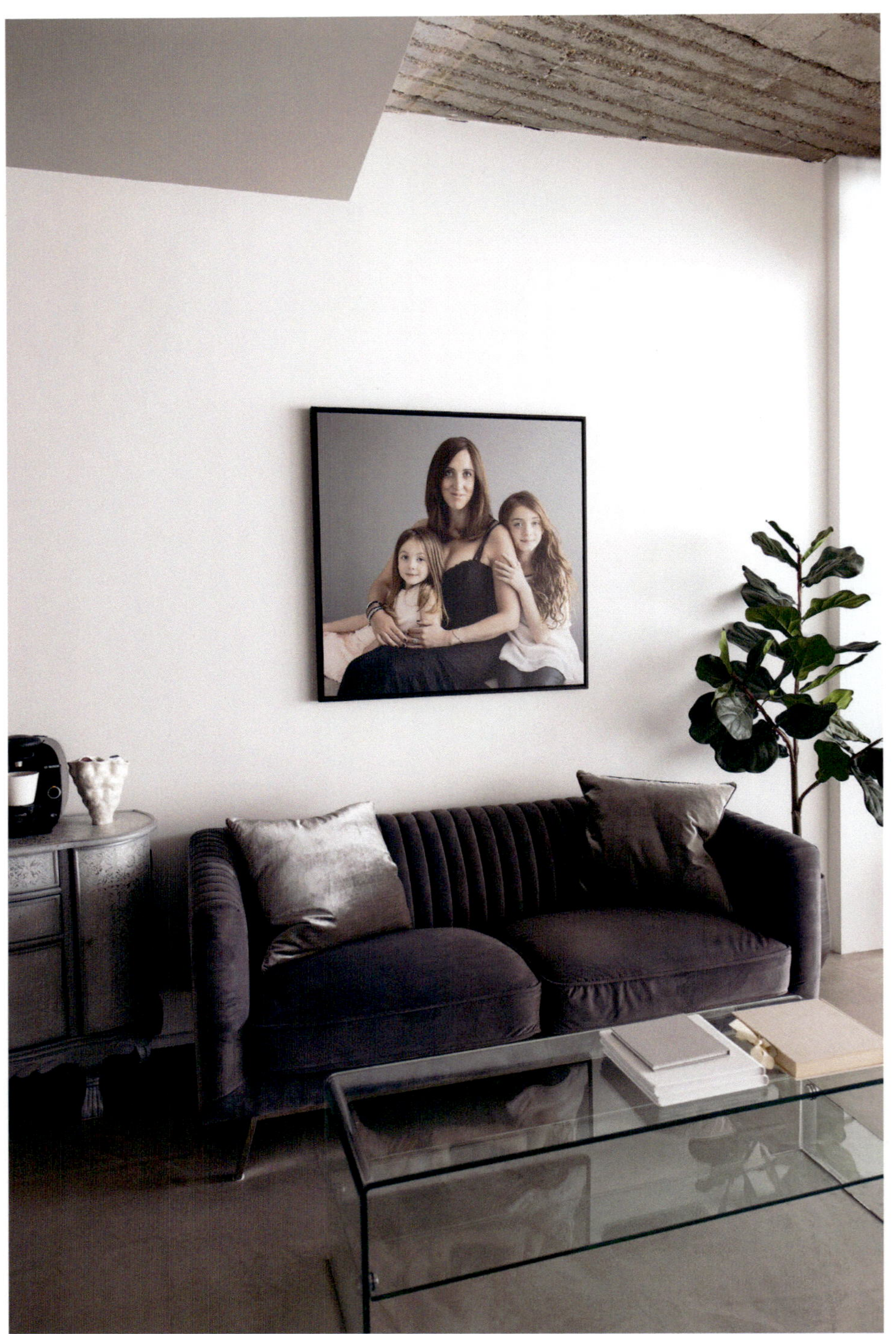

When you start, you might be overwhelmed by the amount of equipment and accessories you need. I always recommend buying something only when you know why you need it, so start simple and build up the rest over time.

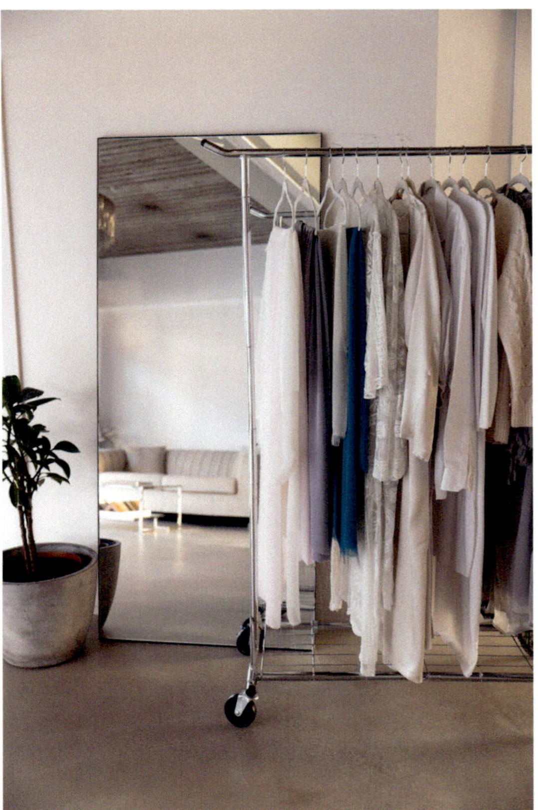

1. A sofa for your clients to relax on while you photograph their baby or for pregnant clients to sit on and rest.

2. Water, tea, coffee and snacks. It depends on you how much variety you want to offer.

3. For maternity photography, you don't need much. You are good to go as long as you have your camera and light (whether natural or artificial). However, to make your life a lot easier and to create more flattering images, I would recommend getting:
   - A fan. I use it every session to add wind to the hair or to blow fabric.
   - A few wardrobe staples. I have an oversized white shirt, a tight black turtleneck dress with long sleeves, a long tube skirt, a cosy knitted jumper and a few tops.
   - Fabric. Most of the time, I use silk chiffon, but I do also have some thicker jersey fabrics.
   - A steamer. To steam your fabrics and clients' clothes – 'ironing' clothes in post-production is very time-consuming.
   - Clips to clip clothes or fabric.

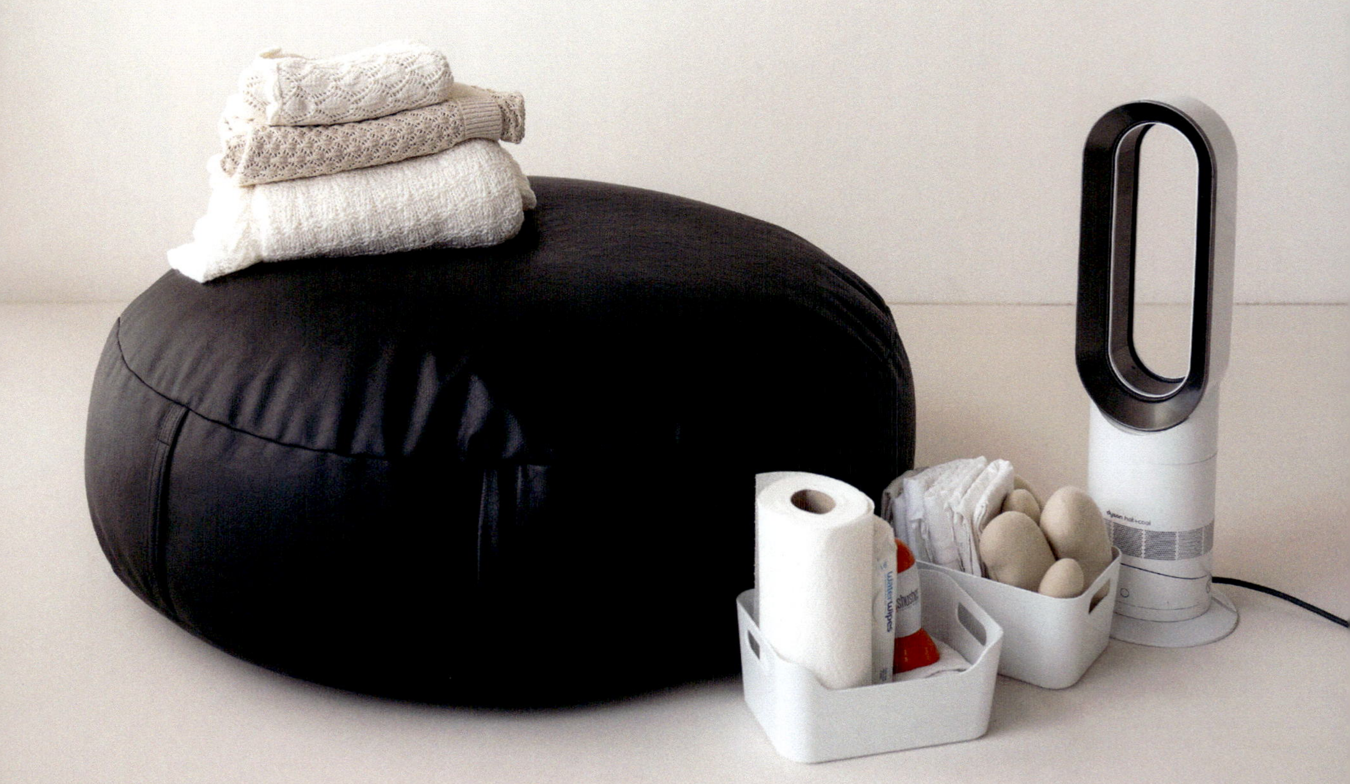

THINGS YOU WILL NEED FOR
NEWBORN PHOTOGRAPHY

For newborn photography, you will need a few more bits. Apart from all the big things like a camera and light, you will also need:

- A beanbag and possibly a beanbag stand.
- Beanbag fabrics.
- Small blankets for swaddling.
- Accessories like hats, bonnets, headbands, cute toys and outfits for a baby.
- Baskets, buckets and other props if you are planning to use them.
- Either small pieces of fabric like muslin or posing beans. You will need them to tuck under your blankets to support a baby.
- A fan heater.
- A white noise machine. I use a little device called Baby Shusher.
- Baby wipes. I only use natural water wipes. Babies' skin is sensitive, and many parents will not want you to use wipes with chemicals or added scents.
- Kitchen roll for quick absorption of bodily fluids. Accidents happen more often than you think when you work with babies.
- Hand sanitizer.
- Pacifiers. I always keep individually wrapped pacifiers in the studio. Most parents bring their own, but there have been times when they've left them at home. I always ask the parents before using it and give it to them to take it home. Never reuse them.
- Posing boxes of various heights (also called apple boxes) or steps for taking family shots with siblings.
- A step stool. I use my step for parent and baby and family photos. I want to make sure I am slightly higher than the family, which is the most flattering angle for portraits.

This list might look daunting, but it really isn't. And apart from the essentials, you don't need to get everything at once, and you can build slowly. Everyone works differently – you might want to add a few things to your list or take some out. The best way to set up your maternity and newborn photography studio is to put yourself in your clients' shoes. I always go the extra mile to ensure my clients have the best experience at my studio.

STYLE: THE ESSENTIALS

Discovering your own photography style is the start of an exciting journey to creating images that reflect your personality. I strongly believe that a unique style goes hand in hand with running a successful photography business. In this chapter, I will offer guidance and strategies to help you find and develop your unique sense of style. It will be your guide and inspiration for creating a style that genuinely reflects your individuality.

Defining your style and who you are as an artist is one of the most challenging aspects of becoming a professional photographer. With so much information and imagery around us, it isn't easy to create a style that is unique to you. Unless you stop comparing yourself to others, you will never be able to find your style. Photography is a constantly evolving creative art. Developing your unique style is a process, and it takes time. Don't rush it – let it evolve and grow as you grow.

What is style?

Style is a distinctive 'look' that reflects your personality, preferences and individuality, making the images you create uniquely yours. So many factors will influence your style, including your upbringing, culture, personal experiences, fashion sense and lifestyle. Your style will allow you to create photographs that reflect your unique perspective; it will not only set you apart but will also give you the freedom to create.

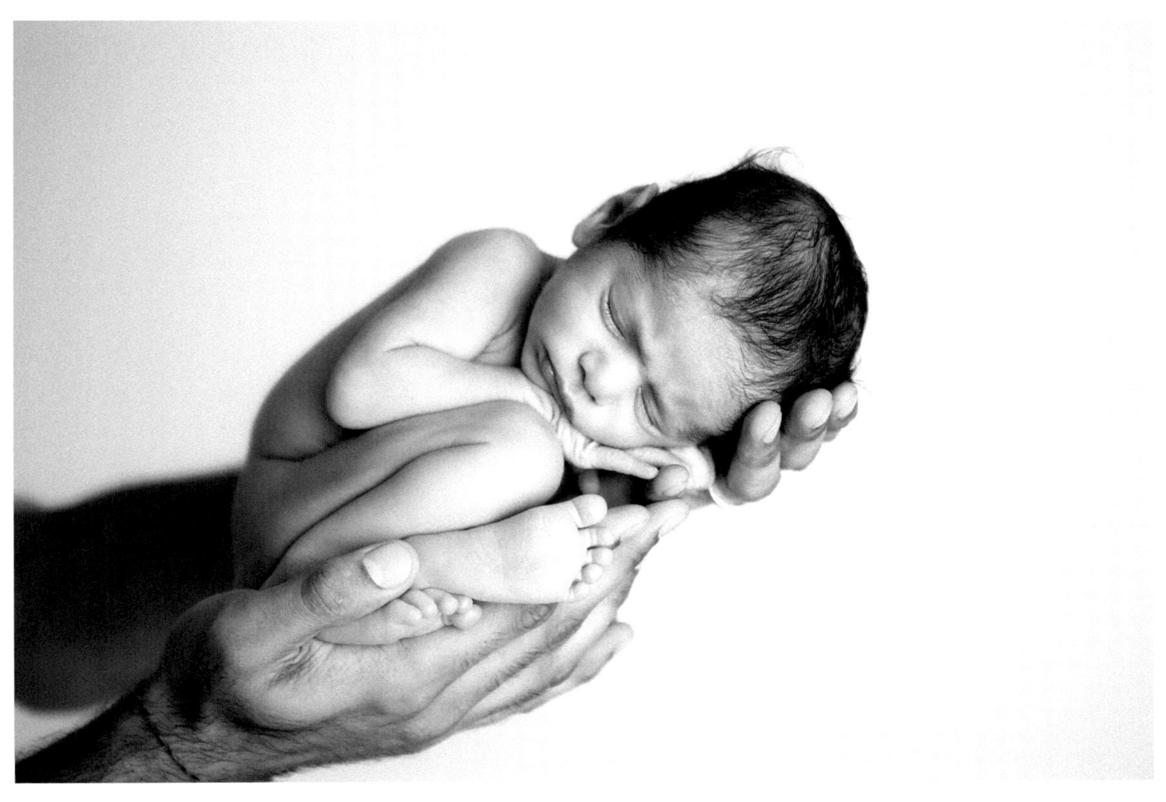

'I describe my style as simple, elegant and timeless. I aim
for my images not to age. This image is more than 11 years
old, and I still love it as much as I did when I took it.'

WHY IS IT IMPORTANT TO FIND YOUR STYLE?

There are so many reasons why it's important to develop a unique sense of maternity and newborn photography style:

1. Photography is a competitive industry, and having a unique style will help you to differentiate yourself from other maternity and newborn photographers. It can also make your work more recognizable.

2. Your photography style should be an expression of your own tastes, preferences and personality. A clear understanding of your style will allow you to create images that truly reflect your identity.

3. A well-defined style will help you instantly stand out from the crowd and become known for a particular 'look'. It increases the likelihood of attracting clients with similar tastes and values; most clients will contact you because they adore your style.

4. It is easier to create work you love by having a clear understanding of your style. You will also feel much more confident, which will make your everyday work as a maternity and newborn photographer a lot more pleasurable. Creating images that genuinely resonate with you will in turn create a vast amount of joy.

5. A lack of clear style will make your images look incoherent; your final gallery of images might appear like a bunch of mismatched and disjointed photographs. However, by staying true to your own aesthetics and style, you'll be able to create a cohesive selection of images.

Find your style

If you are at the beginning of your journey as a maternity and newborn photographer, you might find it tricky to define your visual style. Creating images that feel authentic to you can be a challenge initially. The exercises below will help you define your style. However, figuring out your style is not something that will happen overnight – it will evolve naturally.

Stop looking at other photographers working in the same field. You will never find your true style if all you do is recreate others' work. Photography is a creative art and by copying others' work, you are simply learning to imitate rather than develop your own style.

The first step in creating a visual style that reflects your personality is to identify your tastes. Start broad and finish with unique little things that speak to your personality. Your reflection in a mirror, your wardrobe and your home will give you a lot of clues. The style of clothing you're drawn to is probably the best indicator of your tastes and style. What is in your wardrobe? What types of clothes are there? What fabrics, textures, colours and patterns are you drawn to?

Once you've examined the contents of your wardrobe, look around your home. What is the decor style? What colour are the walls? Is it light and airy or dark and moody? Is it minimalistic, classic or maybe boho?

Now, put your wardrobe and home together – what is the overall mood, tone and style? Writing down a clear description of your aesthetics and preferences will give you a good idea of what truly appeals to you. This is your unique style.

My style

If you look at my home and wardrobe, the places I go to on holiday and my photography, you will find similarities. I don't have a single vivid colour in my wardrobe. Instead, it consists of neutral, muted colours, natural fabrics and a little bit of texture. Most pieces are elegant, timeless and minimal. My home is similar: modern yet classic, light and airy, with minimal decorations, but with art pieces that create focal points.

My photography style is the same: light and airy, mainly soft and neutral colours, with a few low-key black-and-white images mixed in to add a sense of mood, focus on the form and emphasize the purity of the subject as a work of art. My images are uncluttered (I use very few props), crisp and modern.

I would describe my personal style as simple, elegant and timeless.

CREATING MOOD BOARDS

An inspiration board or a mood board is a brilliant tool to help you define your style. Images, textured materials, colour palettes and anything else you can think of can be added to your mood board. There is only one rule: be true to yourself, concentrate on your vision and stick to the imagery that resonates with you. Allow yourself to use images taken by other maternity or newborn photographers but limit the number to just a few. Instead, find inspiration in the work of photographers from different genres. A mood board is so much more than a collection of pretty pictures – these carefully selected images will help you recognize, define and visualize your style.

You can create a physical or digital mood board, depending on your preferred format. It can be a folder on your computer or images arranged on a sheet of digital 'paper', you can use various websites or software for it, or you can have a notebook with images, materials and objects stuck to the pages or pinned to a board. Whether you decide on a digital or physical mood board, you must organize your inspiration together in one place, as this will highlight the style you tend to naturally gravitate towards and help you identify trends and start to find and visualize your style.

Step back and look at the images and items you have collected – they will tell you an even bigger story when grouped together. To make the most of the mood board, we need to start curating it, so select images and arrange them to see what fits together. What speaks a thousand words to you and what might not make the cut after all? Notice details such as colour, texture, style and feel.

The imagery around you, especially if you follow a lot of maternity and newborn photographers on social media platforms, will take your focus away from your personal style and make you question your work. Don't forget to refer to your mood board, as it will help you stay true to your unique style and not be influenced by other photographers working in the same niche.

By having a well-curated inspiration board, you'll also be able to create cohesiveness across your entire photography business, from styling, creating and capturing images to client communication, social media presence and website. It is the visual identity of your style, and it will help you to build and maintain a cohesive brand.

Visual stimulation feeds your eyes and brain, so I recommend always keeping your mood board visible. Everything that is visualized or written down will more likely become a reality.

Remember that making a mood board is a creative process – there's no right or wrong way to do it. It is also a good idea to update your mood board as your style develops.

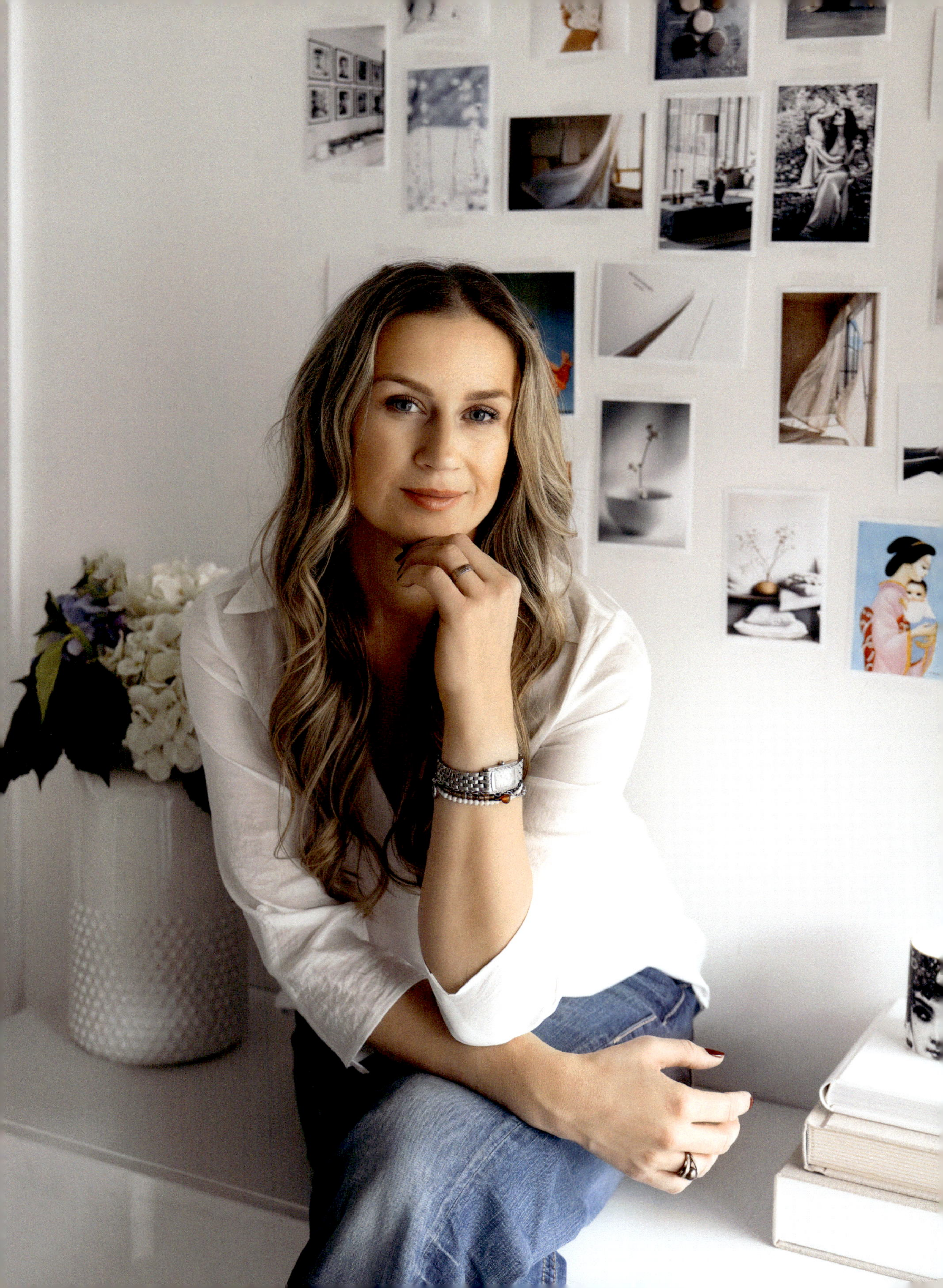

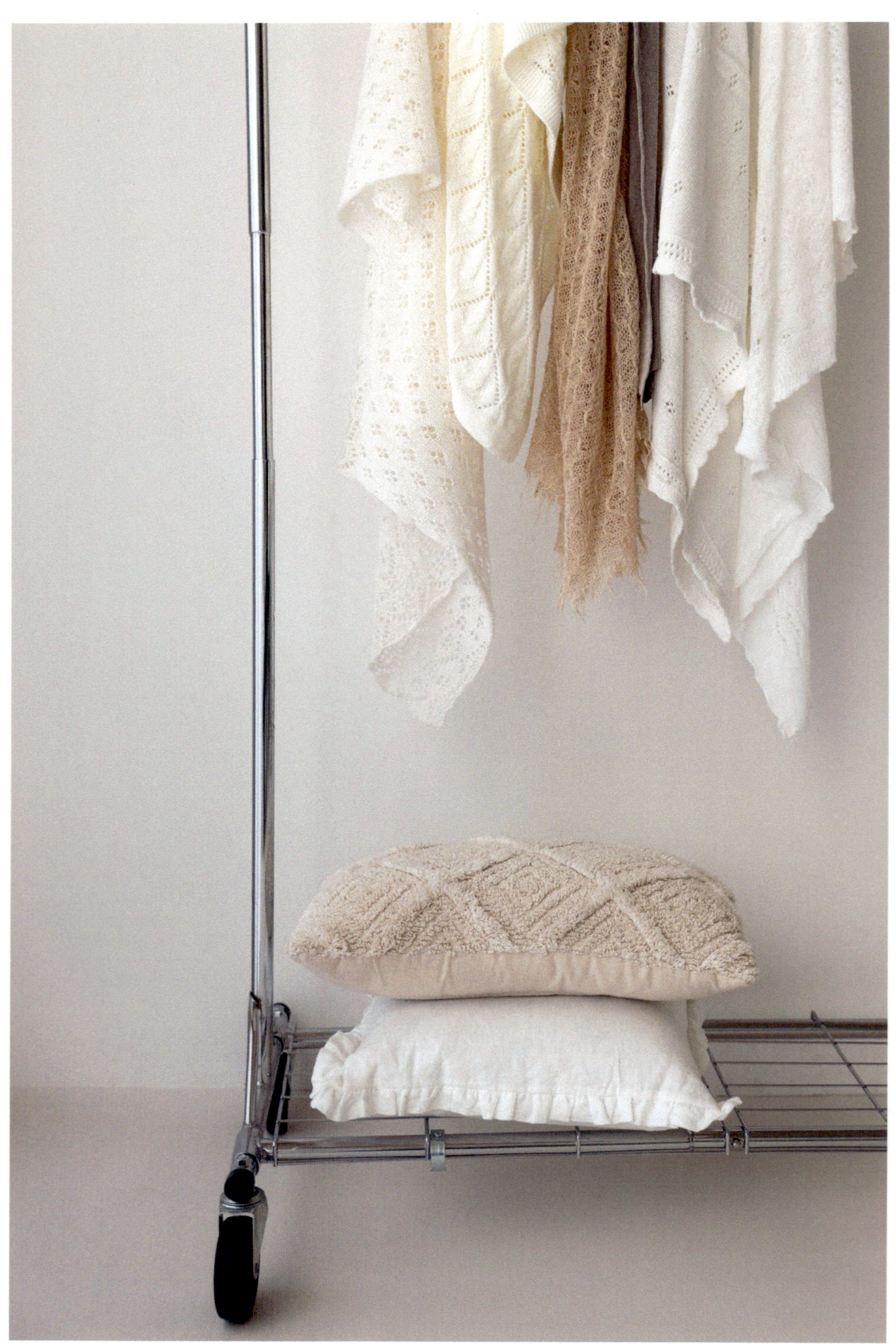

Trends/fashion

Like other visual forms of art, photography has its trends. They can be inspired by current fashion or by a popular photographer using a particular prop or editing style. By taking inspiration from fashion and current trends, you can create visually pleasing, popular, trending and perhaps desirable images at that time. However, if you decide to always keep up with the trends, not only will your images have a very short lifespan, but you will also struggle to develop your own style.

If a current trend resonates with you, then stick to it, but in my experience, this is rarely a great idea. I remember a time when a lot of newborn and maternity photographers were using pampas grass as a prop. I even came up with a saying, 'Don't be a pampas grass', meaning don't be the same as everyone else. As time passed, the pampas grass trend faded, and fewer photographers used it. If you decided to ignore trends, would you really choose what's currently popular?

I don't hate trends and I don't begrudge or resent anyone who enjoys being on trend; it's just not for me. I never worry about following what's popular. Instead, I focus on what feels right to me. A clear understanding of personal your style can be the most effective way of creating images that stand the test of time. As Coco Chanel once said, 'Fashion fades, only style remains the same'.

Stay inspired

Inspiration is essential to the creative process; you must be inspired to be able to maintain a creative flow, to produce your best work and to avoid burnout. There are many ways to spark creativity, but the most important thing is to be open to it. You will see and experience many inspiring things in your everyday life. However, sometimes, inspiration lurks in the most unexpected places. Pay attention to it; let it surprise you.

You can be inspired by the texture of a blanket, a fruit bowl or the cover of a fashion magazine. You can find inspiration in paintings, art books, films and museums. Watching your kids play in the garden or the light peeking through a window might inspire you even more. Inspiration is very personal – something that resonates with me might completely bore you – so select what speaks to your soul, learn from it and fuel your creativity with it.

I am in awe of how women's bodies change shape and grow new life inside. The smell of a newborn baby, the little noises it makes, its wispy hair, and the unimaginable love that the baby brings inspire me and make me want to capture it all.

Avoid seeking inspiration from other newborn and maternity photographers' work – there is a fine line between being inspired and copying someone else. If you recreate someone else's image, you are not just taking away the chance to exercise your creativity and find your own unique style, but you are stealing and disrespecting another person. Take the idea, be inspired and make it your own.

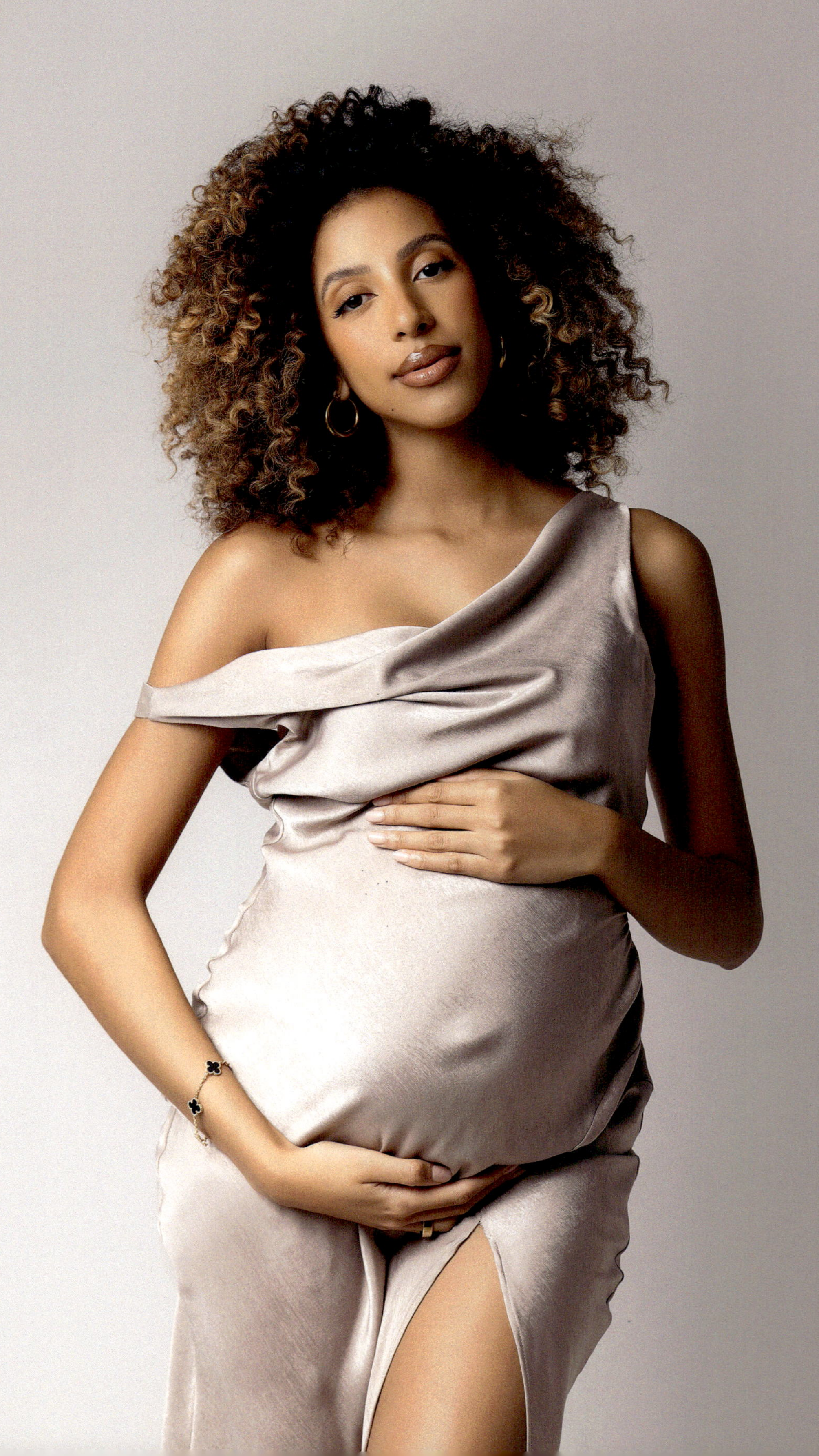

MATERNITY

Motherhood opens an entirely new chapter in a woman's life. Everyone talks about how special motherhood is, but I don't think one can understand it until that miraculous life starts growing inside you. It is a blend of so many different feelings: excitement, uncertainty, perhaps fear and anxiety, but at the same time, you burst with joy; your heart is filled with more love than one can describe with words.

The months before the baby is born are simply magical. A growing belly is proof of the miracle inside; everything starts to become real. This is the beginning of the most amazing experience of your life. The love a pregnant woman experiences is a powerful and mythical force; the ability to grow a new life inside is a magical power; the changing body is graceful and unimaginably beautiful.

All this is what I aim to capture when I photograph mothers.

THE SESSION: TIMING & PLANNING

When it comes to maternity sessions, preparation and planning is very important. For many mums, this will be the only pregnancy photo shoot they will have in their life. Pregnancy can be a very emotional time, so be very sensitive to and respectful of your subject.

There could be many reasons why a client hires you for a maternity session. I often hear stories of women miscarrying a baby and wanting to finally celebrate their pregnancy. For some clients, it will be their final pregnancy and the last chance to capture their pregnant body. The client may wish to fulfil something she wished she had done the first time around. Some might be encouraged or inspired by others, and some just want to capture the baby bump. Regardless of the reasons, they all want to feel beautiful and to have the best experience. It is our duty as photographers to capture our subjects in a flattering manner. It is not simply about a belly but the woman carrying the miracle inside.

Maternity sessions are best captured between 29 and 36 weeks. It will vary from client to client, so yet again, communication is very important. Here are three important questions to ask when scheduling a session:

- How do you carry? In other words, how big is your belly already?
- Is this your first pregnancy?
- How big would you like your belly to be in the pictures?

Pregnant women are all different. If it is the first pregnancy, most likely, the belly will start showing a little later. In this case, I often schedule a shoot around the 34th week. If it is the second or third pregnancy, your client will likely be showing a lot earlier, and you might want to schedule a session around the 29th or 30th week. Bear in mind that everyone has different tastes. Some women will prefer to have a small baby bump showing, while others might like a much bigger bump on show.

Don't leave it too close to the due date. Not only do babies sometimes like to arrive earlier, but most women feel very uncomfortable and swell towards the end of their pregnancy. You must take all of this into account when scheduling a session.

It is essential to talk to your client before the session. You don't have to do it over the phone – an email is perfect if you and/or your client prefer it this way. Likewise, if you meet your clients in person before the shoot, this is absolutely fine too.

You need to find out not only how your client feels and what she likes but also how she would like to be photographed. Although pregnant women are glowing and beautiful, and more often than not, they are proud of their pregnancy bodies, there might be some areas they would rather not highlight. Styling and clever posing can be employed to create images that will meet the client's expectations.

Don't forget the location. You might have your own space or studio, or you might plan to shoot at the client's home or a preferred outdoor location. If neither is an option, renting a hotel room might be a great solution.

Talk to your client about hair, make-up and nails. Some women are more comfortable getting it done themselves, some might not wear any make-up at all, some might like to be pampered. If a client requires it, I offer hair and make-up services at the studio. I have a few make-up artists that I work with, so I book one of them if a client requests.

People often overlook details like nails. I've had clients arrive with chipped nails, which takes time to retouch in post-processing. I always recommend clients choose neutral or timeless nail colours. Little details like this add to the final result.

Is your client coming alone or is she bringing her partner? Does she have children already? If so, will they be joining her for the shoot and how old are they? Before the shoot, you want to have a clear plan of what you are doing. A shoot where the client comes alone and a shoot where she will bring a partner or toddler will be very different. Don't forget, this might be the first time your client has hired a professional photographer. She will be unsure what to bring and what to expect, so the more questions you ask, the better prepared and confident she will be.

We all imagine things differently, and the same description or word might create completely different imagery in our heads. Therefore, I always ask how my client would like to be photographed. I ask if there is anything specific that she loves or has in mind. To help us both prepare better for the session, I always ask the client to send some inspirational images, either attached to an email or a link to a Pinterest board. This helps me understand what kind of look and style they envision and to make sure I can create images that they will be happy with.

Outdoor sessions

If I'm honest, maternity sessions on location are not my favourite. I prefer to focus on my subject, and I don't want the background to detract from the pregnant mum. However, we are all different and you might love to shoot on location. Outdoor sessions can add variety to your images and create something unique, especially if your clients have a location that has meaning to them.

Deciding the time and location of the session is essential. Sunrise or sunset are two very common times to photograph outdoor sessions. If you are photographing in the middle of the day, make sure you can find shade or a tree to defuse the light. You need to know the location you plan to photograph at.

Once I know what style and look my client wants to achieve, we can start planning the wardrobe. Is my client after some cosy, soft, intimate images or more fashion or editorial images or a bit of both? We can start planning what she needs to bring and what I have in the studio.

Clothing and styling play a huge part. When I started photographing maternity sessions, I only had a few large pieces of fabric. As I became more experienced, I slowly started building a studio wardrobe. I don't believe that one needs lots of bits – a few essentials will give you enough freedom to create stunning images. During my sessions, I usually use a combination of things that my client brings and a few bits from my studio wardrobe. However, if you want to take the pressure off the client and offer a large selection of fabrics and clothes, go for it, but know that it is not essential.

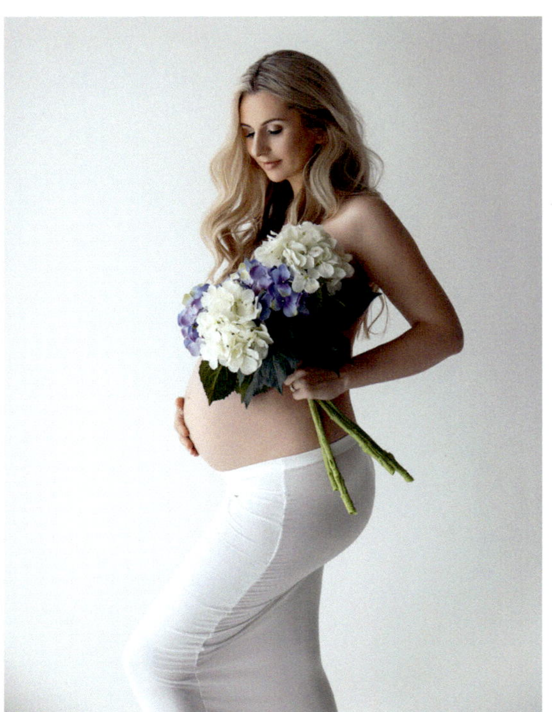

What you keep in your studio wardrobe will largely depend on your style, as discussed in the previous chapter. Be true to yourself – you don't have to buy every option possible. If you love maternity gowns, collect a few of them. If you are more of a romantic boho-style person, include a few lace gowns. There are so many options.

You can mix fashion trends when styling maternity sessions too. What are you personally inspired by and drawn to, and what fashion trends are you attracted to? Maternity photography and fashion trends are linked, so always keep an eye on the fashion industry.

Take the images your client shared with you, pick them apart and analyze them. What are they portraying? Are they edgy or soft? Are they light and airy or dark and moody? Are they intimate and full of feeling or are they powerful and feminine? Are they minimalistic or do they have tulle gowns and flower crowns? Is the light natural or artificial? All this information will help you style the shoot and capture what your client envisions.

Backdrops and props are a big part of your styling. If you are working in a home or commercial studio, you will likely have some backdrops or a plain wall that you use. For home sessions, a bedroom is often a great place to shoot maternity portraits. I like to keep my backgrounds simple and uncluttered, and I seldom use props. However, if you like, you can create flower walls and boho-style set-ups with draped curtains and wooden benches.

Items like baby booties, baby grows, ultrasound pictures, teddies and crowns are great to use as props. I recommend asking clients to bring their own, so they have a meaning and are in the pictures for sentimental reasons.

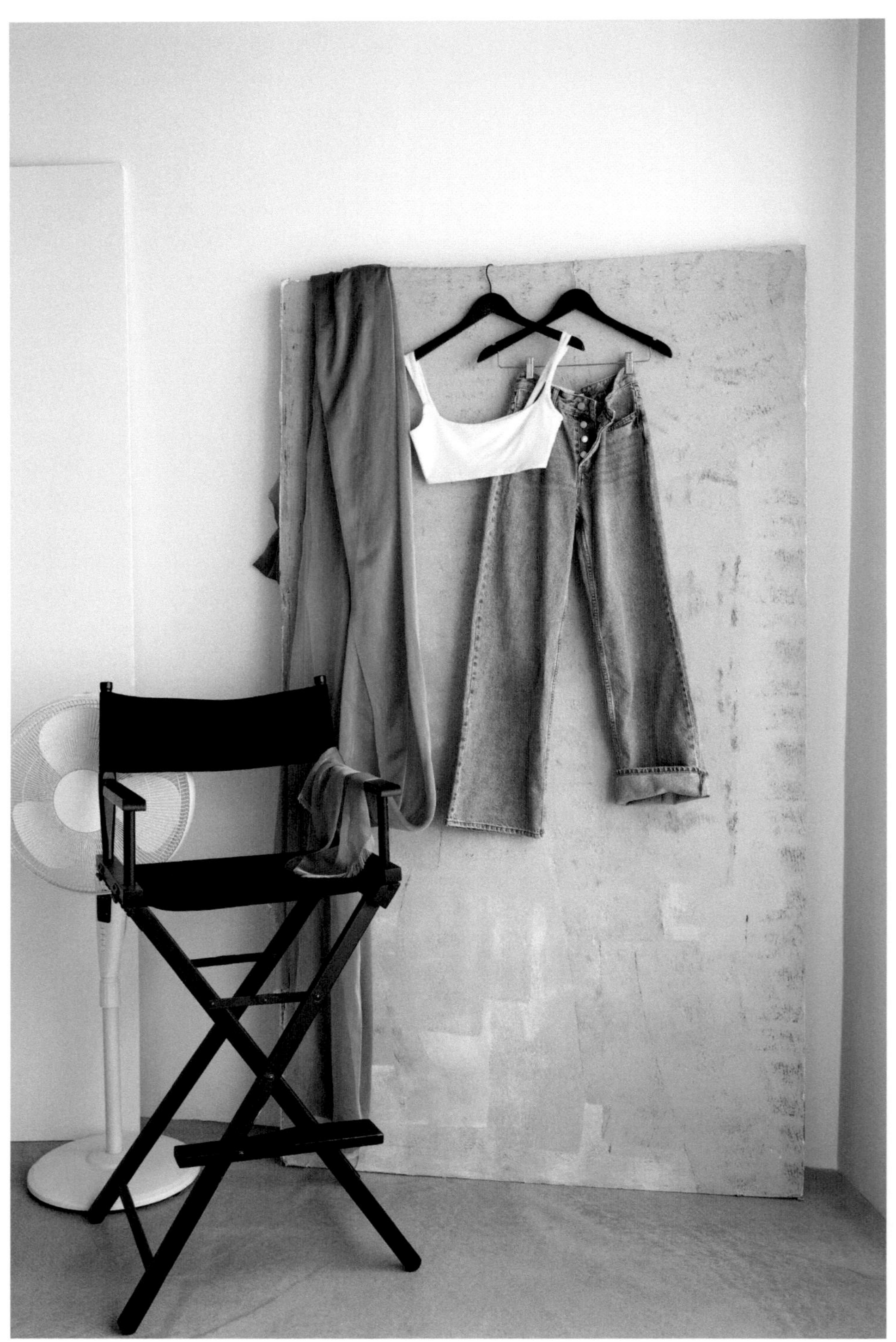

In my wardrobe

I like to keep my wardrobe and styling very simple and minimal. I mainly use plain backdrops, basic clothing items, fabric and a couple of trendier pieces. I prefer a classic wardrobe that will stand the test of time. Most of the things I own, I have in two or three sizes to make sure they fit clients.

In my wardrobe, I have:
- White shirt
- Cosy knitted jumper
- Black turtleneck dress
- Black-and-white vest tops
- A few lace gowns
- Silk dressing gown
- A few tube dresses and skirts
- Silk dress
- A few trendy tops
- Long pieces of fabric, such as silk and chiffon
- Artificial flowers

I also have a list of essential and optional items that I always share with my clients.

Essential items:
- Strapless nude bra – especially if a client wants to create images using fabric
- Light- and dark-coloured underwear – matching tops and bottoms

Optional items:
- A pair of jeans or trousers – ideally, not maternity; as long as she can squeeze into them, they don't need to zip up
- Tops – crop tops, blouses or vest tops
- Tight dresses
- Silk or lace dressing gown
- Beach dresses
- Cosy jumper or cardigan
- Jewellery – statement jewellery can add a lot to the pictures
- Anything else they think might work

When a client arrives at the studio, we put all the pieces together and plan our shoot, deciding what we will use. Some pregnant women might only want to shoot nude images, celebrating their bodies – in this case, they won't need to bring anything at all.

If a partner or children are coming to the session, I recommend bringing simple outfits that coordinate well together. A partner or children must find something to coordinate with mum's chosen style and outfits without being overly 'matchy'. For a partner, I always recommend bringing both light- and dark-coloured tops.

Photographing and posing mothers-to-be can feel intimidating and somewhat challenging. During this time, women are glowing and usually very proud of their baby bump, but at the same time, the body is changing, and they are not necessarily happy with that new look. I often get emails from potential clients saying they would love to book a photo shoot to document this very special time in their lives, but they don't know how to pose and don't necessarily feel their prettiest. Women often feel insecure, worried and uncomfortable in front of a camera, whether they are pregnant or not. So, when a client is pregnant, not only do we need to find a flattering pose, capture great expressions and think about lighting, camera angle, exposure and focus, but we also need to make sure our subject is relaxed and comfortable.

Most of my clients are ordinary women who have never stood in front of a camera and have no idea how to pose and what to do. During maternity sessions, I always direct them and offer guidance and tips on posing. I often show them how to stand, how and where to place their hands and where to look; I do everything to ensure my client is comfortable in front of the lens. My aim is to not just show a beautiful baby bump but also to make sure my client looks her best.

When I photograph an expectant mother, I want to give her adoration and words of encouragement. I pay her genuine compliments and tell her how gorgeous she looks. I give specific directions on how to pose, tweak hair and bra straps, and show her how to emphasize her curves and baby belly by arching her back. This not only gives her faith in me but also makes her more relaxed, knowing what to do. I want to make sure she feels beautiful and trusts me.

There are only a few base poses that I use and build on. By slightly changing the placement and position of your subject's hands, head tilt, gaze and expression, you can create a great variety of images. You can also play with clothing, accessories, light and angles. Once you master a few basic poses, you will have endless possibilities.

'I want to make sure she feels beautiful and trusts me.'

- **Double chin**. The chin should be out and down to avoid or minimize a double chin. This is a fantastic trick for graceful necks and strong chins. However, watch your client's neck – make sure she isn't straining her neck and looking unnatural and stiff. If she is, have her try again and ask her to breathe in and out to release tension.

- **Shoulders**. Often, a pregnant woman is tense and worried, especially at the beginning of the shoot. Ask her to breathe in and out to relax the tension from her shoulders. Make sure she is not hunching – you want shoulders to be back and down to slim the back and give more elegance to the neck.

- **Slouching**. Ask your client to stand tall – poor posture makes people look shorter. While there is nothing wrong with being short, in pictures, we want to elongate our subject.

- **Arms**. Keep your subject's arms away from the body as much as you can. Arms placed next to the body will not only make your client look wider, but an arm pressed firmly to the body will look wider itself. Keeping arms away from the body creates negative space and will add beautiful curves to your subject. Another option is to use arms to contour the body. In maternity photography, this will mostly mean wrapping arms around the belly to emphasize the baby bump.

- **Hands**. Make sure your subject's hands are soft and relaxed. I often notice my clients' thumbs pointing up and separated from their fingers, or fingers straight and tense. Ask her to shake her hands or to wriggle her fingers and then gently rest them back on her belly.

- **Legs**. The leg closest to the camera is usually bent to add shape. I seldom have my clients standing on both feet with their weight distributed equally. If my subject's body is facing me, then I ask her to cross or partially cross over the leg. This will elongate and slim the body as well as adding beautiful curves.

- **Feet**. I always ask pregnant women to either place their foot, usually the one that is closest to me, on their toes, to turn their foot out or to point their toes. Flat feet don't just look unflattering, but instead of adding elegance and lightness to the photographs, they make the body look stiff and square.

There is a lot to look for and to think about, but trust me, this will become second nature, and soon, you will train your eye to spot every little detail and perfect your posing.

I must mention one more thing before we dive into posing. There have been many times when my clients have told me, 'I don't like posed images – I would like natural, candid shots.' Posing is often associated with stiff body positions, uncomfortable expressions, forced smiles and sometimes cluttered or over-styled images. Bear in mind that a client rarely means they actually want candid shots as per the true definition. Most of the time, it is their way of saying they want a relaxed, authentic image with genuine expression. This is why it's essential to learn how to pose your clients, so they feel comfortable.

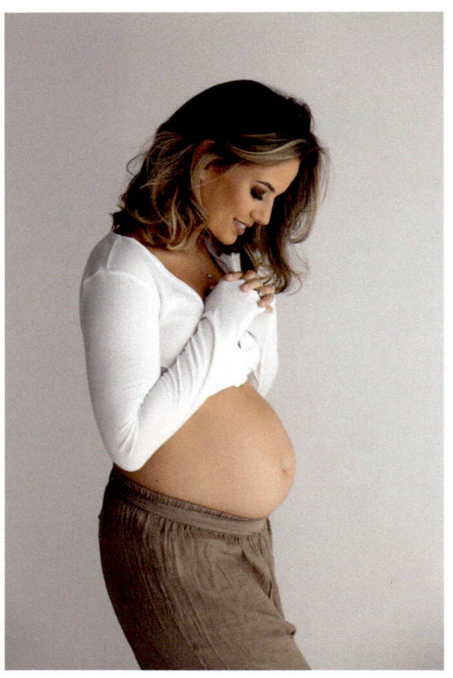

BASIC POSING

During both maternity and newborn sessions, I use flow or transition posing to bring variety to my photographs. How do I do that? First, I pick a few base poses and build on them. The core of the pose remains the same, but by moving my client's arms, hands, feet and face, I create different poses. By directing her gaze and changing her expression, I create new looks. There are numerous combinations and variations. To add even more variety, I shoot from different angles and crop images differently. Remember, it's not all about just changing the pose – the same pose can look very different when shot from different angles.

These are the base poses I use, however, you can always come up with your own list of base poses.

My favourite pose. You can get a wide variety of images from it, and it is really easy to pose. This is one of the best poses to showcase a baby bump too. Simply turn your subject to the side, either half or three quarters of the way. I usually start with my client standing in complete profile, and as I shoot, I either slowly rotate her towards me or move myself. Remember, we are always adding micro-movements to create variety.

When posing our subject sideways, we want to use arms and legs to help us flatter the shape of a pregnant woman's body and to create even more contours and curves.

The first thing I want to ensure is that the leg closest to the camera is bent and the foot isn't flat on the floor. This will emphasize the curve of your subject's thigh and bum. Pay attention to the knees – you want to make sure they are pointing either straight or a little inward. If your client is struggling to bend her knee or to keep her balance, use a small box to raise the leg. We want to make sure our mother-to-be is comfortable.

There are so many different ways that you can position her arms and hands. I will cover arm placement in more detail later (see page 65). I always start with hands resting on the baby bump; the hand that is furthest away from me goes on the top, and the one closest to me goes on the bottom of the belly. I always ask my clients to pull their arm closest to me back to create negative space between the arm and the body. This simple movement makes a pregnant woman look more slender and adds another beautiful curve.

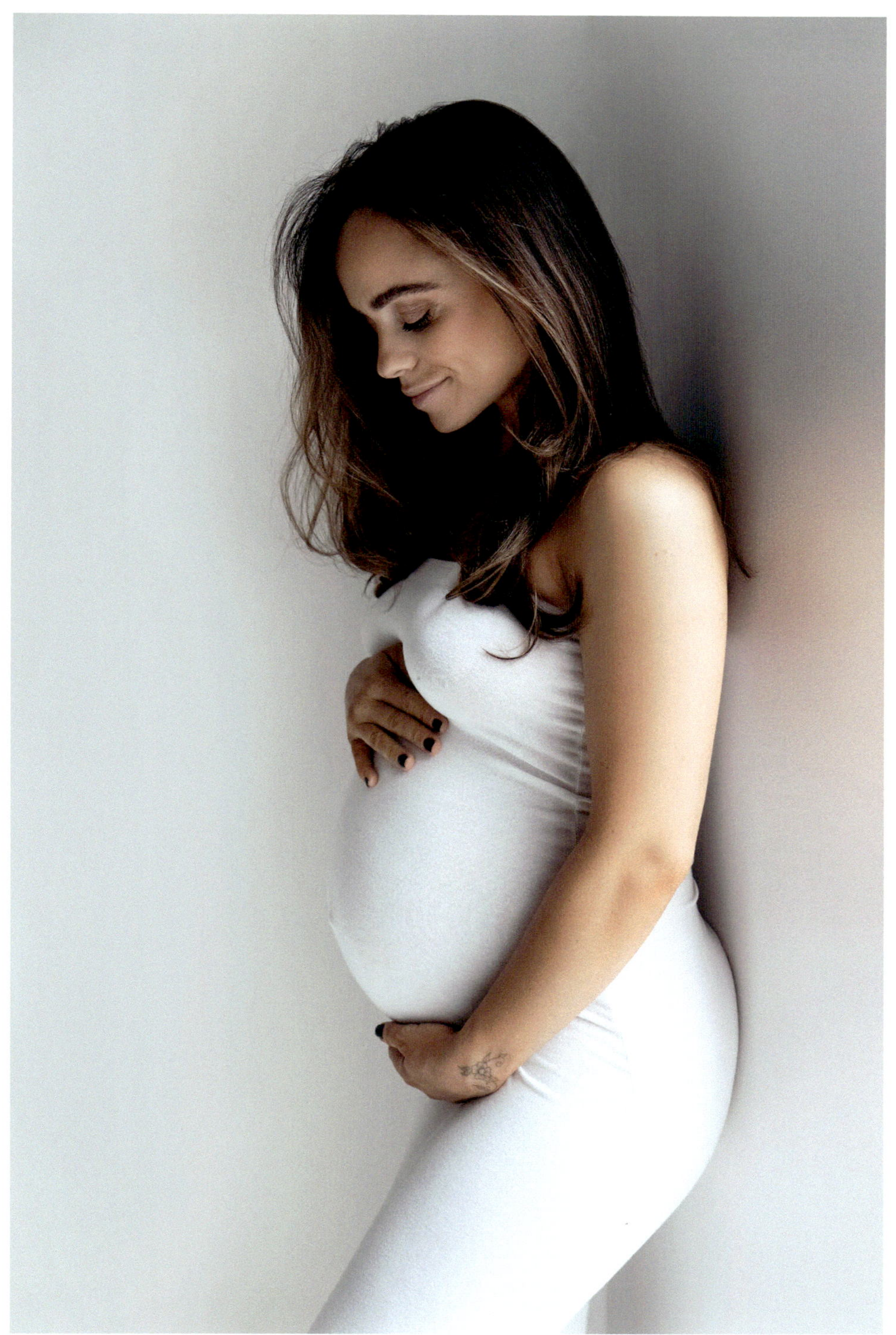

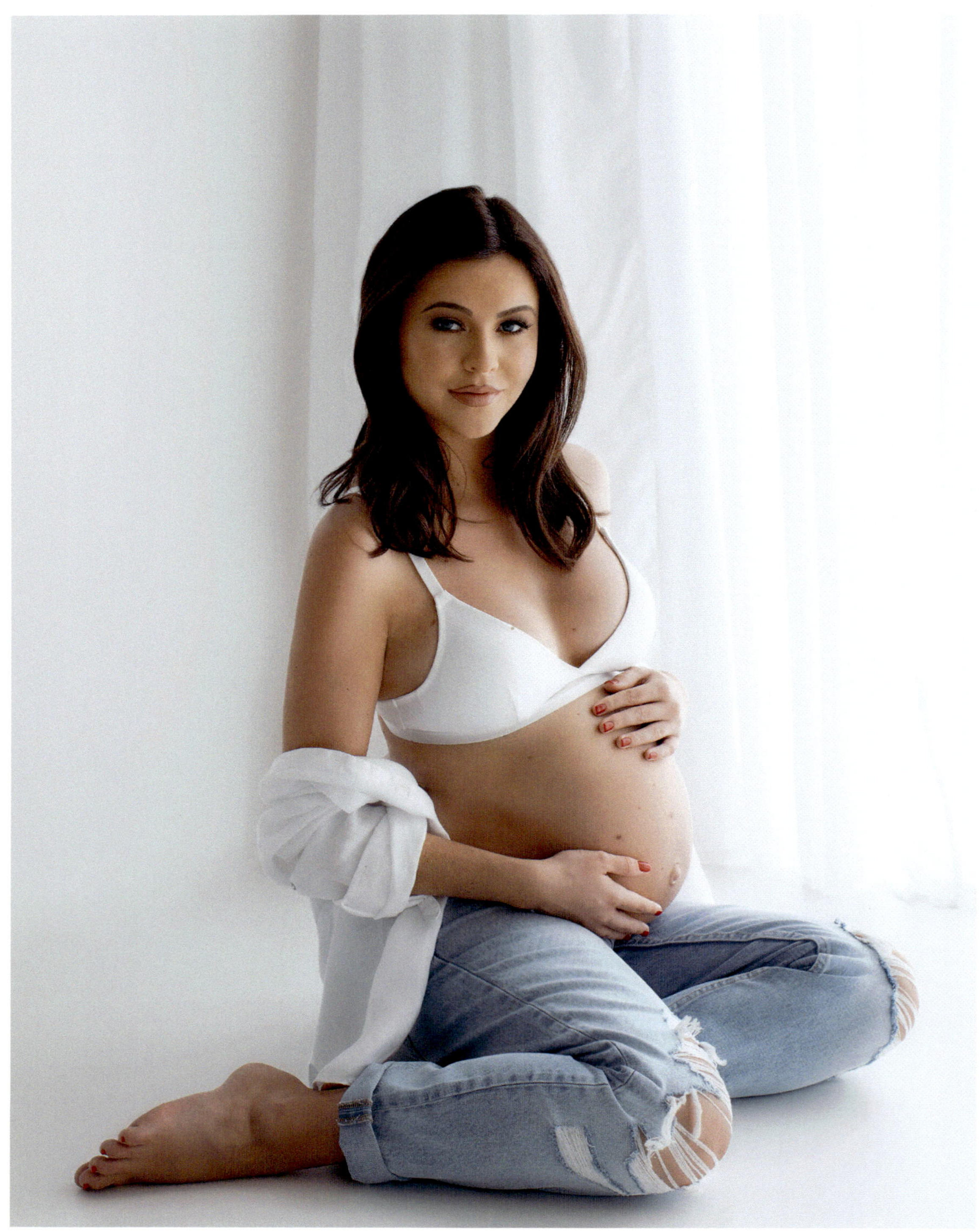

Sitting pose

This is another simple pose. Either have your subject sitting cross-legged on the floor or bed (if clothing allows) or ask her to kneel and then sit back on her heels. In both these sitting positions, make sure your client is sitting up straight. Good posture will help her belly stick out and make her look taller. I usually start photographing this pose with arms cradling the belly.

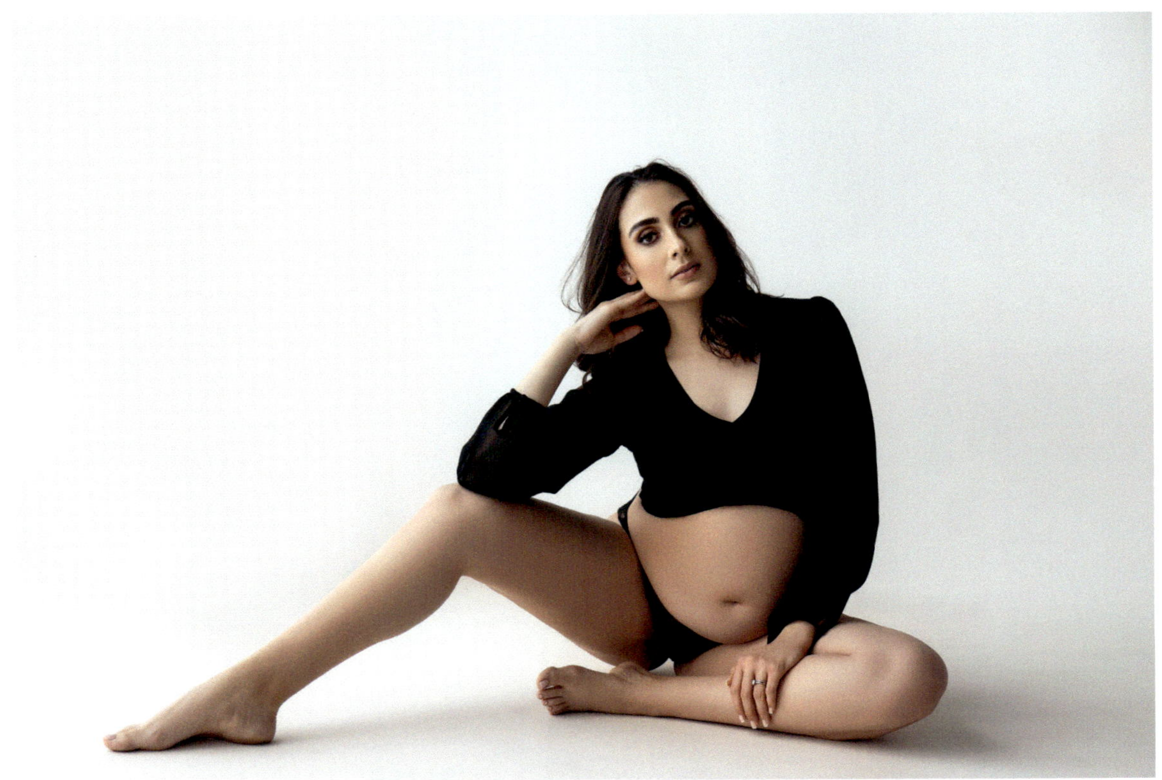

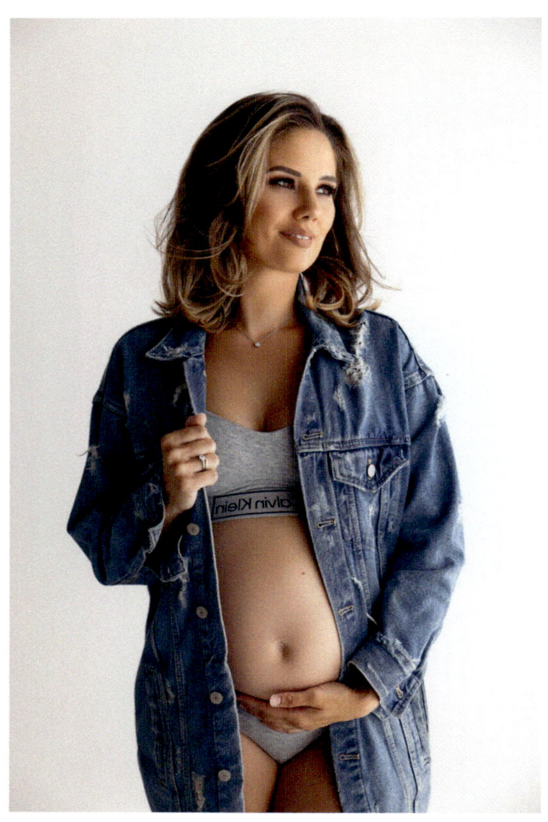
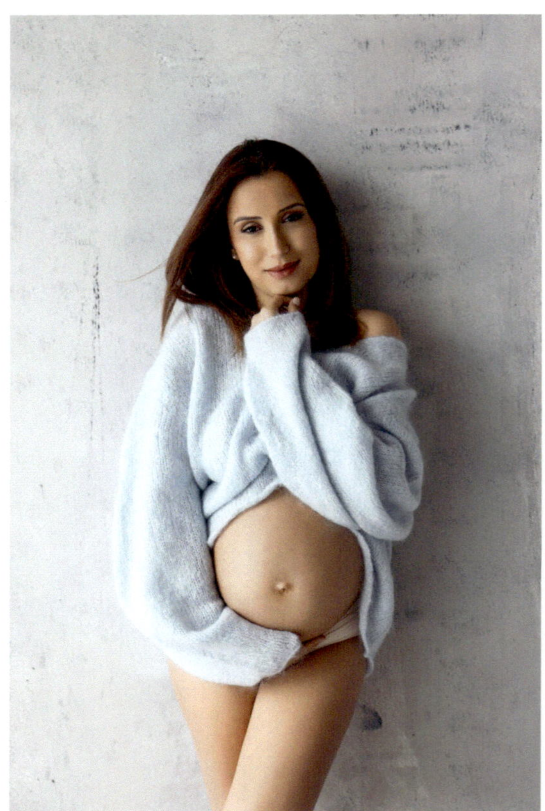

Belly facing the camera pose

This pose won't work for every woman. If the bump is tiny or my client is wearing dark, belly-covering clothing, I never photograph her in this pose. It is hard to see the curve of the baby bump when shooting straight on. To emphasize the pregnant belly and draw attention to it, use arms and hands to contour it. The position of the hands will help to define the beautiful shape. You can start by placing one hand on the top and one on the bottom or place both hands at the same level on the bottom of the belly. Ask your client to partially cross her legs. Photograph your client in this pose when she is wearing clothes that expose her belly.

Laying down pose

A pose that both my clients and I love, especially if I am photographing a pregnant woman nude. You can simply lay your client on her back or her side. If your client is lying on her back, ask her to arch her back as much as possible. The gap between the floor and her back will create a beautiful curve (don't forget the leg closest to you must be bent). For nude images, leg placement becomes even more critical. Have her lie on her side and start by asking her to place her forearm or hand on the floor to support her weight. Her leg should be bent and partially crossed over.

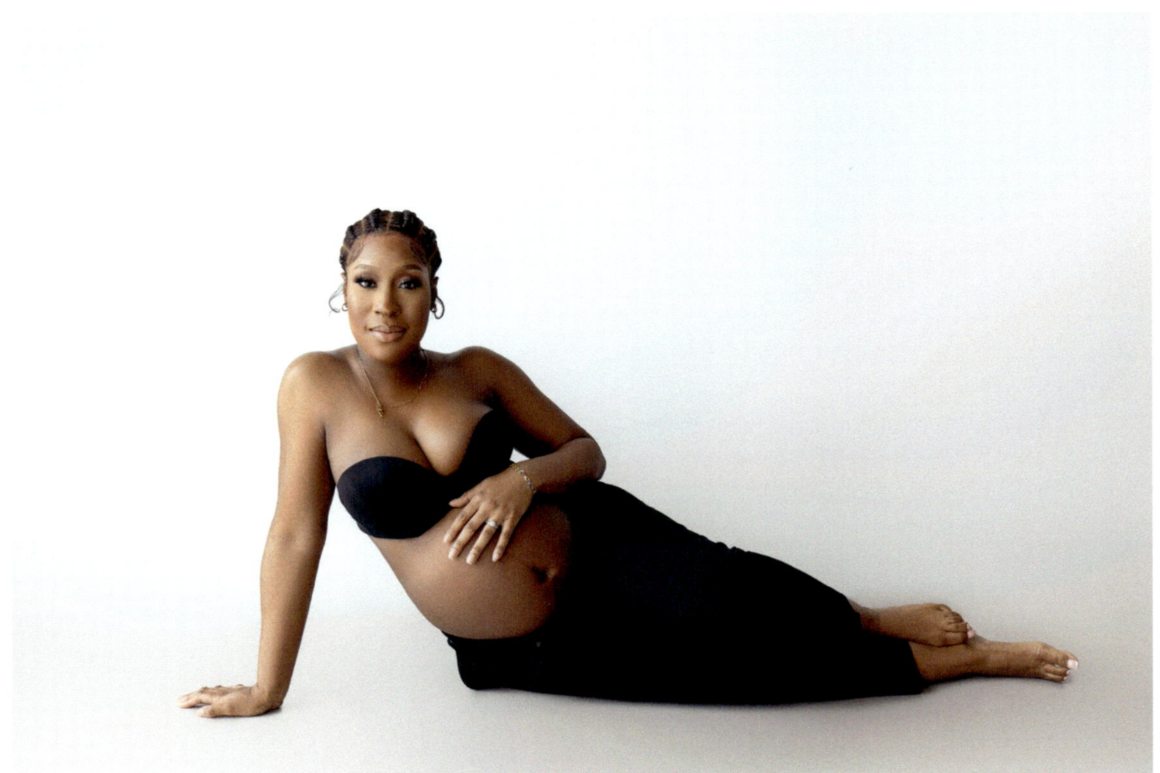

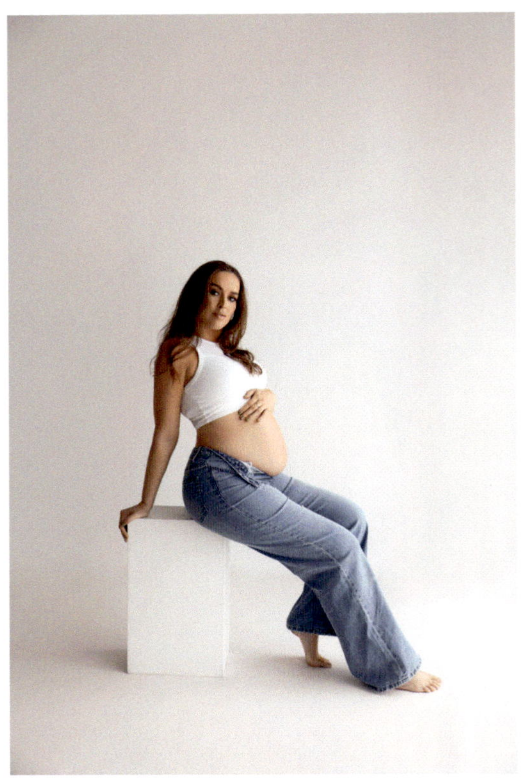 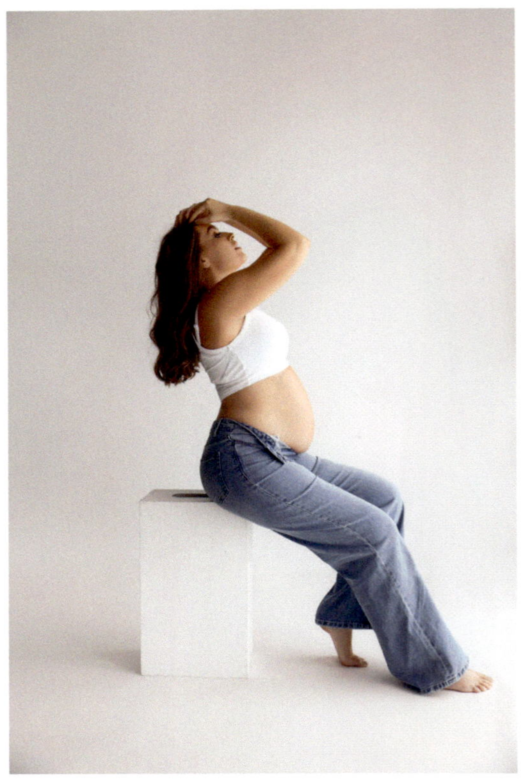

Sitting on a chair, bed or posing block

This pose is effortless, and most mums feel very comfortable in it. Sit your client on a chair or a posing block, either facing you or sideways. Start with her legs stretched out and one leg bent slightly more than the other. Don't forget to ask her to point her toes to make her legs look longer. Start with arms cradling the baby bump and then direct her to change hands and legs position.

Don't forget to maximize every pose. Change hand placement, the position of your subject's legs and the direction of her gaze and expression. Also, change your angles and crops to create different looks and a variety of final images.

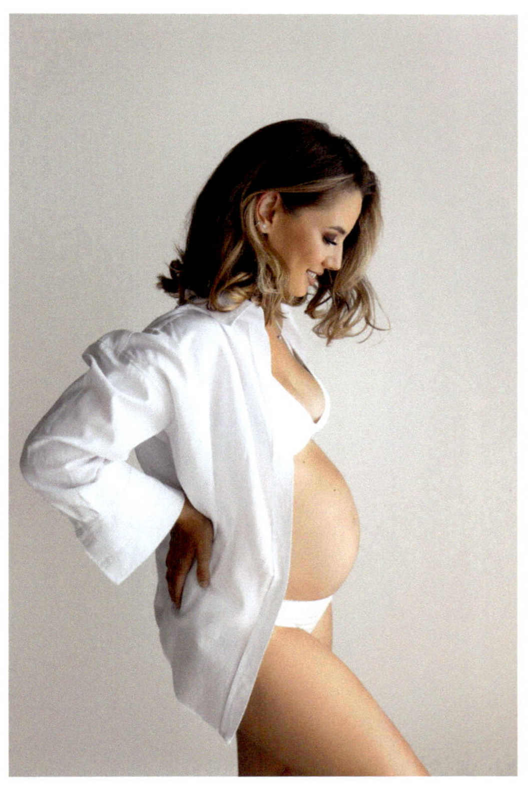

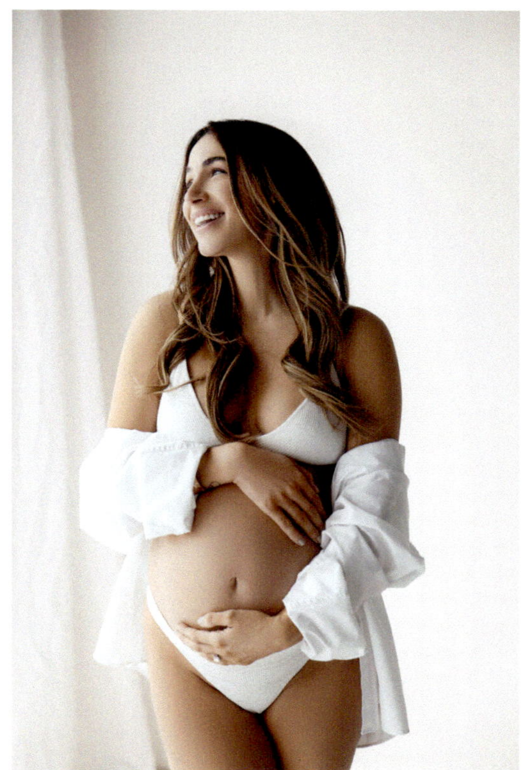

To smile or not to smile

Expression is arguably more important than perfect posing. You can have a perfectly posed and composed image, but if the expression isn't there, the image won't look right. We humans are drawn to expressions, emotions and feelings. If I have one image with a perfect pose and perfect light but a less than perfect expression, and a second with somewhat poor posing and imperfect lighting but a great expression, I will always choose the one with a great expression. I know that my clients will connect to that image.

However, sometimes, it can be challenging to find a connection between your subject and camera.

I talk to my clients before, during and after the photo shoot. This helps us to connect and also takes my clients' focus away from having to pose or smile. Don't forget to talk to your client and to praise her at all times – being in front of the camera is much easier when you know you are doing a good job. I often ask my clients to give a silly laugh, and I might show them how to do this myself. This might make them feel self-conscious at first, but after a few seconds, I get a genuine giggle and laugh. Feeling relaxed and comfortable in front of the camera can be extremely difficult, but positive reinforcement and honest and real conversation always help.

A FEW TIPS ON DIRECTING YOUR CLIENT'S GAZE AND ACHIEVING THE MOST BEAUTIFUL & GENUINE EXPRESSIONS

1. I often start my session with mum looking at the baby bump. Sometimes, when I ask the mother-to-be to look at her belly, she looks at the top of her bump, which makes her lose her chin and look heavier in the face. To create a gorgeously defined chin and graceful neck, I ask her to look at the edge of her belly or a point in front of it. Instead of looking straight in front, I often ask her to turn her chin slightly towards me.

2. Looking out the window or towards the light source, keep a relaxed face and small smile.

3. Looking at the camera. I do love images where my clients look at the camera, and more often than not, they love them too. I seldom start a session with my client looking at the camera, but after a few 'looking at the belly' or 'away from the belly' shots, most clients are relaxed enough, and look at the camera with soft eyes and genuine smiles. If I see tension in the face, I ask my client to tilt her head to the light, which usually relaxes the neck and softens the face.

4. Closed eyes. It might sound silly, but I often ask my clients to close their eyes, mainly if I photograph nudes or slightly more artistic and creative images. Most of the time, I ask them to lift their chin up and close their eyes. However, you can do the same with the chin pointing down and the mother-to-be 'looking' at the belly.

5. Looking up. I often ask my clients to look up in the poses where I have them playing with their hair.

6. Looking towards her shoulder. You need to be careful not to lose the chin line when the client looks in this direction.

During my sessions, I aim to create a variety of images – looking at the camera, towards the belly and away from the belly.

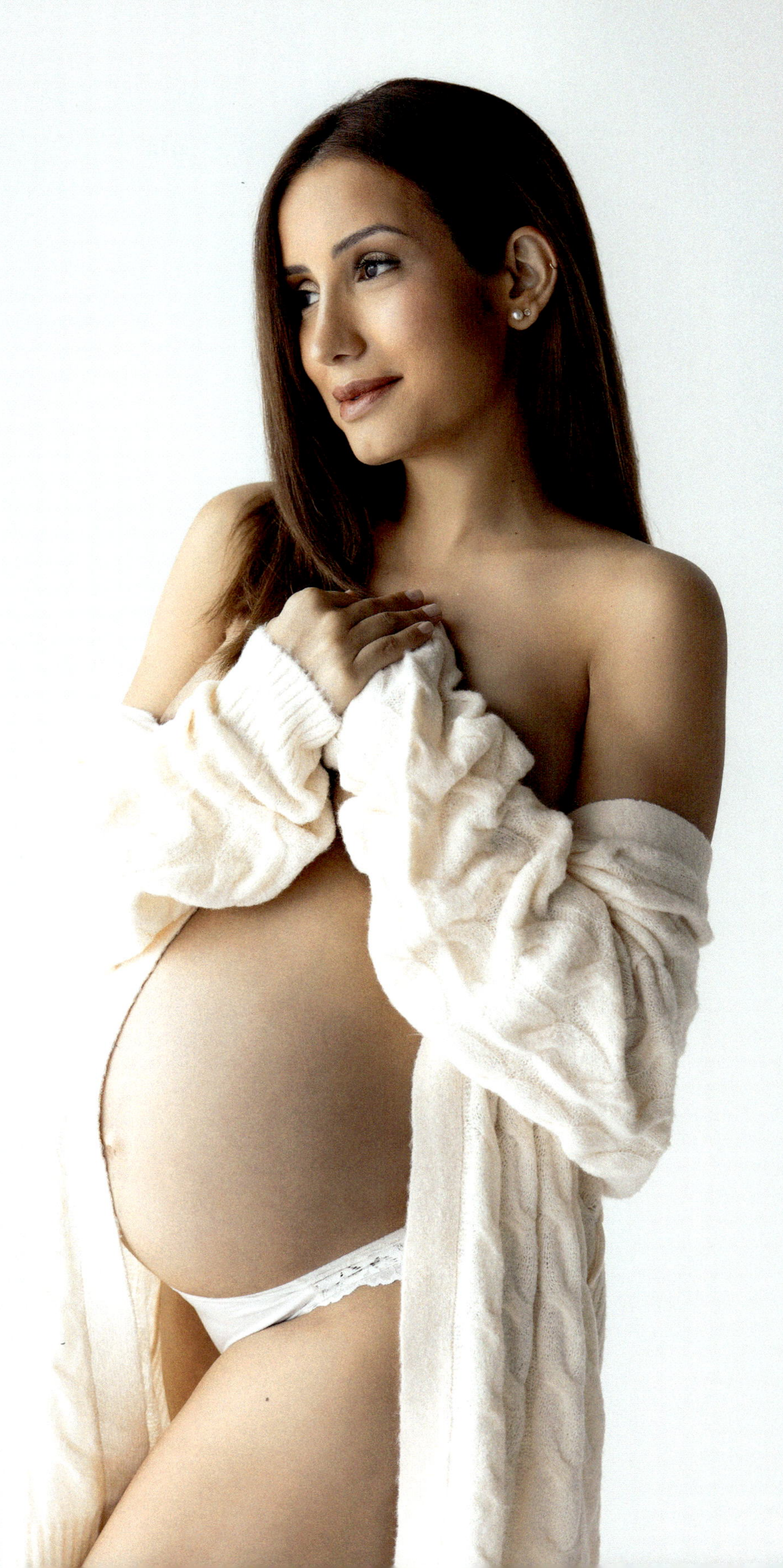

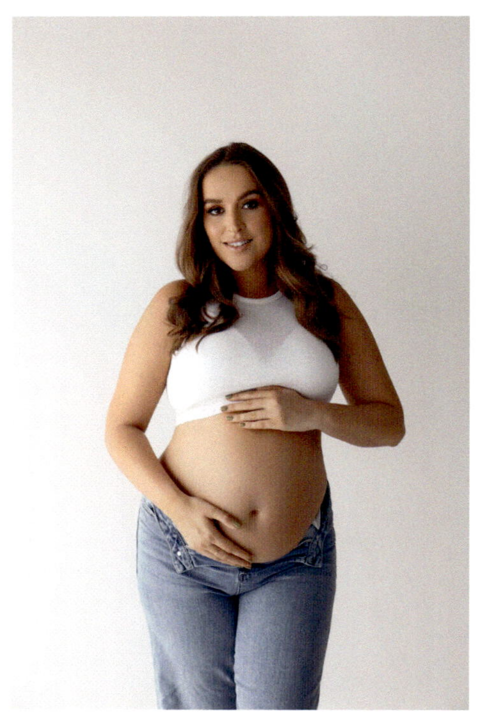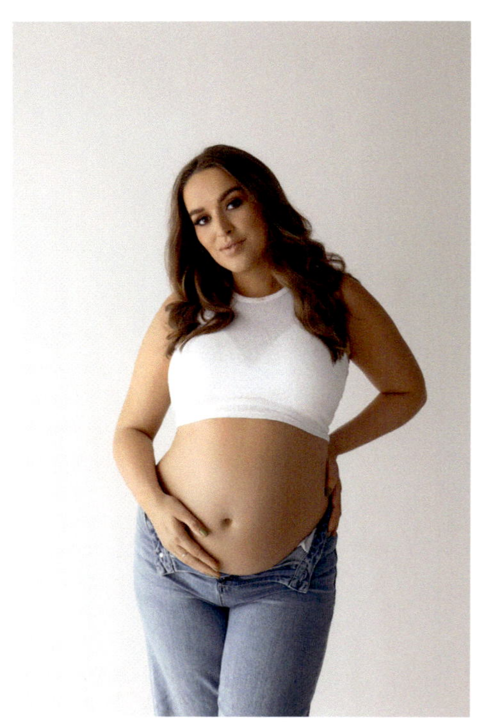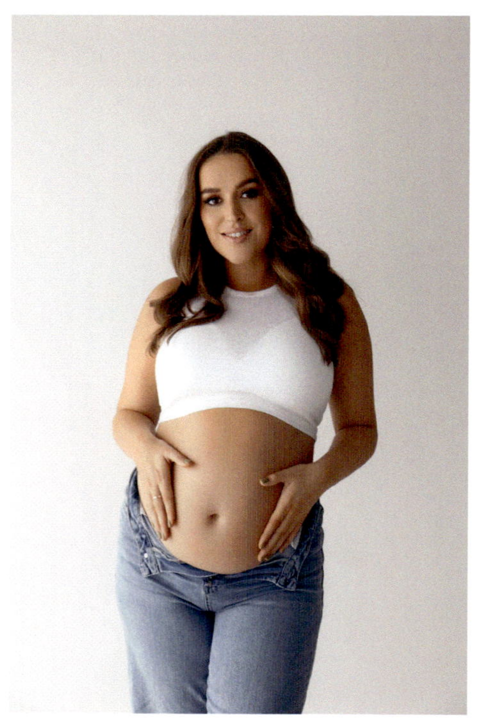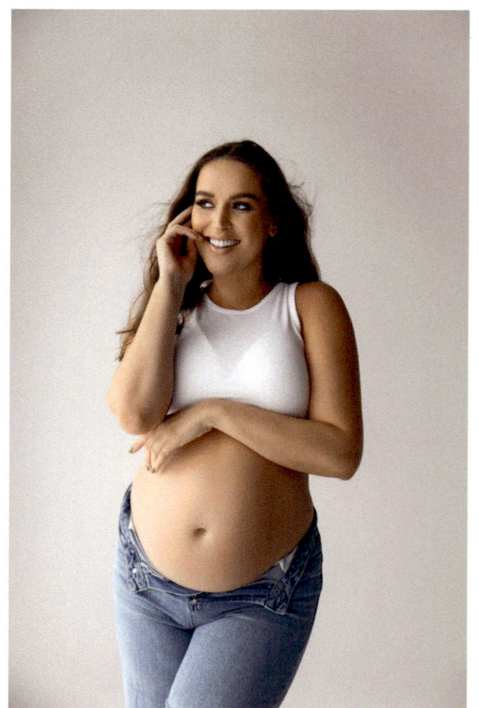

Arms & hands

Sometimes, it might be hard to think of what to do with your client's hands. During maternity sessions, the baby bump is the obvious and easiest place to rest hands on.

Below are a few ideas of what to do with the hands. Some of these hand placements will help to create more intimate, motherly shots; some of them I would use to create more editorial, fashion-style images.

- One hand on the top of the belly, one on the bottom of the belly
- One hand on the top of the belly, one hand resting on a leg
- Both hands on the bottom of the belly
- One hand on the top or the bottom of the belly, the other one on the back or the hip
- One hand on the belly, the other one playing with hair or resting on the side of the face
- Both hands resting on her chest or holding a top (when a client wears something loose)
- One hand on the breast, one hand on the bottom of the belly.

These are just a few options. Be creative and I'm sure you will come up with some excellent hand placements of your own. You can also have your subject playing with her hair with both hands, throwing or swishing her dress or even dancing. Remember, to create intimate images, you will most likely have your client's hands cradling her baby bump. Whatever you decide to do, ensure your client's hands are soft.

My last – but not least – important posing tip

If your client seems tense, ask her to take a deep breath instead of asking her to relax. Sometimes, if a client keeps being told to relax, it might stress her even more. She might think that she looks stiff and, instead of relaxing, will become even more rigid and conscious of her appearance. A deep breath and exhalation usually help to relax even the tensest person. I often take a deep breath myself in a situation like this, and even shake my shoulders on exhale. When a client sees me being involved, relaxed and a little silly, it makes her feel much more comfortable in front of the camera.

Adding partners or children creates not just more meaningful images but also adds more variety. Whether photographing opposite- or same-sex couples, I pose partners the same way. I usually start with photographing mum on her own and then add her partner and/or children. I still give everyone guidance and pose them, but now, instead of directing just mum, I direct them all. I also show them where to stand and what to do, pretending to be the partner. I ask them to giggle, look at each other, Eskimo kiss (rub their noses), place their foreheads together and take a deep breath or ask a partner to kiss the baby bump. I also like photographing mum looking at the camera and her partner whispering something sweet in her ear or kissing her head. I will always place the partner either behind or to the pregnant woman's side, never in front. The same goes for hands. I place the partner's hands on the baby bump first and then add mum's hands on top. While the mother will remain the focus of the image, the partner's body language will show affection and support.

Most men don't want to be at the photo shoot. As soon as they walk in, I usually ask them to sit down and relax while telling them they have nothing to worry about: 'The star of the show today is the pregnant mother.' Most of the time, after sitting and admiring their beautiful partner while I photograph her on her own, they are very happy to join in. Every couple has a unique relationship; sometimes, I stand back a little, stay quiet and capture their connection. Just remember that all posing rules discussed earlier still apply!

I always encourage siblings to be brought to the session. I love photographing them evolving and growing together as a family. If siblings are older, I ask them many questions and try to engage in conversation with them. I ask if they have felt the baby moving, what they think the baby will look like, if they think the baby will cry a lot when he/she is born, if they have helped parents to think of a name and so on. I want older siblings to feel involved. I usually photograph families together and mum with the children on her own too.

If the sibling is a toddler, then photographing the soon-to-be big brother/sister may be challenging. Most toddlers don't understand why mum keeps asking them to kiss her belly and don't comprehend that a baby is growing inside. Whenever I photograph toddlers during maternity, family or newborn sessions, I aim to be very quick. They get bored easily, and before you know it, you've lost them. If mum can lift a toddler, I ask her to sit him/her on her belly, then add a partner to the pose to capture some family images. It is nearly impossible to plan anything with toddlers – I usually just go with the flow and do my best.

Ask parents if you can give toddlers some treats. Sometimes, chocolate buttons or a few raisins can save the shoot.

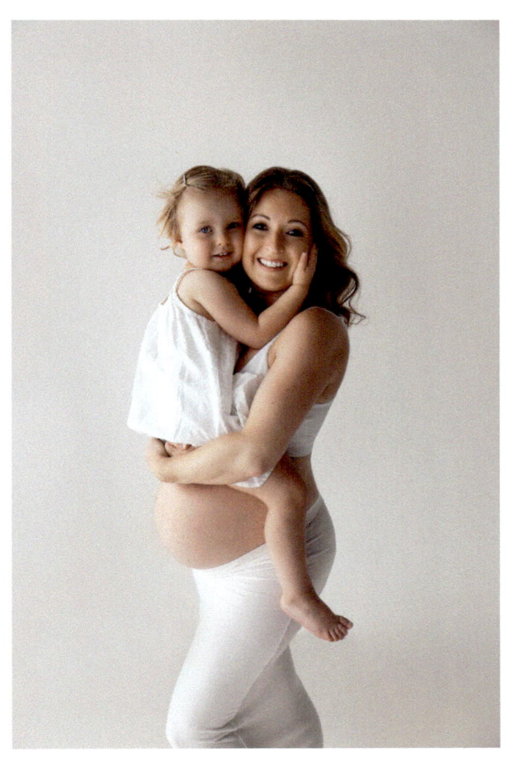
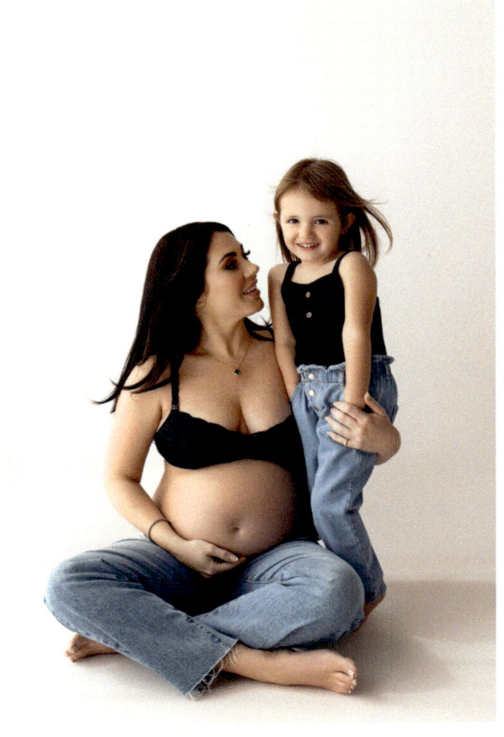
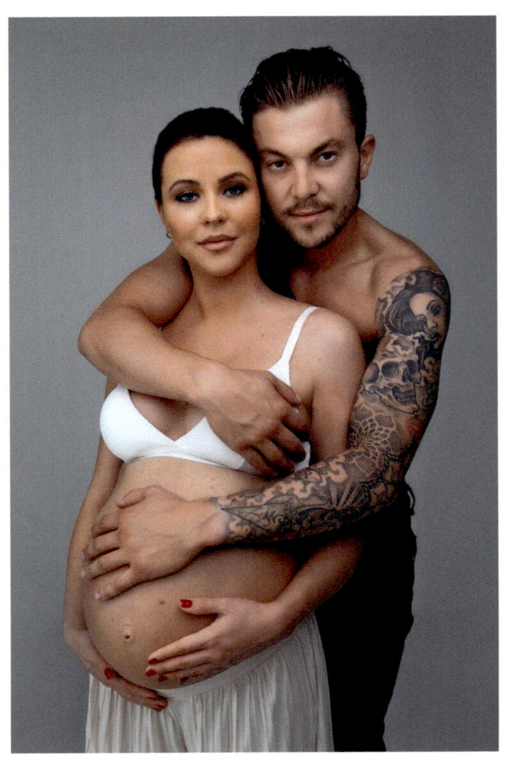
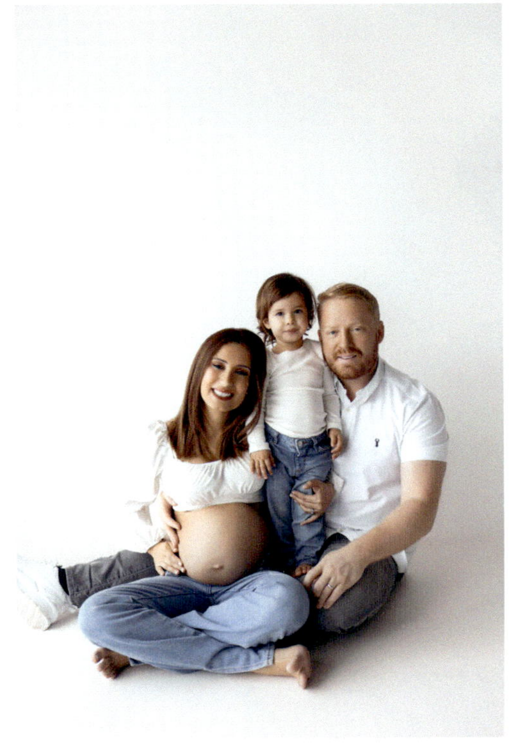

HERE ARE A FEW TIPS ON HOW TO GET A TODDLER TO INTERACT WITH THE BABY BUMP

1. Place a sticker (which you can edit out later) on the belly and ask a toddler to remove it and stick it back. It will look like they are pointing to or touching 'baby'. I have little star stickers at the studio for that. Sometimes, I ask them to kiss the star. They are often keener on kissing the sticker than the belly itself.

2. Ask the toddler to listen to mummy's tummy. Sometimes, I pretend to listen too. I ask if he/she can hear the baby. Can they hear the baby singing or dancing?

3. If mum is lying down, I tell him/her that mummy's belly is a soft pillow and ask them to put their head on it.

Whenever I photograph a pregnant woman with just her partner or older children, I always take breaks. I photograph mum on her own, add a partner/sibling/all of them, then carry on photographing mum on her own and repeat. It doesn't matter how old siblings are, they soon get bored, so when working with toddlers or older siblings, you must be quick.

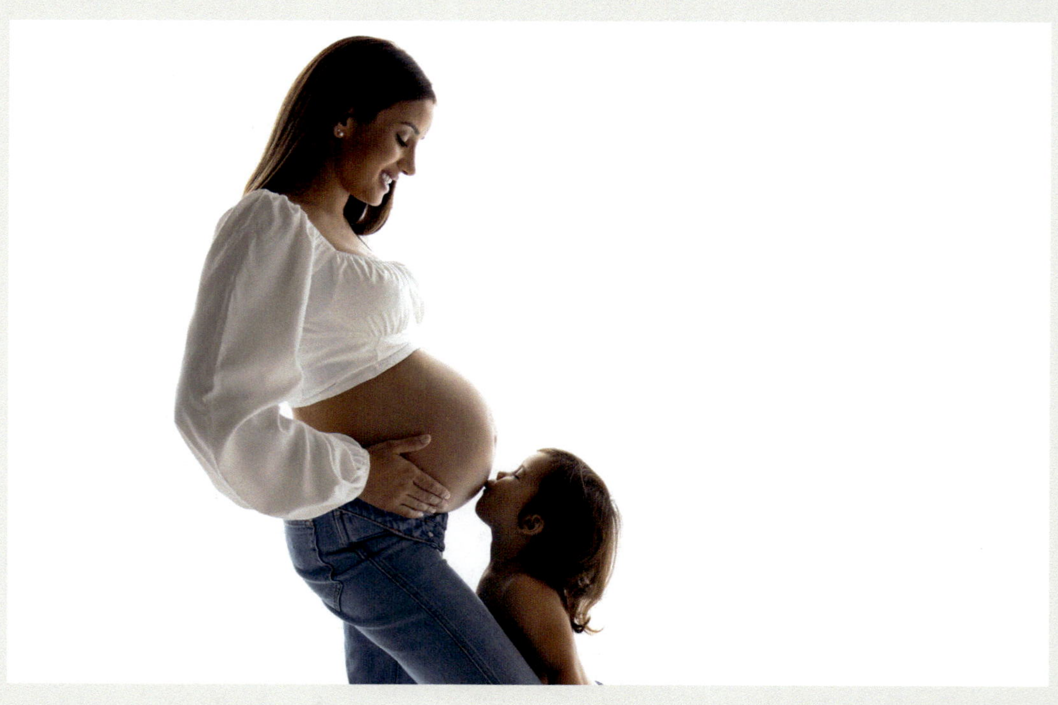

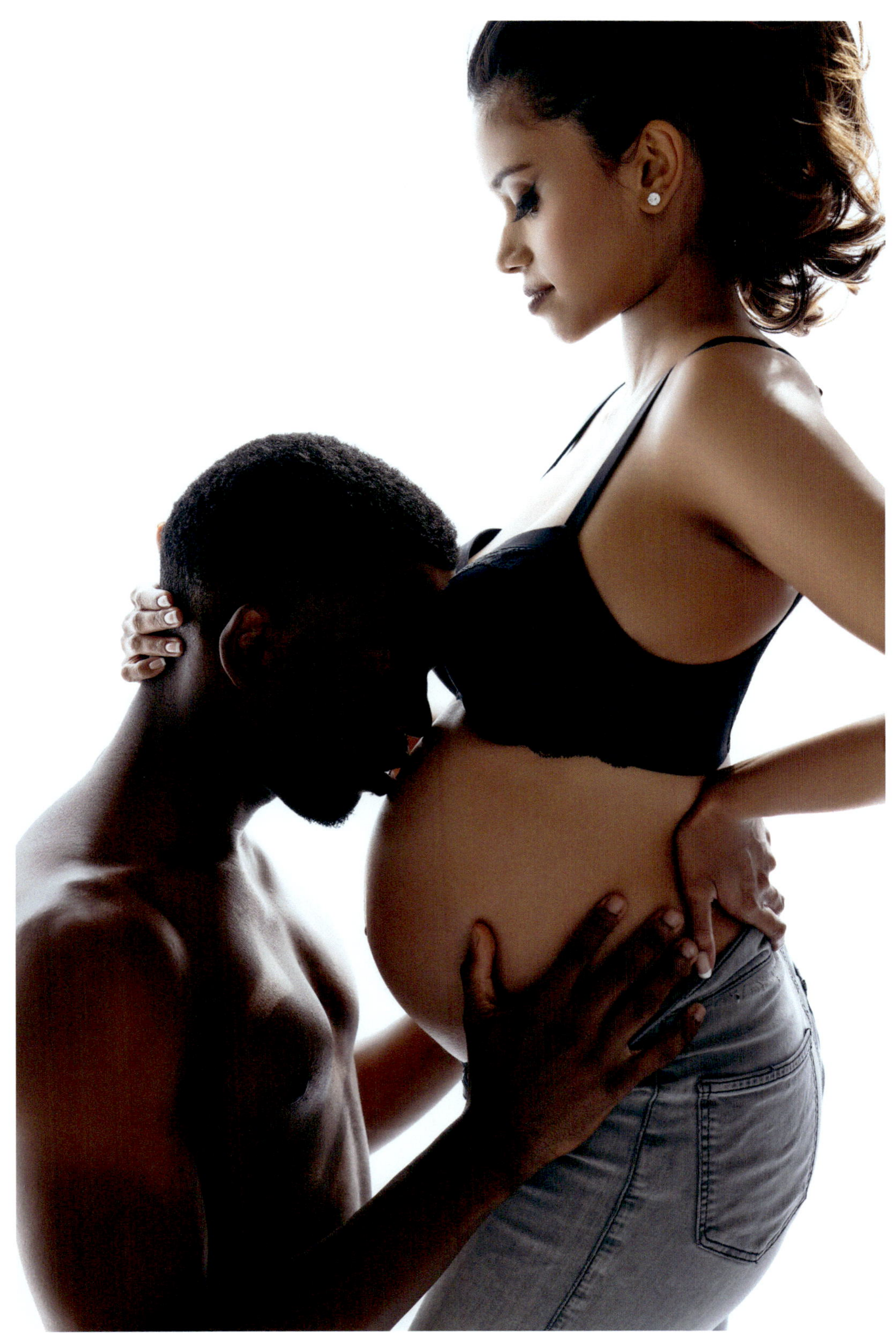

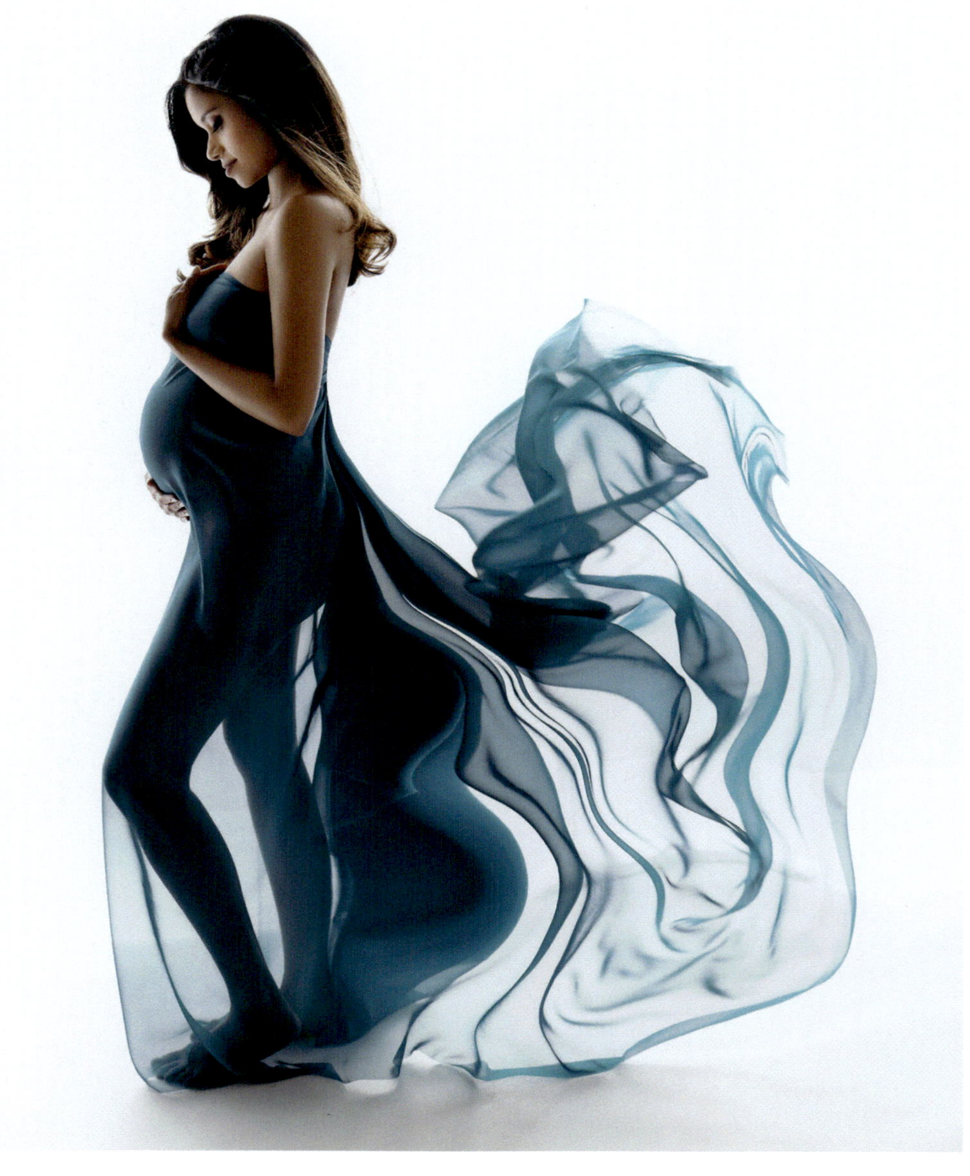

A few long pieces of fabric were all I had when I started photographing pregnant woman. A long piece of fabric allows endless possibilities. You can wrap your client in it, get someone to toss it to create beautiful movement, drape it and get a fan to blow it, and anything else that comes to mind.

You will need someone to help you if you want fabric tossed. If a pregnant woman brings a partner to the session, I usually ask the partner to help me. If not, I make sure I have my assistant to help toss the fabric. You can also ask a mother-to-be to toss it herself, but from my experience, most mums find it very difficult and often, either the pose or the facial expression is compromised. You can also add tossed fabric in post-production. However, this is my least favourite method. Bear in mind that every time you toss a fabric, it will fall differently, and sometimes, you will need many tries to achieve the image that you are looking for.

For images where I use fabric, I ask my clients to bring a nude strapless bra and nude seamless underwear. A strapless bra not only gives shape to the breasts, but is perfect for keeping fabric in place. I use a strapless bra to tuck and style my fabrics. If your client doesn't have a strapless bra, you can use clips to hold the fabric in place.

Silk and chiffon are perfect for draping, tossing or blowing with the fan, while thicker, stretchy fabric is great for wrapping. For tossing, you will need a fabric that is at least 5–6m (16–19ft) long.

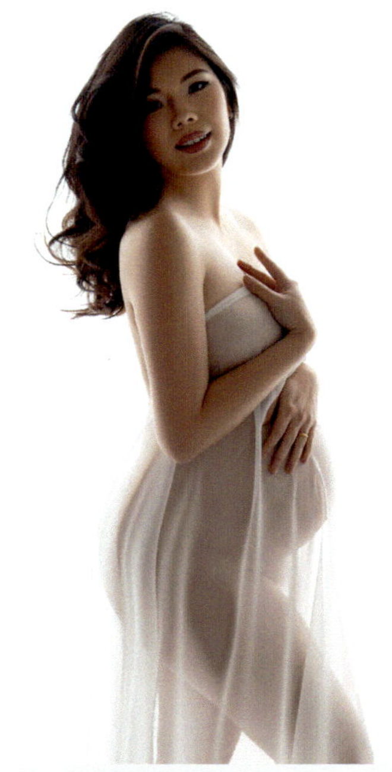

Fan

A fan is essential if you are going to photograph pregnant women. You will use it to move their hair and fabric. I have two fans in my studio: one very powerful industrial fan, which I use to move the fabric, and a regular room fan to move the hair.

Some women are very comfortable with their pregnant bodies and want to create nude images. It is essential for you to be very comfortable with nude bodies too. I love nude images, especially black-and-white nudes, as they portray the pregnant body in the most beautiful, timeless way.

Light plays an extremely big part when it comes to nude photography. I usually use backlight or low-key light to emphasize the body's contours.

Another thing to remember is hand placement and leg position – use them to ensure that parts that you don't want to see are hidden. Most of the time, I leave nude images until the end of the session, when mum is relaxed, and we have built up a trustworthy relationship.

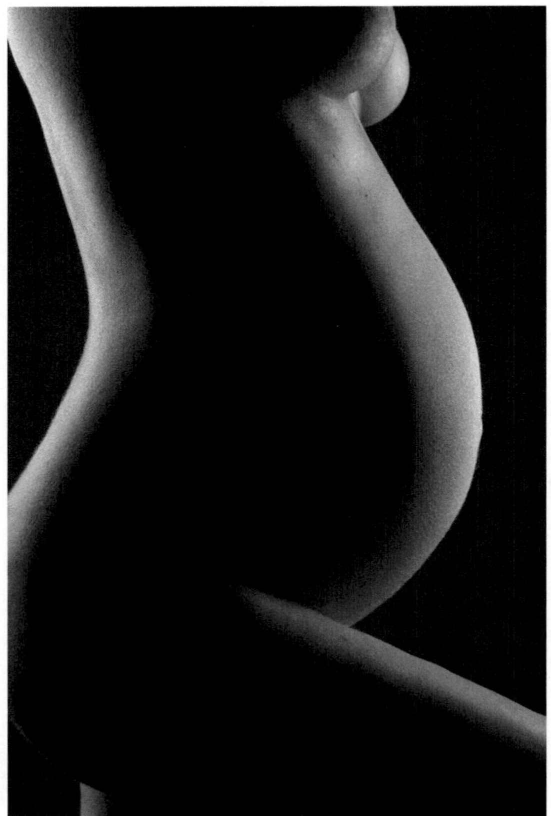

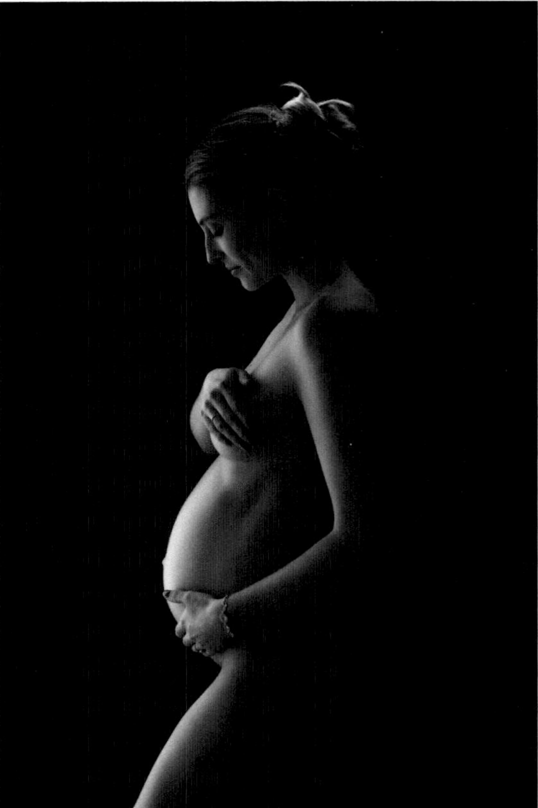

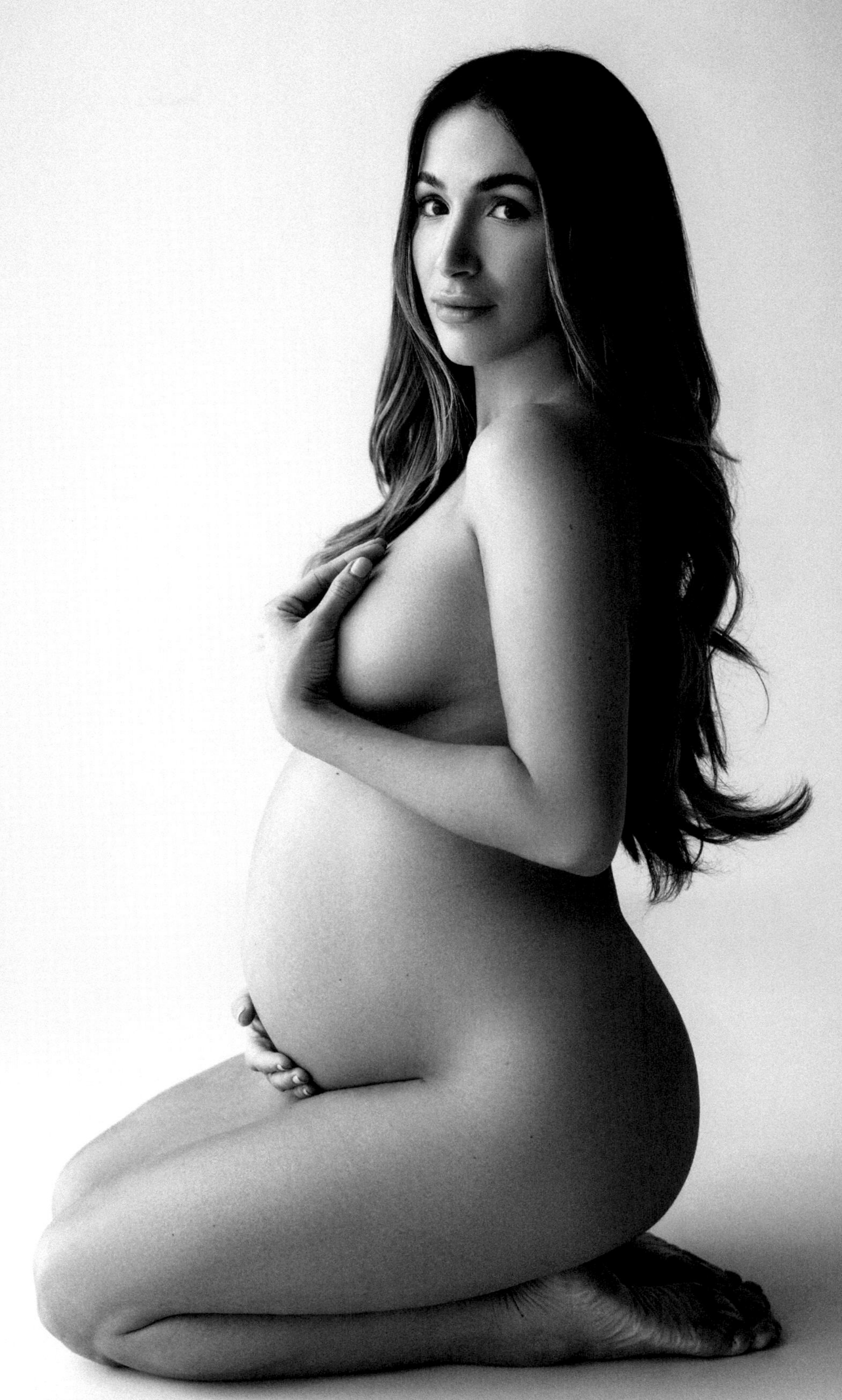

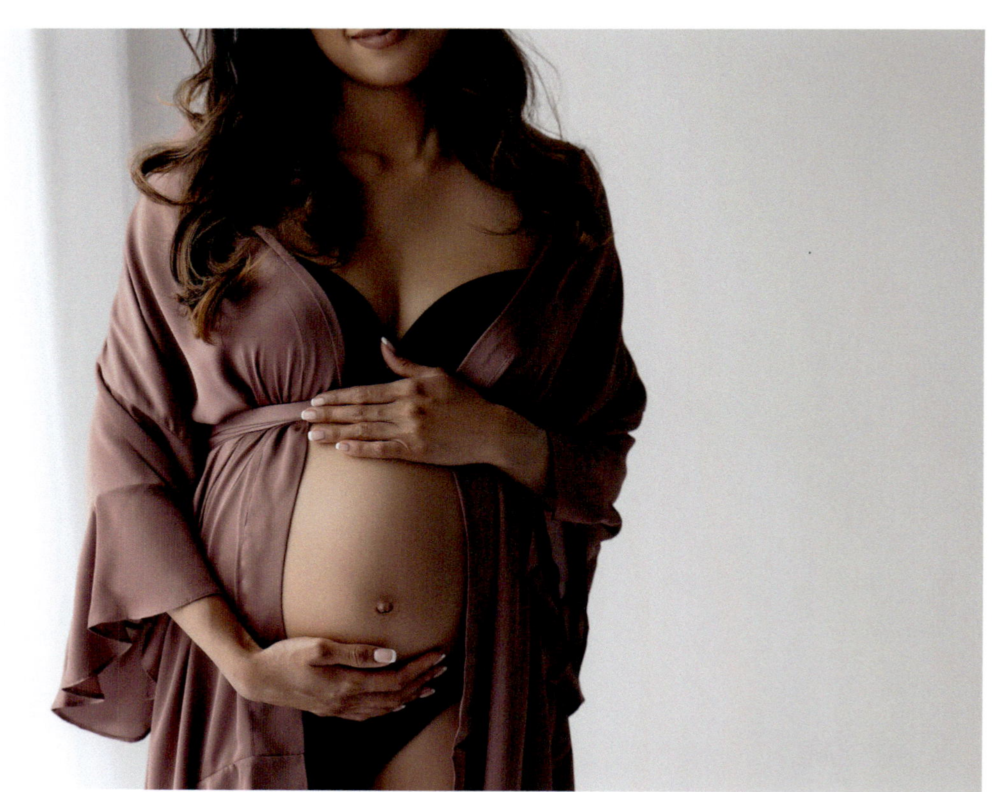

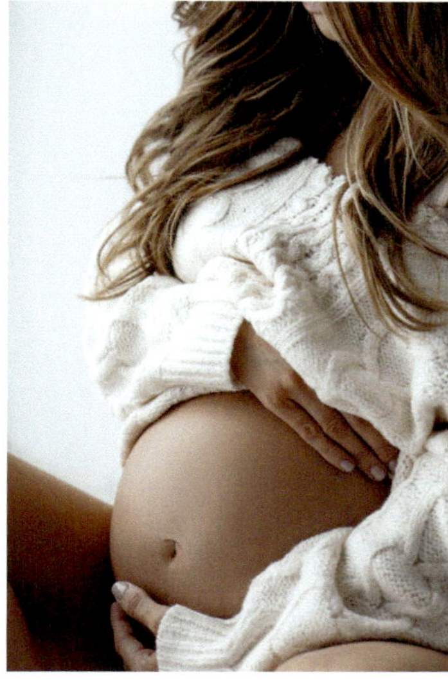

Beautiful maternity photographs are about more than good body positioning. Lens choice, camera angle and crop are also very important. Where each person will need a slightly different combination, some basic rules work for most.

Let's talk about lens distortion. If you have a small space or studio, consider cropping just above knee height instead of using a wide focal length (such as 24mm) and distorting your subject. If you use a wide-angle lens, step back to avoid distortion.

If there are certain parts of the body you would like to give less visual emphasis to, make sure they are further away from your camera. During pregnancy, women can get a little broader around their hips, which they might not want to draw attention to. By asking your subjects to lean forwards slightly and bringing their head and shoulders closer to the camera, the focus will be on their face, making their hips and legs look slimmer.

The angle you shoot from will also make a big difference. If you shoot from a low angle, you will make a person look taller; if you shoot from a high angle, you will make a person look shorter. The focal length and crop will play a part too. If you shoot from a low angle with a wide-angle lens, it will create distortion; the body will look out of proportion, making the images look wrong. However, if you have space and can step back, shooting from a slightly lower angle will make your pregnant mum look a little taller.

When I photograph pregnant clients, I usually photograph them at eye level, and sometimes from slightly below.

Avoid cropping at joints like elbows, wrists, knees and ankles. Also, make sure you don't crop parts off fingers or toes.

Play and experiment with your crops – you don't always have to have the entire head or whole body in your images. I often crop the top of the head off or come in close and crop just above or just below the lip, depending on where I want to direct the viewer's focus and attention. However, know why you are cropping your image in a certain way.

THE MAGIC OF
A WHITE SHIRT

My favourite set-up is very simple: a white wall
with a large window and either underwear and
an oversized shirt or a cardigan or a pair of jeans
with a tank top or sports bra. Select a couple of
base poses, make sure your client is comfortable,
and guide her through flow posing by asking
her to move her arms and gaze. Talk to her to
encourage different expressions and move around
her. Move further away or get closer to create
different crops. Shoot from the side and from the
front. There's no limit to the number of unique
photos you can create with this simple set-up.

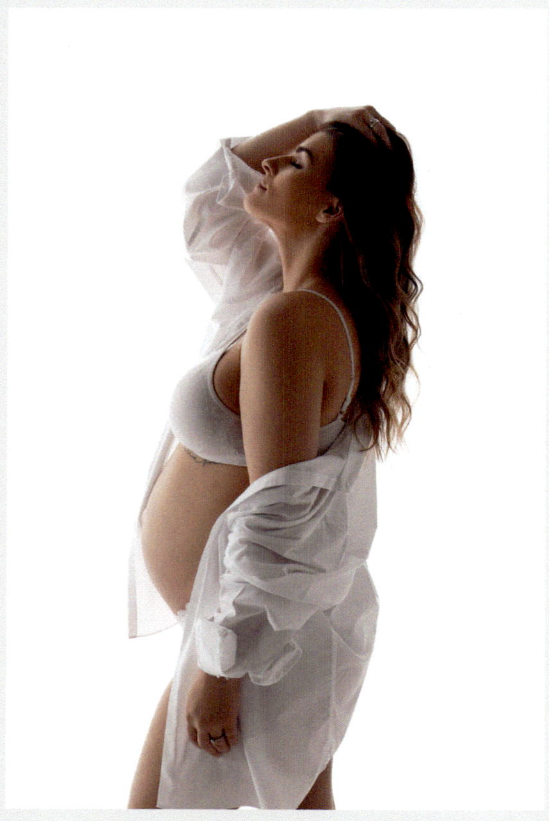

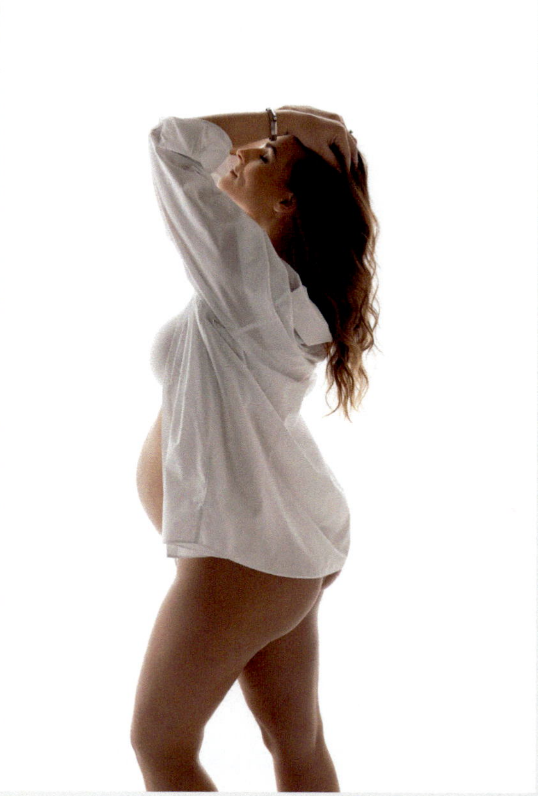

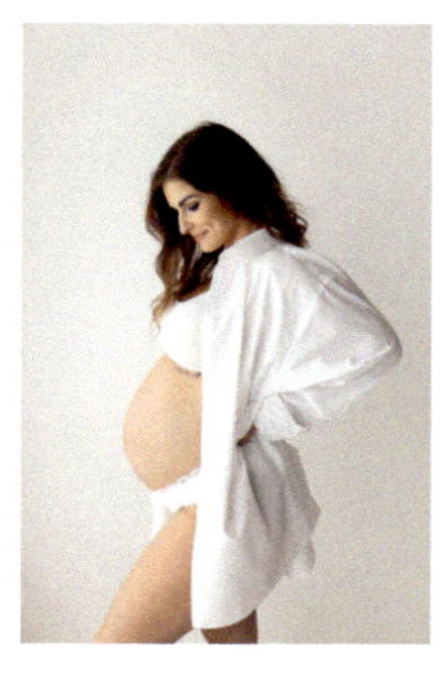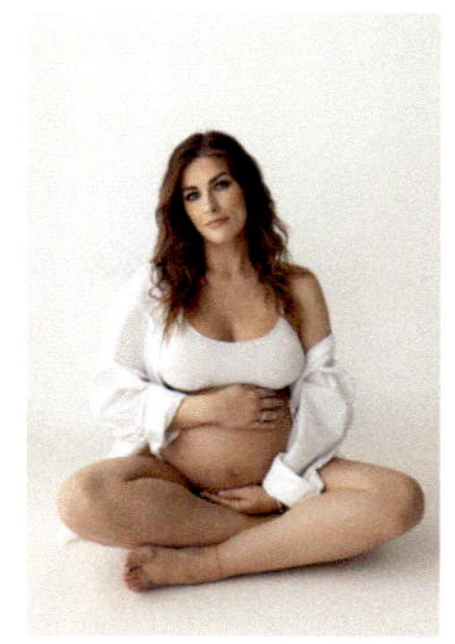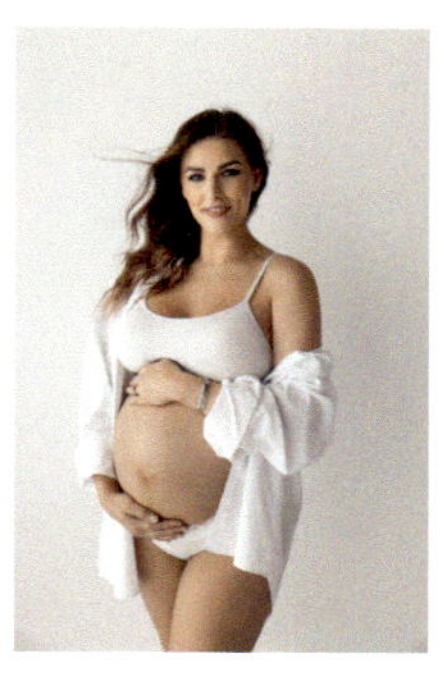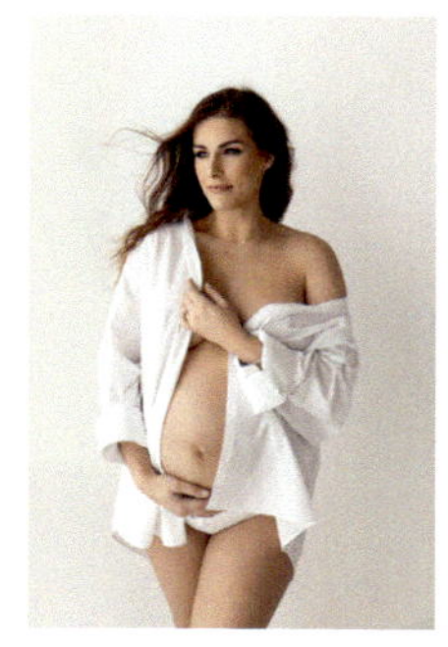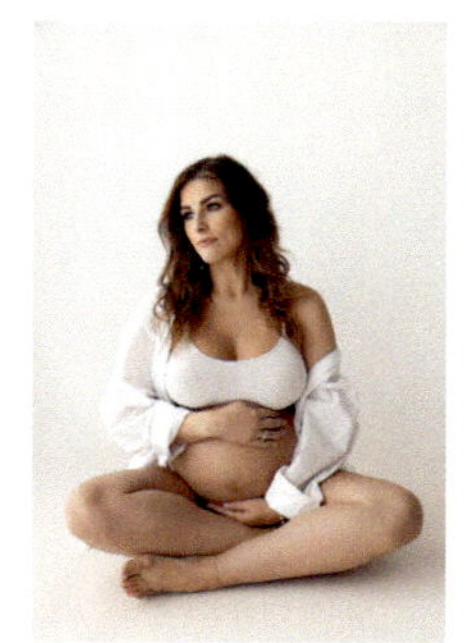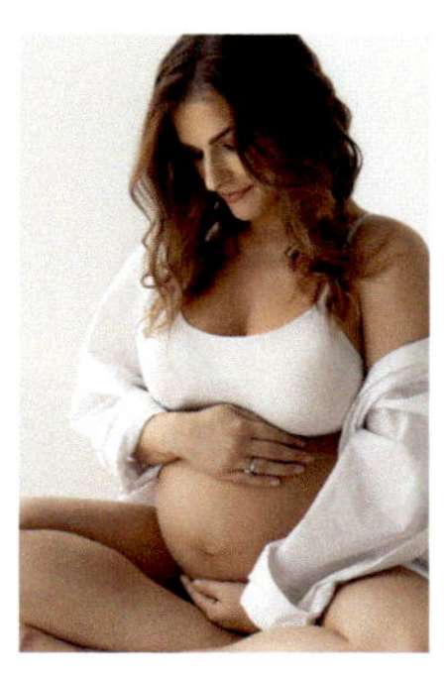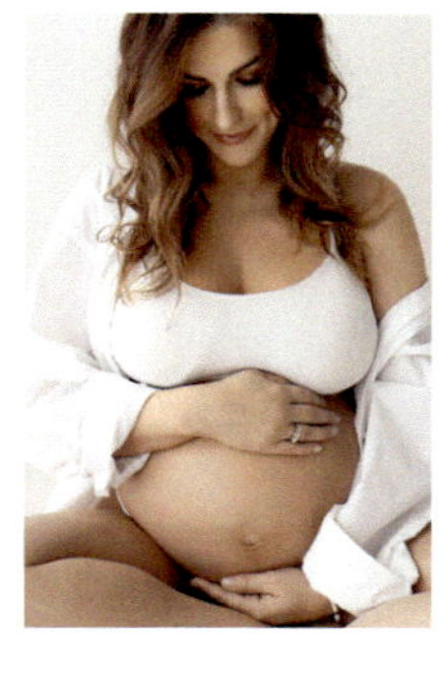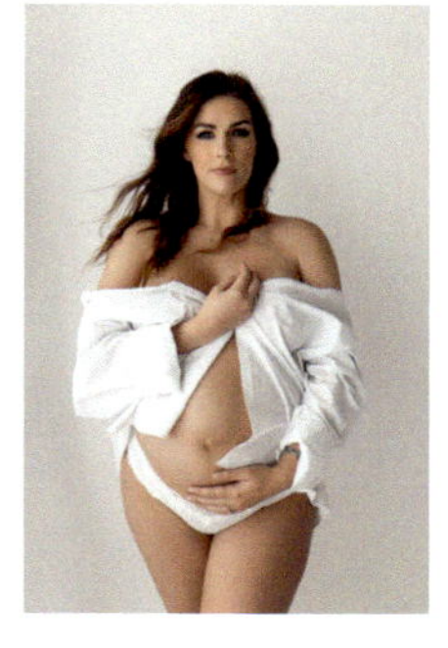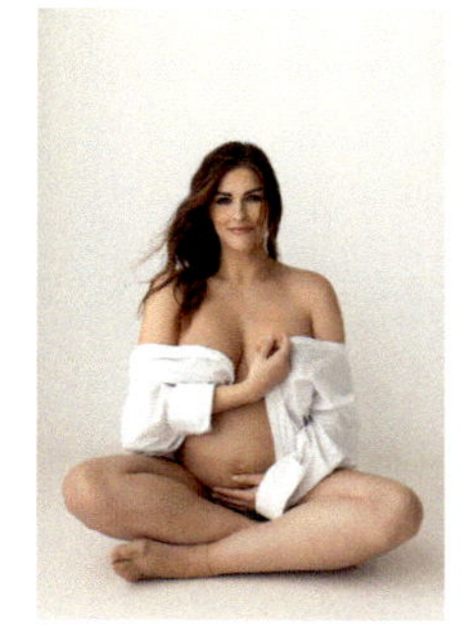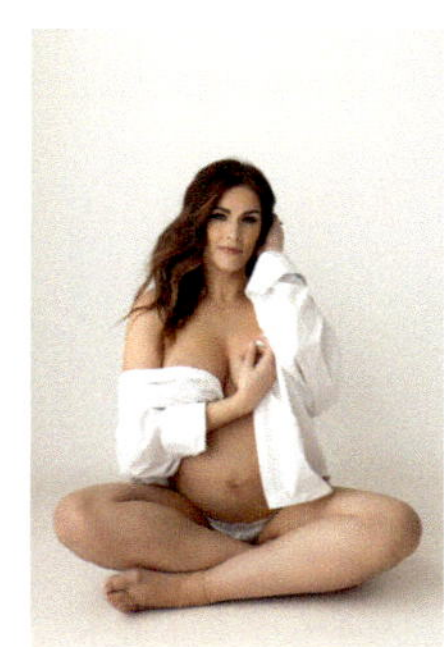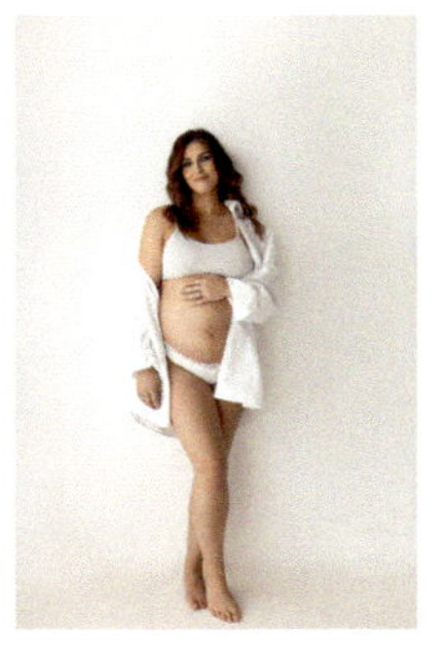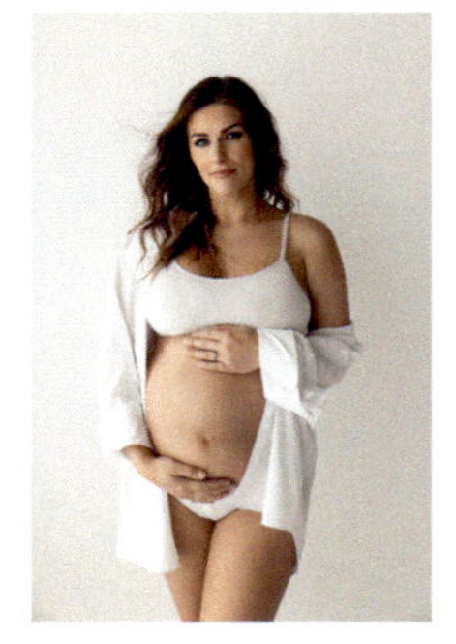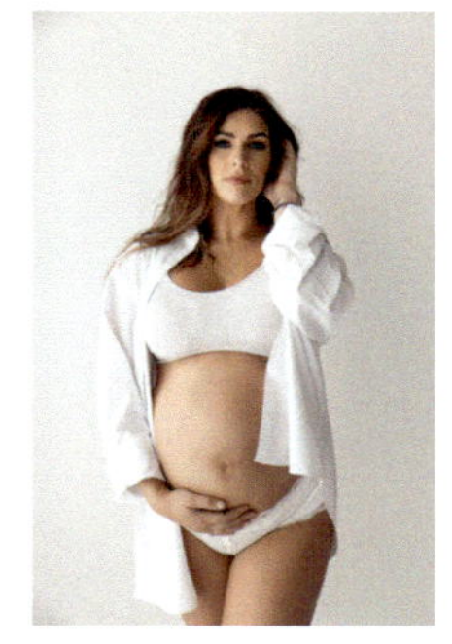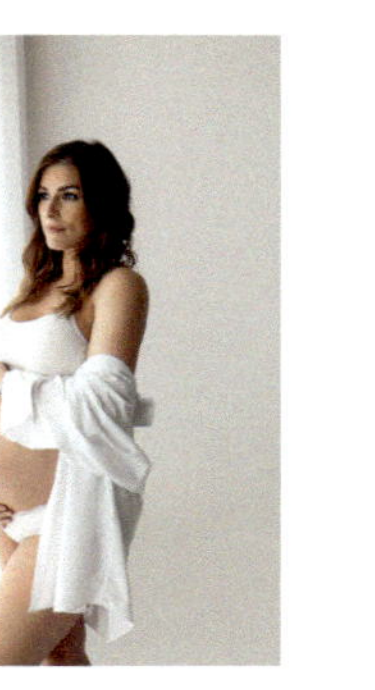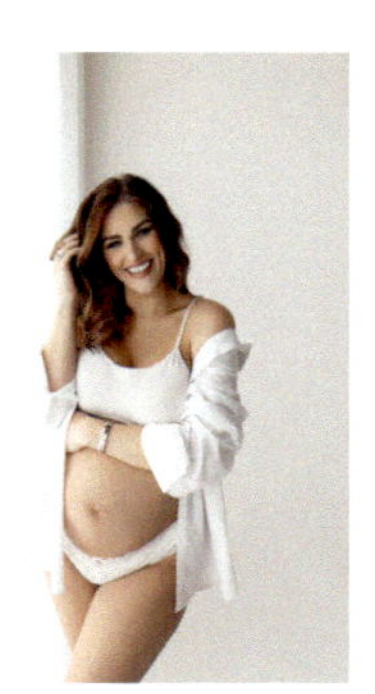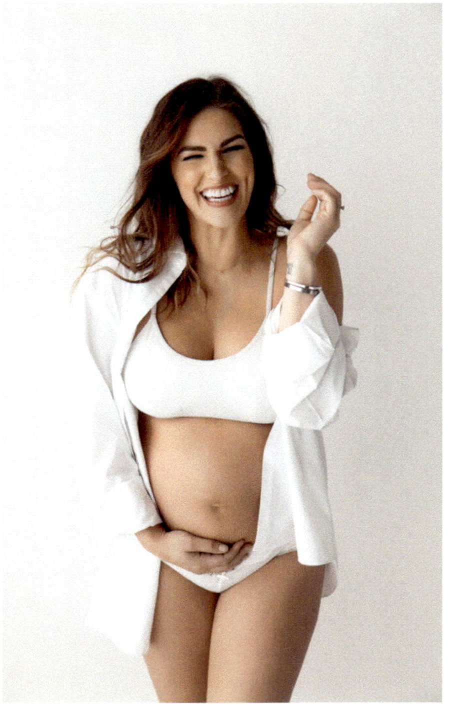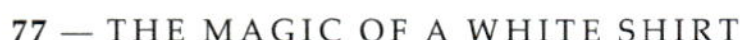

I mostly use natural light during my maternity sessions. However, I use flash if natural light is unavailable or my client wants to create more editorial-style images.

Over the years, I have used many different lights, modifiers and set-ups. It doesn't matter what brand or what kind of lights you use, as long as you know how to use them. Don't forget, the light creates mood and shapes the body.

I used to use an external light meter to measure the light. However, modern digital cameras make life a lot easier, and you can adjust your light by looking at the LCD on the back of your camera.

There are endless ways to light your subject. When I'm feeling creative, I like to play and experiment with the lights. However, during most sessions, I usually use two different light set-ups and try to keep it simple.

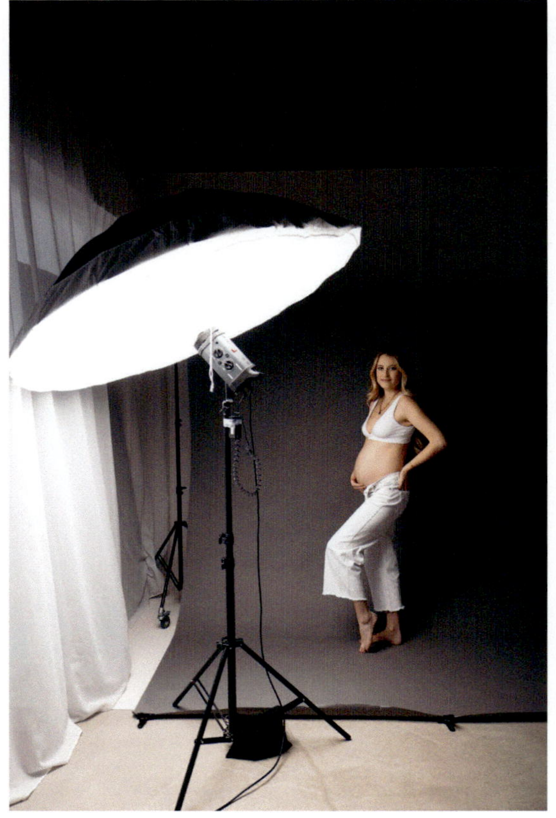
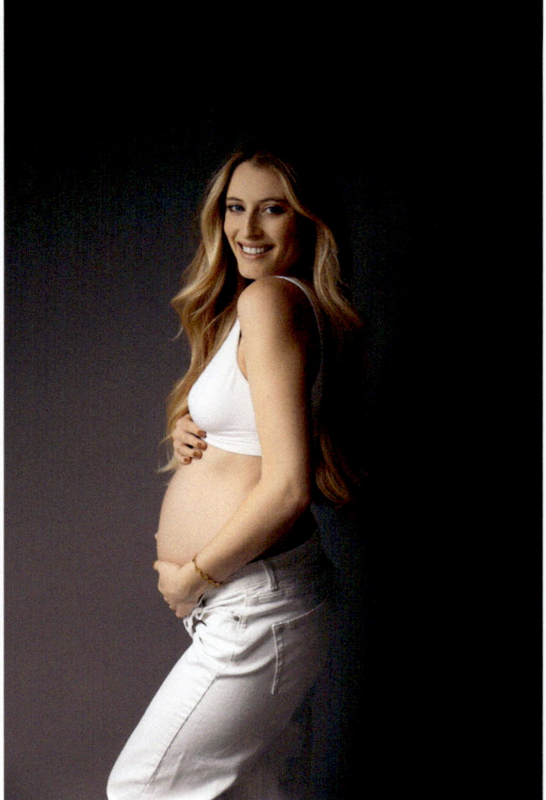

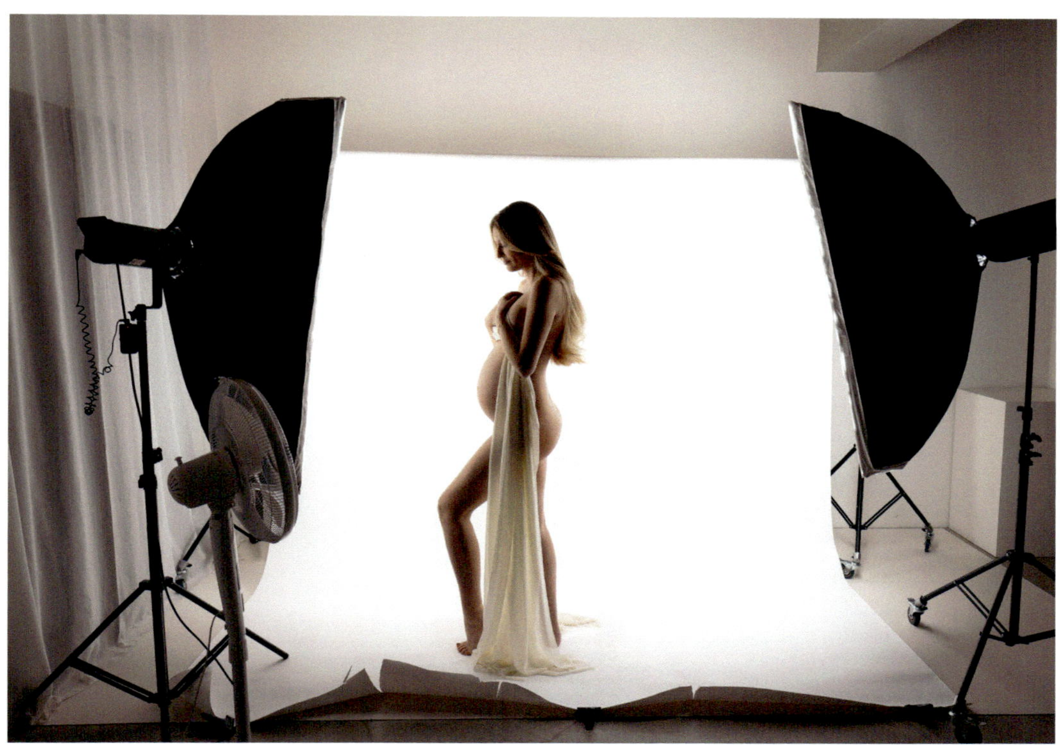

One light

Beautiful results can be achieved with a single
studio light. I mostly use either a wide, reflective
umbrella with a diffuser or a large octabox.
I usually position my light above and slightly
towards the subject's face or side. If my light is to
the side, I place my subject behind it and slowly
move them forwards until the light starts to fall
on their face and body. You can photograph your
subject there, in what is called feathered light,
or ask her to step in front of the light and face
it, which is called direct light. Use a reflector to
soften the shadows if you prefer a softer look.

Backlight

I use this set-up to create silhouettes. Well, sort of
silhouettes – I still like to see a pregnant mother's
face and expression. Depending on how much
light I want on my client's face, I either have two
lights without modifiers aimed at my backdrop or
two lights with tall, narrow softboxes, in the same
line as my subject or a little closer to the camera,
aimed towards the subject.

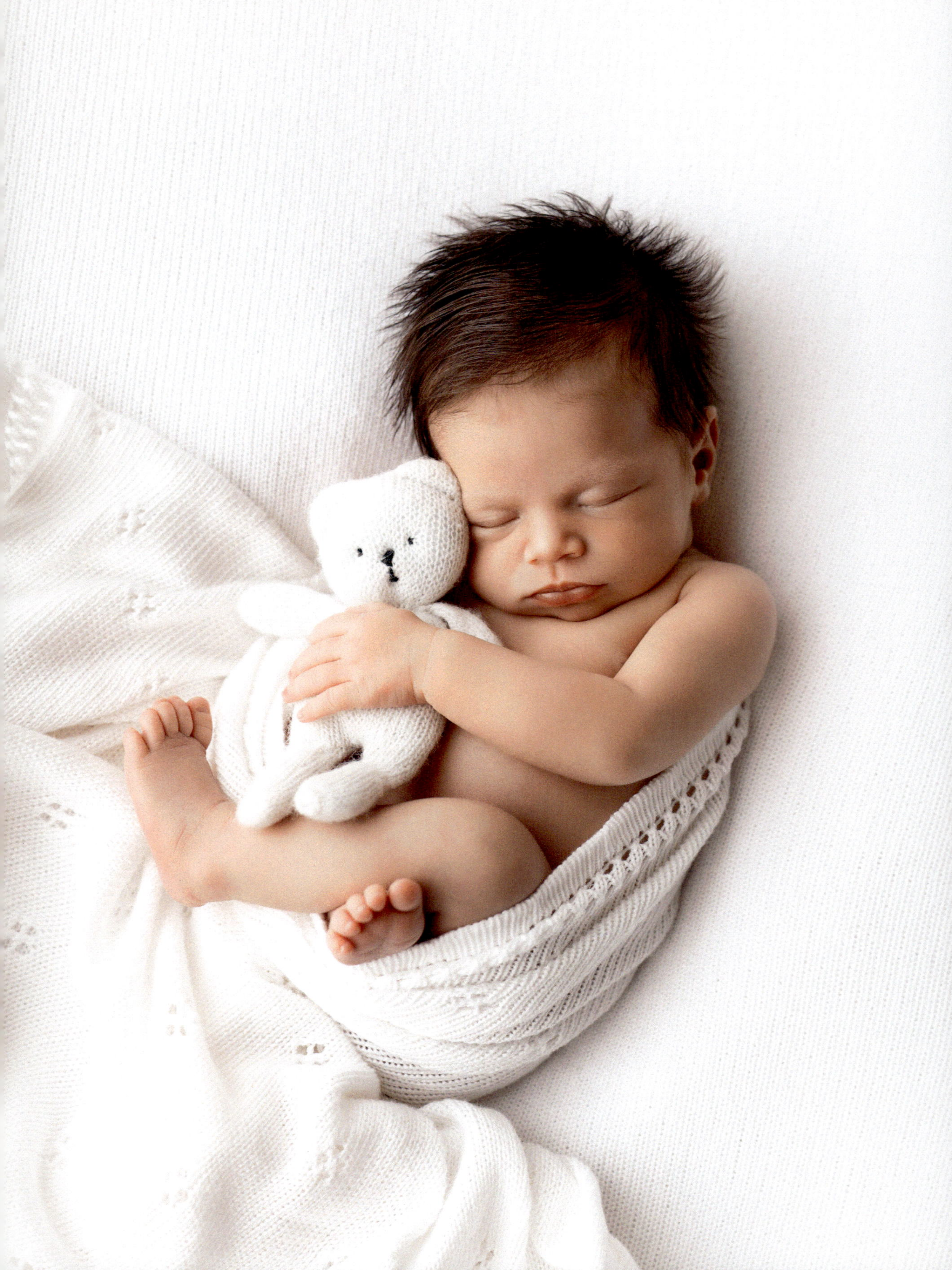

NEWBORN

A unique experience

A newborn baby is an extraordinarily beautiful and most delicate being. They are perfect, pure and the epitome of goodness. Each is unique and created with their little personalities intact from the first minute. They are incredible, miraculous, tiny people loved unconditionally.

No matter your personal style, if you are able to see your subject as a heart and soul, you will be able to create images that connect with your clients and fill their hearts with warmth and the most cherished memories. See the babies that you photograph the same way their parents do – images that speak to your clients on an emotional level are invaluable.

You have the opportunity, as an artist, to create something amazing. Photograph every new life with your heart, and never forget it is a privilege to be trusted to photograph a newborn baby. Document every little detail and help your clients to remember this incredible time in their lives.

Communicating with parents is a vital skill before, during and after the session. This will often be the first photo shoot parents have booked. We as photographers have done this hundreds of times before, and sometimes it is easy to assume that new parents know it all too. However, they seldom do – most of them have no idea what a newborn session is, when it is best to schedule it and what will happen during and after. Also, don't forget the costs and your policies. By communicating with parents before the session about pricing and policies, what to expect (booking, session day, viewing images, etc.), and their expectations, I am able to ensure a smooth and enjoyable experience.

Most of my clients book their newborn sessions while they are still expecting. In my initial email, I explain that newborns are usually photographed during their first few weeks. I usually note their due date and schedule the day of the session when the baby is born. Babies are unpredictable and seldom born on their due date, so I prefer to schedule the actual session date after the birth. If the baby is being delivered by a planned caesarean section, I schedule the session day at the time of booking, usually ten to twelve days after the birth. If mum or baby is unwell, we postpone the session and schedule it when everyone is well and healthy.

Why under two weeks? If you have researched newborn photography, you have most likely heard about the two-week or ten-day 'rule'. Most photographers, especially when starting, have very strict rules on when they photograph a newborn. It has been widely published that a newborn must be under two weeks of age, or it is not possible. However, I don't entirely agree with this.

Yes, you would ideally schedule a session for when the baby is one or two weeks old, while they still sleep a lot and spend a lot of time in a womb-like position. Newborn babies are born with nearly 300 bones (adults have 206 bones). As baby grows, those 300 or so bones start to fuse together into calcified bone, which makes it much harder for them to return to the fetal position. It is much more comfortable for them to be moulded into newborn poses while they still have that flexibility. However, it is important to remember that every baby grows at a different speed. In my experience, most babies retain the curly womb-like position until they are about three weeks old.

I try not to schedule my sessions before a baby is at least five days old. I want my babies and parents to be settled, and they need time to establish some kind of feeding routine. I find that most new parents start feeling less tired and more human about a week after the birth.

Although I prefer to photograph newborns when they are one or two weeks old, I occasionally photograph older babies too. There is a huge difference between two-week-old and two-month-old babies. The latter spend longer periods of time awake, and most importantly, they have lost the fetal curl. With experience, you will still be able to position them in many newborn-like poses. However, there is a possibility that you will not be able to settle the baby. I always tell my clients that the baby will never be this little again and that every age is worth documenting.

Cluster feeding

You can find a lot of information about colostrum and cluster feeding online or in books. If the baby is breastfed, they feed colostrum during the first few days. Mum's milk usually comes on day three or four. Some will say that this is when the baby cluster feeds. In other words, he/she feeds more often than usual. Other sources state that babies have growth spurts and cluster feeds on day ten or fourteen. Personally, I don't think it is possible to predict when a baby will have a growth spurt. As long as a baby is five days old, I don't worry about other potential cluster-feeding dates when scheduling the session.

Premature babies

Premature is defined as babies born before 37
weeks of pregnancy. Most babies born after 37
weeks are fully developed and not classed as
premature. I schedule these sessions when a baby
is between ten and fourteen days old. If the baby
is born before 37 weeks, I wait until the baby has
gone home and settled into a routine. If everyone
is healthy, I typically schedule premature baby
sessions a week after they've come home.

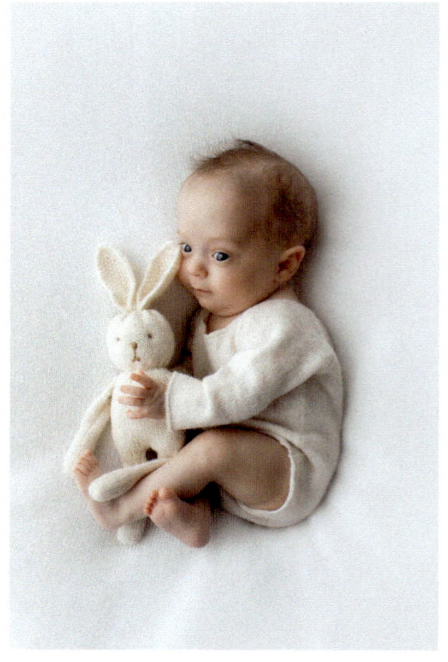

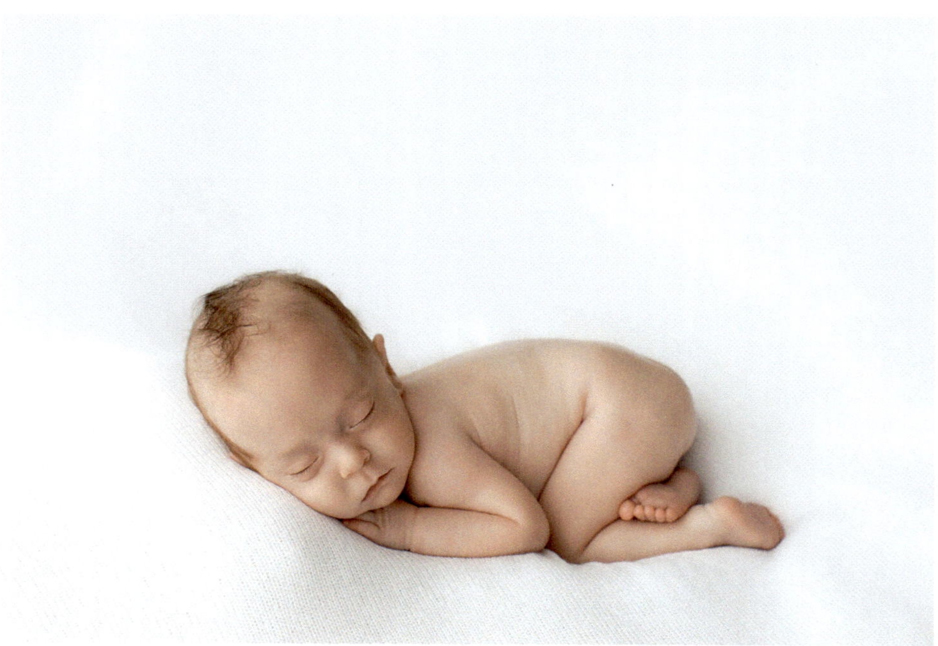

Meet Hugo, born at 26 weeks and photographed when he was five months old.

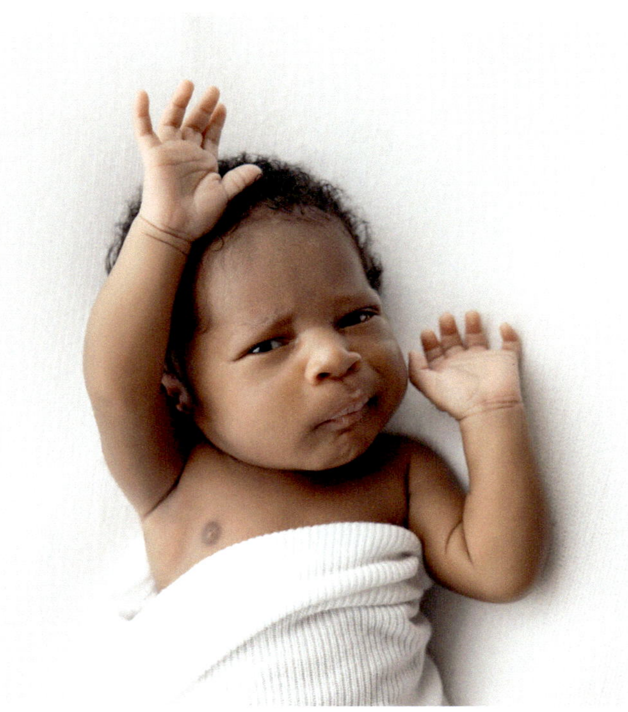

Time of day

I try to schedule my newborn sessions in the morning. Babies are often unsettled at night and very sleepy in the morning. If I have two sessions in one day, I usually schedule my first session at 9 a.m. and the second just after midday. Clients with older children that go to school often ask if they can have their session late afternoon. The latest I would schedule a newborn session is 1.30 p.m., as babies usually become more unsettled as the day progresses. Have you ever heard of the 'witching hour'? It is a time when an otherwise content baby is extremely fussy and unsettled. The witching hour usually starts in the late afternoon, so you want to ensure you have finished photographing well before then.

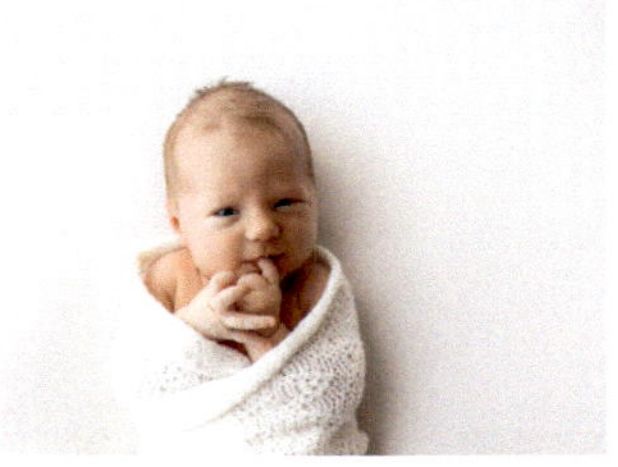

TIP

If you are at the beginning of your journey as a newborn photographer, I recommend scheduling your sessions in the morning if the baby is eight to nine days old.

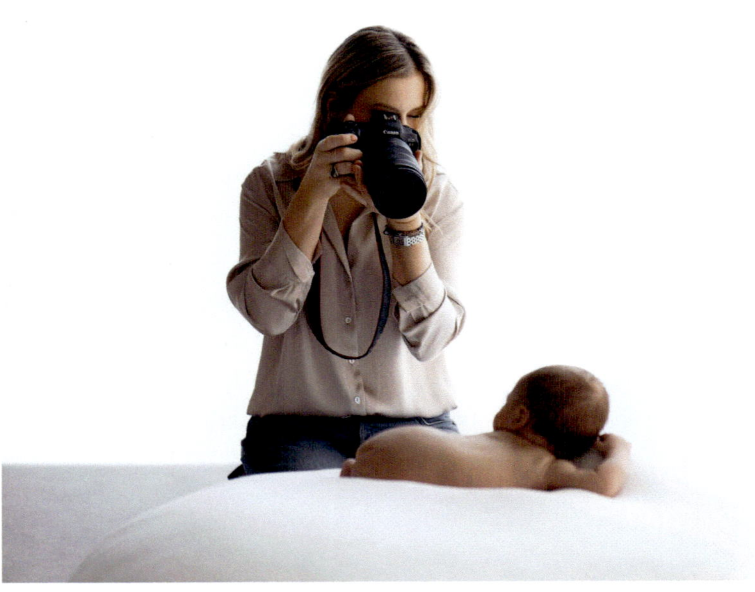

Session length

Most of my sessions last two to three hours. It usually takes me 30 to 45 minutes to photograph a baby on his/her own and a similar amount of time with parents. If there is an older brother or sister who is not too keen on being photographed, family and sibling images might take slightly longer. I find that three hours gives plenty of time to photograph, feed, soothe and comfort the baby. Lot of photographers spend four to five hours on newborn sessions. In my opinion, this is way too long, as everyone will get bored and overwhelmed.

How to prepare and what to bring

Client preparation is essential for a smooth session. Unless your clients have had a newborn session before, they will have no idea what to bring and what to expect. The more you prepare your client, the easier the session will be and the better experience your clients will have. A few days before the session, I send a short email with clear instructions explaining how to find the studio, where to park, how to prepare and what to bring. If you prefer, you can post them a printed guide. I like to keep my communication emails short and clear – the longer an email is, the less chance people will read it. Most parents experience sleep deprivation, emotional adjustments and all the other demands that come with a new baby. They are already worried if their baby will be fussy and if he/she will wee or poo everywhere. I don't like to put any additional stress on parents before their session. I want them to be relaxed and enjoy the time they spend with me, so I keep my preparation list as short as possible.

MY PRE-SHOOT PREPARATION LIST FOR CLIENTS

1. I ask my clients to feed their babies to a very full tummy just before leaving home. If they mix breast and formula feeding, I ask them to formula-feed their baby before leaving. I aim to start photographing as soon as the baby arrives, and often, the baby begins to get hungry as I finish the shoot. Sometimes, the baby can get hungry halfway through the shoot, and sometimes they need to feed more than once. Remember, newborns are unpredictable and every baby is different. Some photographers prefer to feed the baby upon arrival; see what works best for you.

2. Wear comfortable, lightweight clothes. The studio is very warm to make sure the baby is comfortable.

3. Bring a change of clothes in case of accidents.

4. Bring a few extra nappies.

5. Bring an extra feed if the baby is bottle-fed.

6. Bring a pacifier. Some parents might be reluctant to use one. However, I always say even if they are not planning to use one going forwards, a dummy can sometimes work magic and can be a great help to settle the baby, especially for those babies that are light sleepers or have a strong sucking instinct.

7. Dress the baby in a front-opening baby grow. I want to be able to easily undress him/her and not disturb the baby if it arrives asleep.

You can also ask your client to try to keep their baby awake for an hour or two before the session – this might give you more chances of a baby being sleepier. However, if you give too many instructions to the new parents, you will stress them out and they simply won't follow them.

After I greet, congratulate and welcome the parents to my studio, I briefly explain the plan for the day. There are a lot of 'ifs' when it comes to newborn photography, and it is not easy to predict or control it. I always ask parents a few questions:

- Is baby breast- or bottle-fed?
- When did the baby feed last?
- How often does the baby usually feed?

Once I know the answers, I can guess when the baby will feed next and have some kind of plan.

I offer parents tea, coffee or water and suggest they sit back and relax while I take care of their baby. I further communicate that it is their time to relax and that I will let them know if I need their help. When clients are with me, I want to take care of the baby as much as I possibly can.

If the newborn arrives in a car seat or pram, I am the one that gets him/her out so that their sleep isn't disrupted. I undress and swaddle the baby in a blanket; if the baby has a dirty nappy, I clean and change it. If the baby is bottle-fed, I feed the baby. I wind both breast- and bottle-fed babies myself. If the baby is unsettled, I explain the benefits of being the one to soothe the little one. I always remain calm to make sure the baby is settled and the parents are relaxed.

Most issues and concerns can be resolved before they happen by effectively communicating with parents prior to the session.

Creating the right environment

From the moment a client steps into your studio, you want them to feel both welcome and secure in bringing their baby there. My studio is always warm and clean and smells of lavender to instantly create a feeling of calm; I aim to create an almost spa-like experience for my clients.

If you can achieve this despite the inevitable challenges, your client will feel this way as well. Having calm and joyful parents will greatly improve your chances of having a calm baby.

Paint your walls with warm and embracing colours – light neutral colours or a simple white will create a welcoming atmosphere and be a perfect space to photograph in.

Inside the studio, I have a comfortable sofa that parents can use to sit on and relax, and watch while I photograph their baby. Mum can also use this area to feed.

I also have a little drinks and snacks station, where clients can help themselves to tea, coffee, bottled water and snacks. Newborn sessions can take a while, and keeping everyone comfortable and entertained dramatically enhances the experience.

Often, a newborn baby will arrive not just with parents but also with a big brother or sister. Siblings often get bored very quickly, so I have a few basic toys, such as blocks, wooden toys and books. The toys I keep are fun yet a little boring, so when it is the siblings' turn for pictures, they happily leave the toys behind.

The perfect environment must be created for the newborn baby to fall into a deep enough sleep, which is essential for posing. Baby's former 'home' was a balmy 35–37°C (95–99°F). Although I keep my studio warm, it is not sweltering. Instead of heating the entire room, I usually have a small heater pointing at my beanbag and blowing pleasantly warm air towards the baby. This way, the baby stays warm, and the parents don't get too hot. When wrapped in a blanket, babies are being held by parents, so I turn my fan heater off. I don't want anyone to get uncomfortable and overheated.

White noise is another way to create a peaceful setting. You can use a small speaker, your phone or a special machine. The womb is a very loud place, so replicating that volume is great for sleep. White noise reduces background noise and also aids in relaxing newborns. Also, having this extra noise allows the parents to feel freer to talk and chat with me without waking the baby, which leads to a better connection with my clients and a more relaxed environment for everyone.

While creating a perfect environment is a necessary factor for keeping a baby content and happy, the most essential component to a successful newborn session is the level of confidence the photographer has in handling newborns. A great deal of patience and hands-on experience is the only way to master this skill. Like a tiny shark and the scent of blood, babies can smell stress. If you are unsure what you are doing, and there is stress or irritation in the air, then babies will cry and fuss. Knowing how to handle newborns will not only help you manoeuvre your subject into eye-pleasing positions but will also help put apprehensive parents at ease.

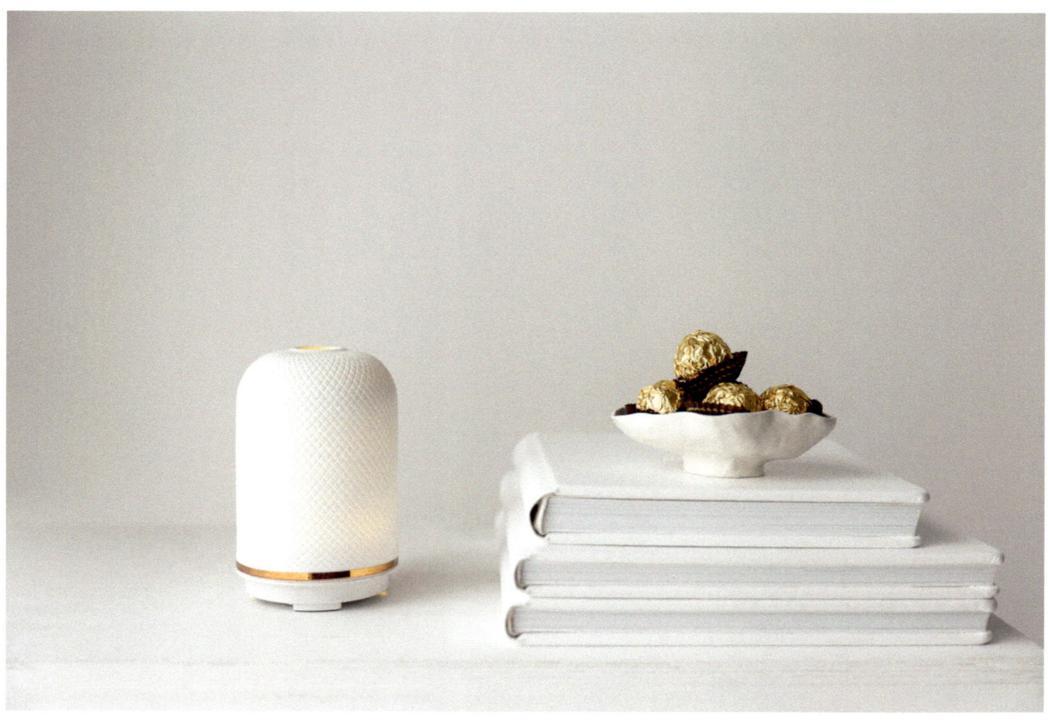

Style a newborn shoot the same way you would put together an outfit. If you have a clear idea of your style, as discussed in the previous chapter, it will be much easier to style a session.

I am very picky about background fabrics, blankets, wraps, headbands and clothing items. I like to create timeless images and keep the attention on the baby, so I use white, cream or neutral colours. I mix and layer different textures to add interest to my photographs. If I use a smooth backdrop fabric, I might swaddle the baby in a knitted woollen blanket with a lot of texture or frayed edges.

Choose fabrics that suit your style in terms of pattern, colour tones and textures. Whatever colour or style you decide to use, make sure your chosen colours work nicely together.

I look for blankets, scarves (you can use them as a swaddle) and accessories everywhere, not only in newborn photography prop shops but also home stores, secondhand shops, general clothing stores and fabric shops. The first question I always ask myself when I find something is, does it suit my brand, and does it complement items that I already have? I buy it if the answer is yes.

Talking about buying, it is very easy to get carried away when shopping for newborn props. I buy new stuff only when I need it, to replace something that has perished or, if I absolutely love the item, whether it is a blanket, headband or newborn outfit.

I like to use small pillows and cushions during my sessions. Parents are always welcome to bring a little toy with them, but if they don't, I also have a few cute toys at the studio that I use.

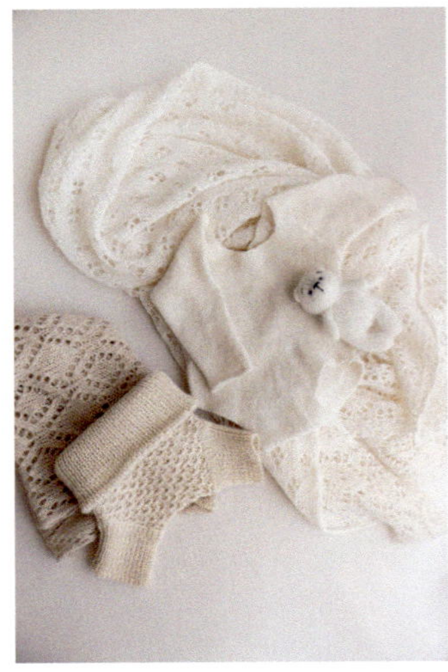

I seldom use props like baskets or buckets during my newborn shoots. I only have a handful of baskets, vessels or posing cushions, all complementing my brand and style. If a client requests it, I am happy to use it. I usually go through fazes when it comes to props. If I am in my prop-using faze, I still take most of my images on a beanbag and use only one basket during a shoot. I'd never like my session gallery to resemble a catalogue of various newborn props, and I recommend you avoid it too.

Don't feel that you need every prop out there to become a great photographer. There was a time in my career when I thought if I could only have this particular blanket, outfit or bucket, I could create the most amazing images. I know many photographers feel this way, but we all know that a specific prop will not improve your work.

When choosing a prop to photograph a newborn in, I recommend keeping it simple and, most importantly, safe. Never use anything made of glass or other material that can break and harm the baby. Avoid anything that has sharp edges or wicker poking out. If a prop is lightweight,

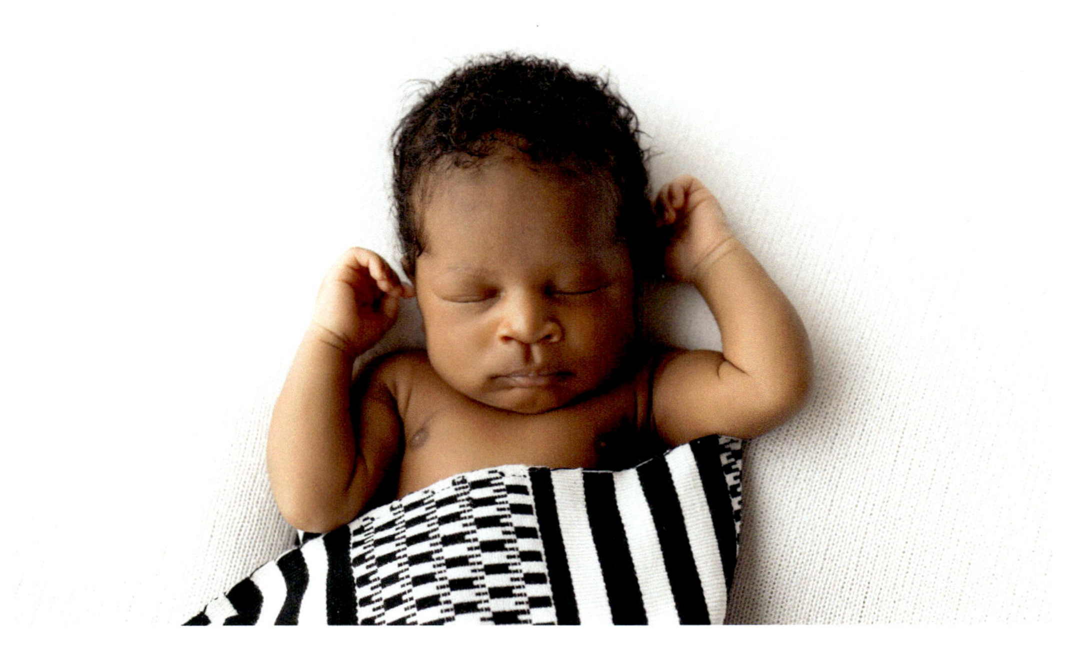

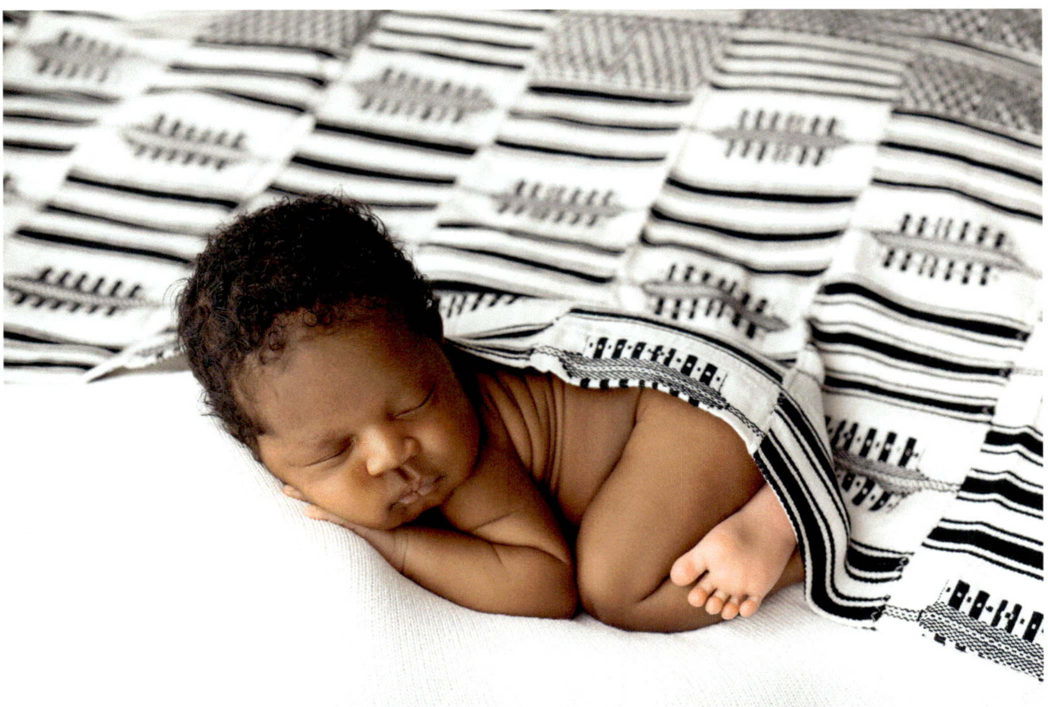

Baby wrapped up in a Kente cloth that my clients brought to their session.

put a weight at the bottom to prevent it from tipping. Large baskets or bowls, wooden crates, tree stumps and traditional baby items like Moses baskets and small beds are all great to use as props. Ensure that a prop is large enough for a newborn baby, and never leave the baby unattended in a prop. Baby's safety must be your top priority at all times.

My clients occasionally bring a special item that they would like to be photographed. This can be anything from a sentimental blanket, toy or jewellery to a silly outfit. If the item doesn't complement my style or brand, I try to convince my clients not to use it. However, if these shots must be taken, then I will take them, but they will not appear on my website or social media.

Most of the time, I love the items my clients bring – they often have a story and a special meaning. I feel honoured that clients trust me and often share very personal and intimate stories with me. One of my clients brought a Kente cloth to their session. Kente cloth is a handwoven cloth, and its colours and design have a special meaning. The cloth is worn by kings, queens and other important figures in Ghana. I loved being educated, hearing its history and finding out its importance to my client. Conversations like this make this job very interesting and also build a beautiful relationship between me and my clients.

Safety first – anatomy & safe practice

Baby safety should always be your first priority, and everything must be done to ensure that the baby is safe while you are photographing him/her. Whether you are photographing a baby on a beanbag, in a prop or with parents or siblings, safety should come above any pose or shot. I treat my babies with respect, and you must too. I try to stick to poses and props that are simple.

I never leave a baby unattended when posed, whether on a beanbag, in a prop or with siblings. I always stay close and never take my eyes off the baby. If I need to look away to pick up my camera, I place my hand on the baby to make sure he/she is safe. If I have to walk away, I always ask the parents to sit by the baby.

Clients sometimes collect ideas for the newborn shoot from Pinterest, other websites or social media. If you are uncomfortable with the pose or the prop, say 'no'. To say 'no' and be safe is much better than regretting it later. Sometimes, even a baby that looks sound asleep can startle and move, so always be ready for that rapid movement.

Although no amount of money will help if something goes wrong, make sure you are insured.

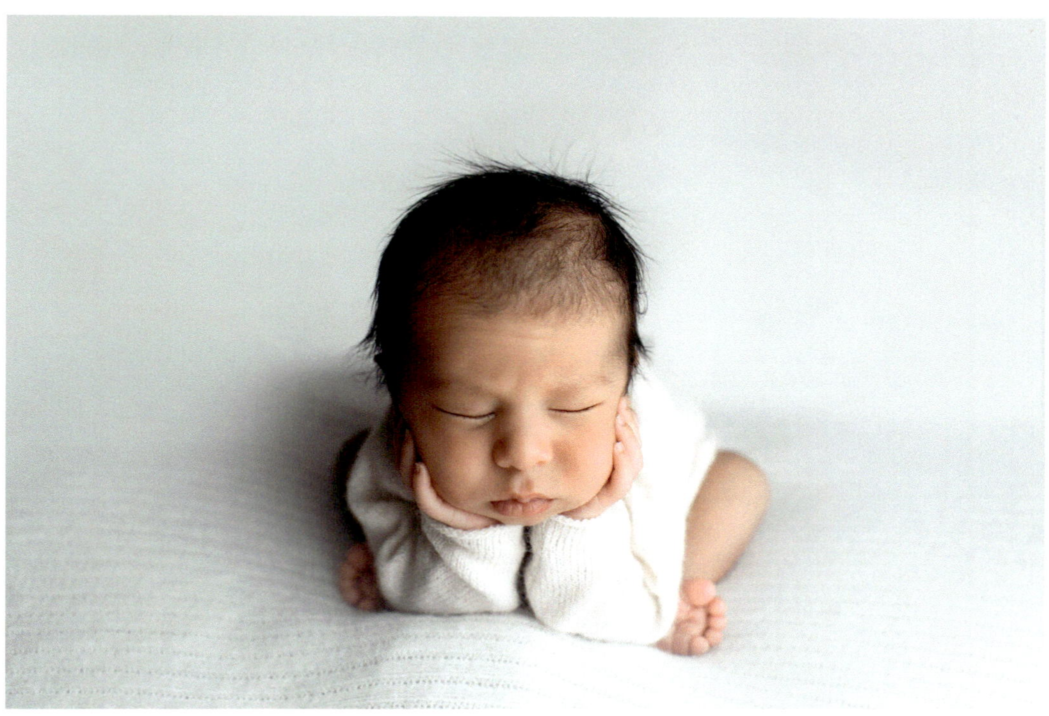

This image was created by merging two images into one in post-production.

COMPOSITE IMAGES

Many parents and beginner photographers do not realize that specific images are created by combining several frames into one in post-production. These images are called composites. The baby is supported throughout the entire set-up, and parents' or assistants' hands are removed in post-production. I can't stress enough how important it is to know how to create images safely. A pose where a baby is 'sitting' and resting his/her head in their hands, also called a 'froggy' pose, is not what you see in the end result.

Do not attempt complicated poses if you don't know how to do it or are uncomfortable. You need to have a lot of experience and be very comfortable in posing to do this safely. I only shoot complicated poses like this on request – they are not part of my regular flow. I also explain to the parents that most babies are uncomfortable – they fuss and wriggle when positioned in these poses. If I see that the baby is uncomfortable at any stage, I move on to the next pose. Baby's comfort and safety is my top priority.

ANATOMY OF A NEWBORN

To become a successful newborn photographer, you must learn how to handle babies. Knowing how to handle and 'feel' the baby will help you pose them with ease. Try to learn as much as possible about newborns – practice and experience will also help. A session's success will depend on your understanding of the baby's cues and your ability to soothe and handle them securely.

Babies are little humans, and their temperaments and behaviour vary. Some babies are more relaxed, and some are a little more dramatic. Even a baby's cry is different. Some have a 'sweet' cry, some loud and intense. You must learn how to understand them and ensure they are safe to have a successful session and happy parents.

HERE ARE A FEW THINGS TO HELP YOU LEARN MORE ABOUT NEWBORN BABIES AND HAVE YOUR SESSIONS GO SMOOTHLY

1. **Temperature**. Babies cannot regulate their body temperature; therefore, the room must be warm. I use a fan heater that blows warm air on the baby. Babies get cold in the same way they can get overheated, so make sure your fan isn't too close and isn't overheating or even burning the baby's skin. Monitor the baby's temperature throughout the session. If the baby is naked, you might need the room to be a little warmer. If the baby is dressed or wrapped up in a blanket, you might need to turn your heater off. I often keep turning my heater on and off during my newborn sessions. If the baby's hands and feet are cold or the skin is blotchy or pale with a blue or purple shade, the baby might be too cold. If the baby is sweating or getting red, he/she might be too hot. Keep the baby warm, but not too cold or too hot.

2. **Immune system**. Although the newborn baby will have some immunity from his/her mother, ensure you are well. If I have a cold, I always reschedule my sessions and never risk anyone's health. It might be obvious, but make sure your nails and hands are clean, and sanitize them throughout the session.

3. **Skin**. Baby's skin is very sensitive. You will often see babies with flaky and peeling skin. I don't have any lotions or baby oils at the studio - I leave it to parents to decide if they want to apply something or not.

4. **Circulation**. Continually monitor the baby's circulation. If you notice the baby's hands or feet turning purple or dark red, you must reposition the baby. If you are wrapping or swaddling the baby, ensure the wrap isn't too tight or restricting airflow, and the baby can breathe comfortably.

5. **Jaundice**. If a baby has jaundice, his/her skin and eyes will have a yellow shade – this is caused by bilirubin. If a baby is severely jaundiced, they will stay in a hospital a little longer; if it is mild, they will come home. If the levels of bilirubin are low and the baby is allowed to go home, you shouldn't worry about the yellow skin – you can fix the shade in post-production.

6. **The startle reflex is an involuntary startle response called the Moro reflex**. A loud noise or a sudden movement might make the baby suddenly extend their arms and legs or arch their back. Try to maintain a calm environment and ensure the baby is safe and secure at all times; swaddling will be a good idea if the baby startles a lot. When moving or handling babies, hold their limbs while applying gentle pressure to help them feel safe – this will calm the baby and prevent startling.

7. **Hip dysplasia**. If a baby has been diagnosed with hip dysplasia, they will be required to wear a hip brace. You can either reschedule the session, photograph babies in a less posed way or have them held by parents.

8. **Overstimulation**. If the baby has been passed around a lot or has been in a noisy and crowded environment, it can get tired and irritated. Create a calm space for the baby and soothe him/her to sleep. Wait for the baby to fall into a deep sleep before you start photographing him/her.

9. **Rooting and sucking**. Baby is hungry if he/she starts turning its head to the sides trying to find something or starts sucking his/her fists. In this situation, I usually feed the baby right away – I don't wait until the baby starts crying for food.

10. **Colic is when a baby cries a lot, but there's no obvious reason for it**. It often happens towards the end of the day. No one knows the reason for it – some think it's due to digestive problems, and some think it is caused by overstimulation.

Crying baby

A cry is a baby's way of communicating with us; it's his/her way of telling us they are unhappy. Most babies cry for almost three hours a day. Some babies cry more and louder than others, and some babies fuss and whinge more than they cry. You must learn to understand why baby cries and try to recognize different cry types.

As soon as my clients arrive, I start observing the baby and reading the baby's body language. I spend some time cuddling the baby to familiarize myself and to see how the baby responds to my touch and movement. I also pay attention to the baby's body language and facial expressions during the session. Looking at the baby's face, you can often see that they are about to start fussing or crying. I never wait until the baby cries – I gently tap their back or rock to soothe them before they cry.

HERE ARE THE MOST COMMON REASONS WHY A BABY CRIES

- Hunger is the most common reason.
- Overstimulation and being overwhelmed. Babies need to sleep; if the baby is too tired, they need to be comforted and rocked to sleep.
- Wind or tummy ache. Rubbing and patting their back to bring up a burp will usually solve the problem.
- Cold or heat. As mentioned earlier, babies like to be warm, but not too cold or hot.
- Pain. If the baby is unwell or in serious pain, parents need to speak to their doctor.
- Stress. Babies pick up on our emotions, so if you're feeling stressed, baby can feel unsettled. Take a deep breath and calm down.

- Inexperienced photographer. If you are moving the baby too much and not letting the baby settle, the baby will cry. Baby will also cry if their limbs aren't held, and can kick or move around freely, unsettling them and prompting a startle reflex. It can also be that the baby doesn't like the position in which you are trying to place them; maybe he/she is uncomfortable.

It doesn't matter why the baby cries, make sure to soothe the baby as soon as possible. A crying baby will also unsettle and upset new parents, and you might lose their trust.

Full tummy

A full tummy is essential – I can't stress this enough. Once the baby is fed and full, they doze off and usually fall into a deep sleep. They are relaxed, which makes the session go smoothly and quickly. Have you heard of the saying 'milk drunk'? Well, you want your babies to be milk drunk. Some photographers dread photographing breastfed babies, but if the baby is full, it will be happy, however it is fed. Often, when a baby is breastfed, it dozes off before he/she is full, and this is why they wake up easily and have to go back to mum for more milk after a few minutes. To make sure a breastfed baby has a good feed, ask mum to tickle the baby's feet, move the baby's arm or wind the baby. I'd rather wait an hour for a baby to have a full feed than have the baby snack every ten minutes. This also gives me the opportunity to relax and chat with the parents.

Settling & soothing

Newborn sessions go much smoother if the baby is asleep, and the variety of images you can achieve is much greater. However, as discussed earlier, babies can be fussy for all sorts of reasons. When working through a fussy period, patience is incredibly important. The first thing I do is feed and burp baby and always ensure they are warm enough. If the baby is still upset after addressing the main potential issues, you can try a few different approaches. Firstly, remain calm. If you are stressed, the baby will feed off your stress, and mum and dad won't trust you with their baby. I am usually a lot better at soothing babies than parents. I am calm and don't tense when a baby fusses or cries. I'm generally much better at reading a baby's body language too. Remember, babies are very intuitive and sensitive to their parents' emotions. They can also smell their mum from a few meters away. Sometimes, having the peaceful presence of an outside person can make all the difference.

I always try a few methods to calm a fussy baby. One approach doesn't necessarily work for every newborn, but one or a combination of techniques will usually do the trick for most.

- Swaddle (preferably in something that can be photographed if they fall asleep). Wrapping or swaddling can miraculously calm a fussy baby. Keep the baby resting on your shoulder or lay them in your arms, curl their legs up and gently sway. Curled-up legs can sometimes make all the difference. If the baby is already swaddled, check it isn't too hot or swaddled too tight.
- Sway, gently bounce or rock the baby. Each baby is different, so you might need to find what works best. Babies love motion, and they will soon close their eyes and fall asleep.
- Gently stroke the baby's forehead from the top of their head down.

- Come closer to the window or the light. Babies' eyes are very sensitive, so if you bring them closer to the light, they will most likely close their eyes and fall asleep.
- Pacifier or dummy. Some babies have a very strong sucking instinct and sucking calms the nervous system. Therefore, a pacifier can work magic. I do ask my clients to bring one to their session and explain that it can comfort the baby. However, some parents may not want their baby to use it, and if that's the case, you must abide by their wishes.
- Shushing or white noise. Life in the womb is loud, and a shushing or white noise machine can work wonders. I always have my 'shusher' on during a newborn session. It not only soothes the baby but also prevents the baby from being startled by environmental noises.

I'm often asked if I've ever had a baby that wouldn't settle. In my professional career, I have never had to reschedule a session because the baby was unsettled. At first, it took me more time to settle the baby, and I would disturb the baby more often when posing. With practice, I learned how to read a baby's body language and gently guide them into a comfortable position, and I mastered burping and soothing. If you are at the beginning of your career and the baby cannot be comforted or settled, offer to reschedule the session. If the baby is constantly crying and unsettled, everyone will get stressed – you, the parents and the baby. Don't ever imply that it is the baby's fault. Babies don't have to perform or behave for you. Don't be discouraged – it takes time to master the craft of newborn photography.

Knowing how to light your subject is crucial. Whether you are using natural or artificial light, you must master your light to create professional images. There are a few different lighting styles that I use during my sessions.

Most of my newborn sessions are photographed using my large floor-to-ceiling window. I schedule most of my sessions in the morning when I have beautiful, soft, indirect light. Even when no hard light comes through my window, I use white sheer curtains to make the light as soft as possible.

I almost always light my babies from the side or the head down between a 45–90-degree angle or from the back. I've found this allows for the most flattering light.

Many factors will affect the final image: your subject's facial features, composition, placement of the light and your shooting angle. While I prefer soft and light images, you might like dark and moody images, so use this guide as your starting point.

The strength of the light

When working with babies, use a soft, filtered light. For natural light, sheer curtains are great; for artificial light, use large softboxes. The closer the light is to your subject and the larger the light source, the softer the light.

To reduce the contrast in the light, either increase the size of the light source or move your subject closer to the light.

The number of lights

For newborn photography, you will only need one source of light. If you are using natural light and the room you are working in has multiple windows, you will have to block the light coming from the windows you are not planning on using. If you use an artificial light, you only need one light. With two or more light sources, you will lose the shadows, and without shadows, the lighting will look flat. Babies have very delicate features, and shadows give shape to their faces.

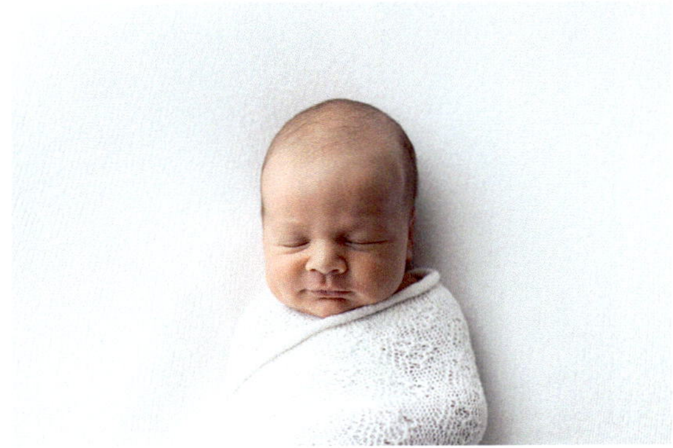

Image taken with a sheer curtain.

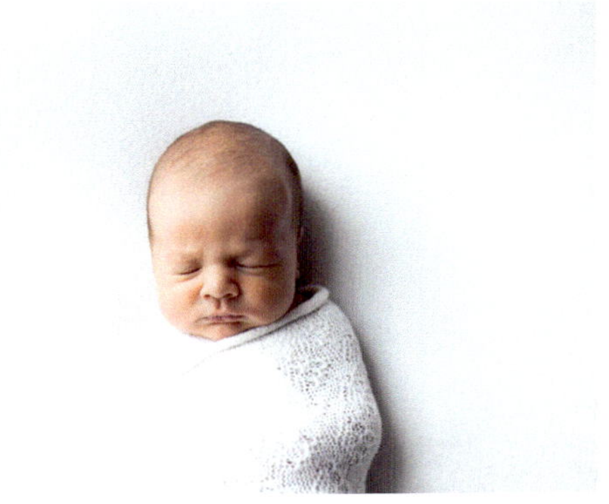

Image taken without a sheer curtain.

Your aim is to create a soft light that falls beautifully on the baby's face. The light should fall down the baby's face – lighting the baby from the opposite direction will create unflattering highlights. We all know the 'spooky face' look when someone places a torch under their chin – this is precisely the look you will achieve if you light your subject from the bottom up. Highlights on the nose and shadows under the eyes create a panda-like circle, which is definitely not the most flattering look. A shadow falling under a baby's nose will give you a clue if your light is correct.

Almost split light

Split lighting is a technique that lights half a subject's face, leaving the other half in shadow. Hard light is often used to create harsh shadows and a dramatic look. To create split lighting, position the light at a 90-degree angle to your subject. When photographing newborn babies, we seldom want harsh shadows, so use soft light or place a reflector on the opposite side of the light.

45-degrees light

This is the technique I use most often. I move my beanbag until the light source is somewhere between 45 and 90 degrees to the subject and I have the most flattering light. The precise angle will depend on the position of the baby and how defined its features are. Look for a shadow under the baby's nose and a slight shadow on the far side of its face. I also look for light in the eye area, even if they are sleeping. You can use supports to lift and adjust the baby's face until it is lit the way you like.

Bottom-up light

Never photograph a baby like this! You can create the most beautiful set-up and have a perfect sleeping baby, but if you shoot your subject with their bottom towards the light, it will look very unflattering. Light will go up the baby's nose, and their cheeks will cast unwanted shadows in the eye areas. As viewers, we tend to focus on the brightest part of an image, and we definitely don't want the focus to be on the baby's bottom.

Backlight

I love backlit images. To achieve this look, you will need to photograph into the light, with the light source placed directly behind your subject. Backlight can give a dreamy look to your images.

Front light

This isn't my favourite type of light for newborn photography. It will give you very flat light, and you will find yourself constantly getting in the way of your light source, as the window will be directly behind you. Babies have very delicate, undefined features, and flat light will create an even more one-dimensional look.

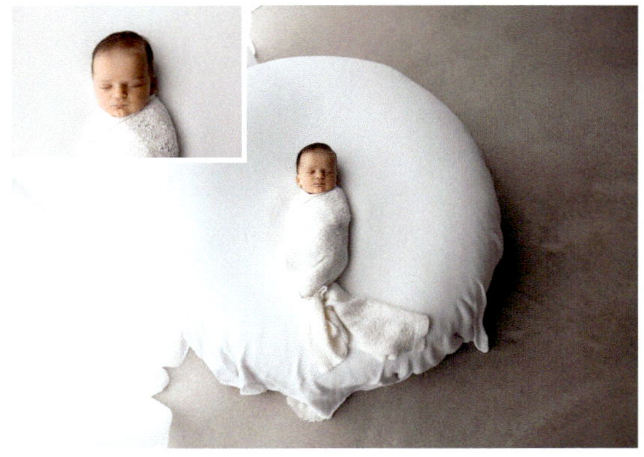

Almost split lighting

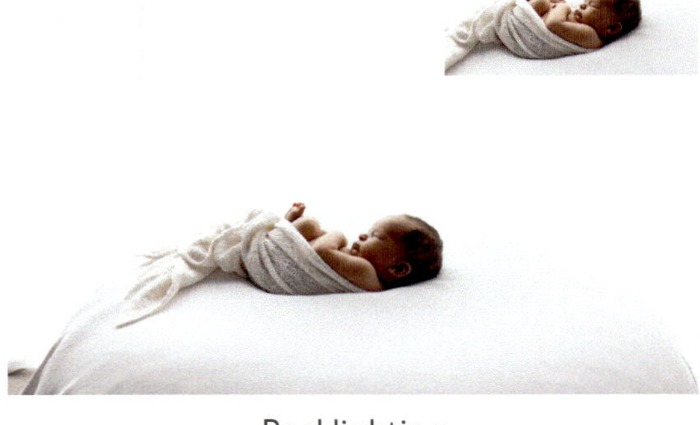

Backlighting

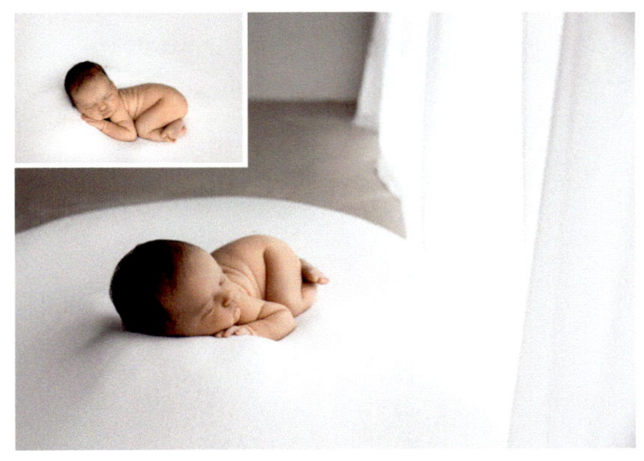

Front lighting

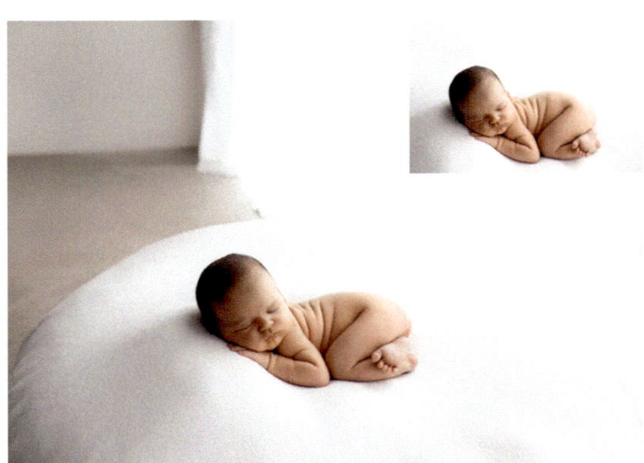

Bottom-up lighting

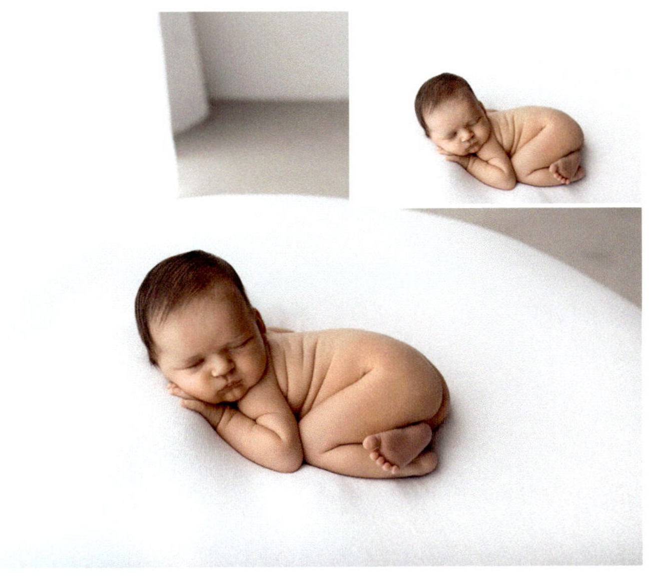

45 or so degrees lighting

As discussed in the Style section (see page 36), there are a great many variations in style and posing when it comes to newborn photography.

While I prefer a more natural and organic style, often called 'unposed' or 'baby-led posing', I find these titles very misleading, as only lifestyle photography is truly unposed. I still pose the babies, but the styling and my approach give the illusion and perception of natural imagery.

There are some easy and some very complicated newborn poses. Also, with posing comes baby safety, which we discussed earlier (see page 92). My favourites are simple poses where a baby is comfortable and natural-looking. The more complicated poses should only be done by a very experienced photographer; if you are unsure of what you are doing, do not attempt them.

Whatever style of photography you prefer, you should learn the basic poses. As with maternity sessions, once you have a base pose, you can build on it and create various images using different angles and props. I take my time while the baby is in each pose and move around to shoot as many angles and details as possible. I take close-ups and wider shots. I fill the frame and include some negative space. I take a picture with a blanket, then I might add a headband or a hat, and then remove both to capture only the baby.

Being very deliberate and getting the most I can from each pose limits handling, so the baby can stay nice and sleepy. We will discuss angles and how to maximize the potential of each pose later in the chapter (see page 122).

Lastly, I never forget that babies are people. They might be tiny, squishy and can't speak, but they are little humans, and they are all different. If a newborn is uncomfortable, I never force them into a position. If I can't make them comfortable in a particular pose, I simply move on. I move around, photograph from different positions, use different camera angles and crops, and create a beautiful gallery of images for my clients.

Flow posing

My goal for every newborn session is to disturb the baby as little as possible, move from pose to pose smoothly and fill a gallery with unique images. Before I transition the baby from one pose to another, I make small adjustments, move their hands and/or legs and add accessories. Often, I don't even know where one pose ends and the other starts. Flow posing helps keep the baby content by minimizing handling while still creating a variety of images.

Babies will become unsettled if you constantly move, pick them up and put them down. Create a flow where you can gently guide them and transition from pose to pose with minimum disturbance. After numerous sessions, my flow has evolved naturally and each pose seems like a natural progression. With a bit of practice, you will create your own flow.

As an example, there are five main beanbag poses (see pages 104–12). You can transition from one pose to another or treat them as individual poses. Learn to transition instead of picking the baby up every time.

Beanbag & supports

There are many different types of beanbags and posing tables available. Mine is a 1m (3ft) wide and 30cm (1ft) high faux leather beanbag. I often shoot from the top, therefore, I prefer a low beanbag. Make sure your posing bag is nice and firm but still malleable. I place a rolled-up blanket on my beanbag to support the baby and provide a sense of security. I put five or six blankets on top of my rolled-up blanket to soften its appearance and provide a smooth surface.

You will also need something to support the baby. You can use posers or supporters like posing beanbags or muslins, towels, small blankets or bits of fabric. You will need these to prop babies up and help them stay in a specific position.

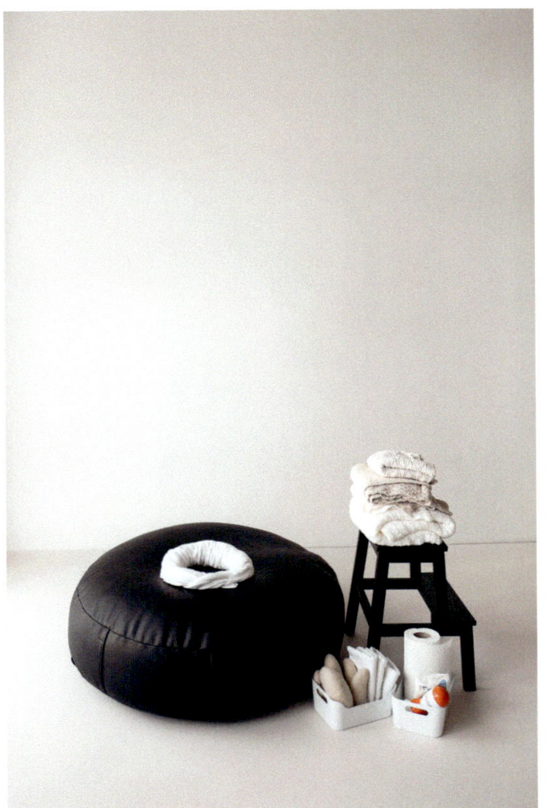

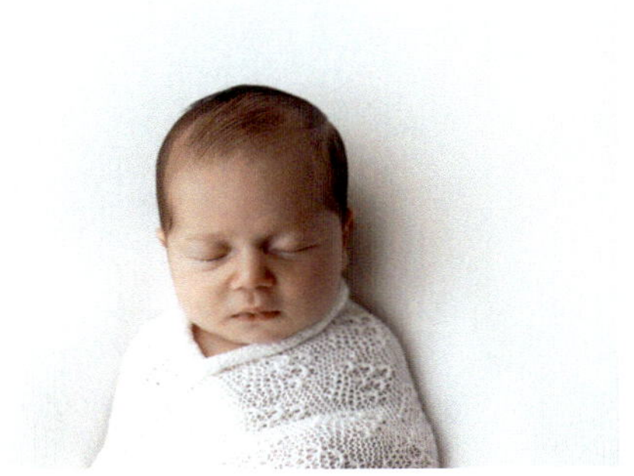

The start

Unless the baby arrives awake, I always start my sessions by laying him/her on the beanbag and swaddling with a nappy still on. (I keep the nappy on as much as possible to prevent accidents.) This allows the baby to get used to its new surroundings and encourages it to go back to sleep, even if it is soon to be feeding time. Posing a baby on its back is one of the most natural and comfortable ways to photograph them. It is also the least complicated pose and can be done without much experience.

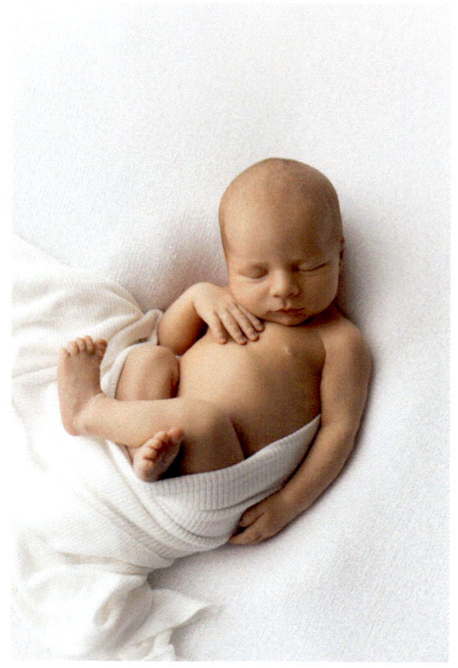

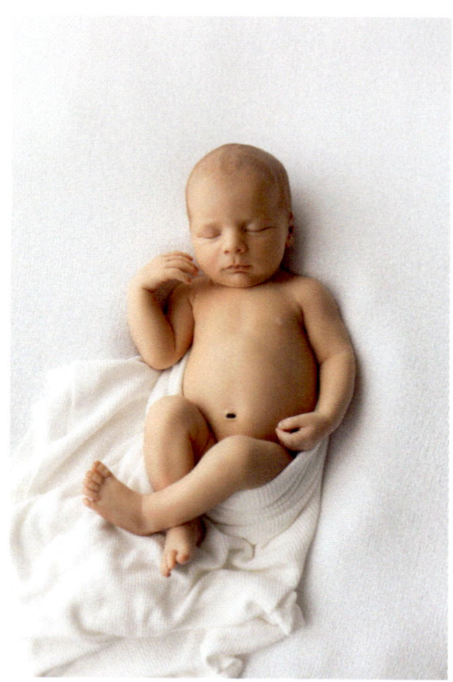

Creating a curve transforms the image.

This is one of my favourite poses. It is very safe and very comfortable for the baby and gives the feel of an unposed image. I like to make the baby look like he/she did in the womb by curling both the head and the bottom half up towards the light source. If the baby is too straight, he/she will appear stiff and uncomfortable. Curling the baby's head and legs together creates a snug, womb-like appearance. I can easily transition from this pose into the tummy pose (see page 106) or side-lying pose (see page 108).

1. When the baby is relaxed and sleeping, I gently start to unwrap their legs and remove the nappy. Having arms wrapped keeps them in place and adds a little extra sense of security while I am using my hands to remove the nappy.

2. Once the nappy is off, I cross the legs. The leg that is further from the light, on the shadow side, goes on top.

3. While holding the legs with one hand to prevent a startling effect, I unwrap the baby's arms. I take the wrap that is on the window side, cross it over and tuck it under the baby's back.

4. Then I take the wrap from the shadow side and tuck it into the opposite side. Make sure the wrap is tight. I have my hand on the baby's arms and legs almost all the time to ensure the baby feels safe. If the baby's head is straight, turn the top of the head towards the light. Adjust the support underneath the blankets so you can see the baby's face.

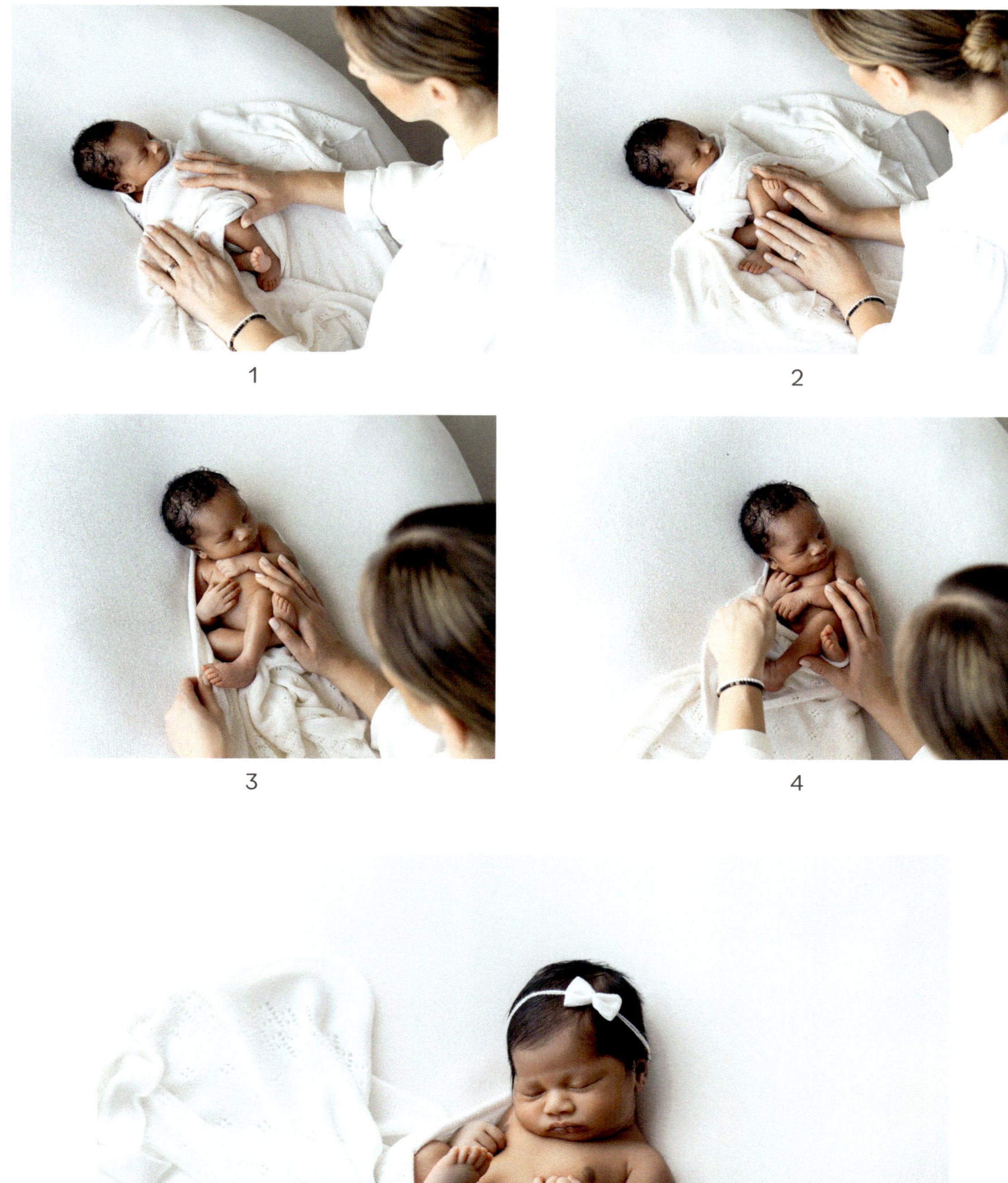

TUMMY POSE

Most babies love being on their tummies, so a lot of them feel very comfortable in this pose. This is also another one of my favourites and a classic newborn pose. It shows off their features, curliness and beautiful back rolls. It also gives you a wide variety of images.

1. When a baby is lying on its back, place the hand that is furthest from the light on the opposite cheek and the leg that is furthest from the light on top of the other leg.

2. Slowly and gently roll the baby onto its tummy while trying to keep the baby's hand on the cheek. I usually rock babies gently into the position that feels most comfortable and natural to them. Make sure the baby's head, not the bottom, is closest to the light.

3. Adjust your posing support so the baby's legs are tucked in. Place a few rolled-up muslins or a posing bean under the baby's head to add curl so as to bring out those sweet little back rolls. Make sure the baby's head is well supported.

4. This pose is all about the curves and wrinkles on the back. There should not be a space between the baby's cheek and shoulder, and the knee should be touching the elbow. If there is a gap between the elbow and the knee, gently bring the baby's bottom forwards. Also, make sure that it is the baby's hand under the cheek, not an arm. You might need to lower the hand to perfect the pose.

If you'd like to lift the baby's bottom up a little to create an even bigger curl, use a few rolled-up muslins. Not every newborn will like their bottom raised higher, so always read the baby's cues. I prefer the baby's bottom not raised, as this looks more natural to me.

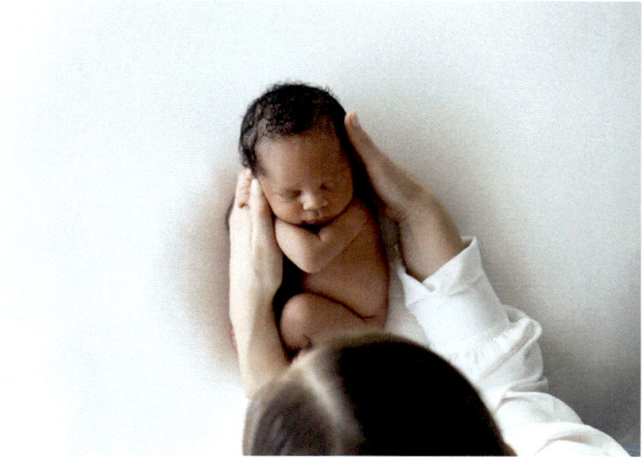

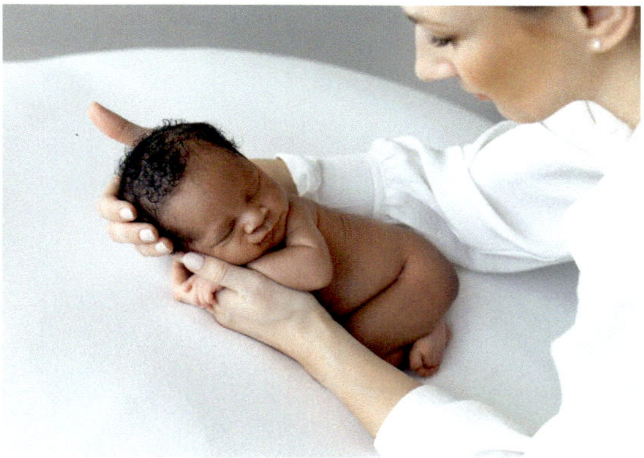

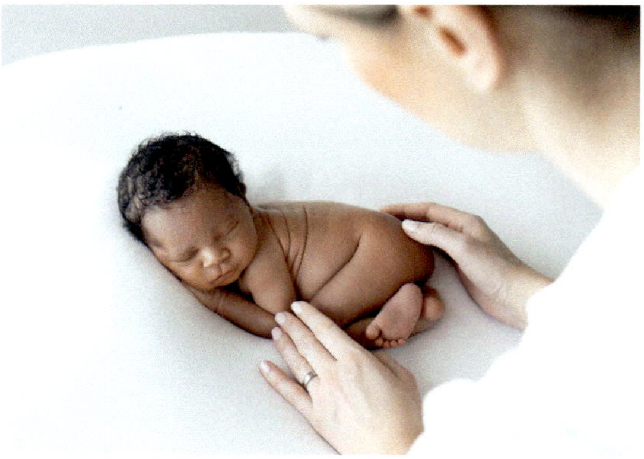

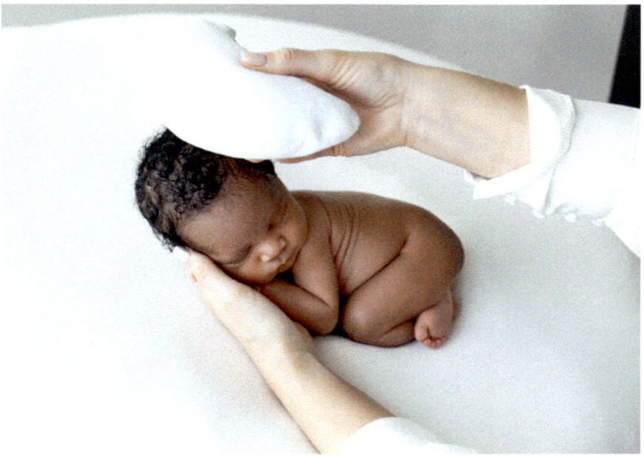

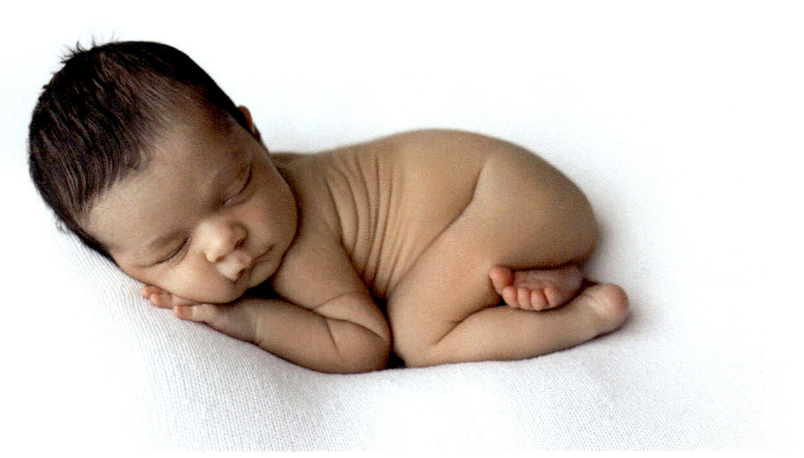

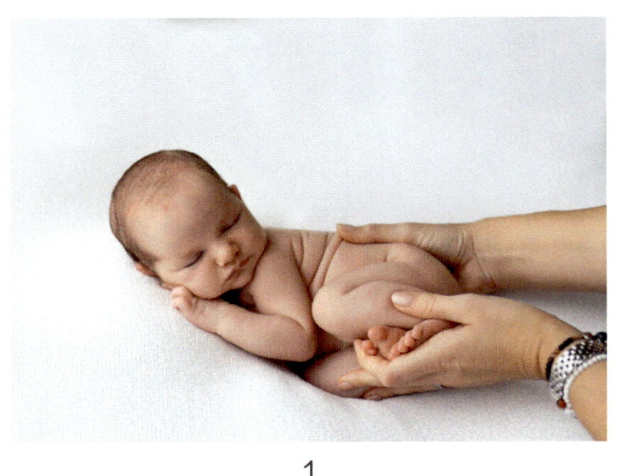

1

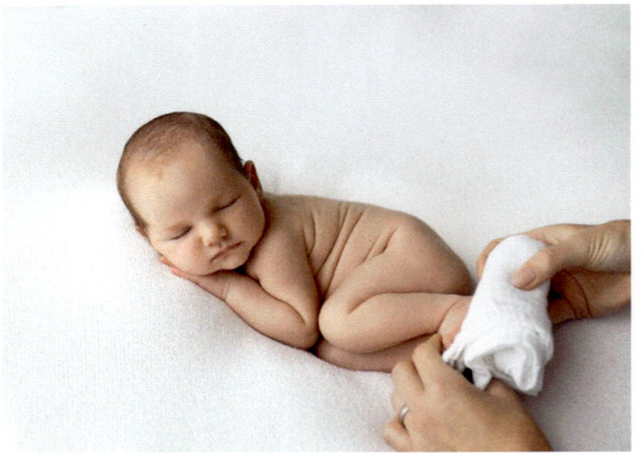

2

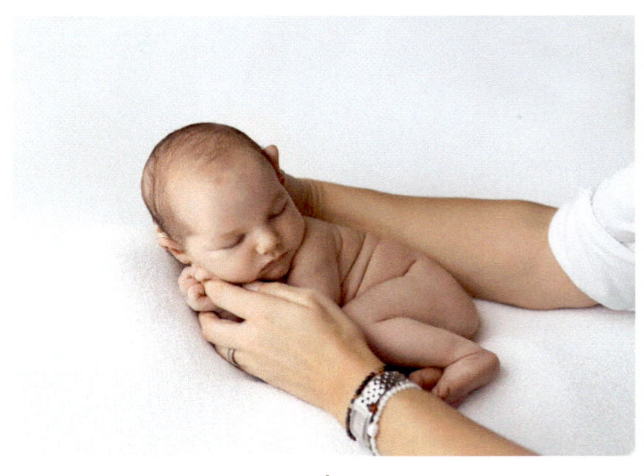

3

4

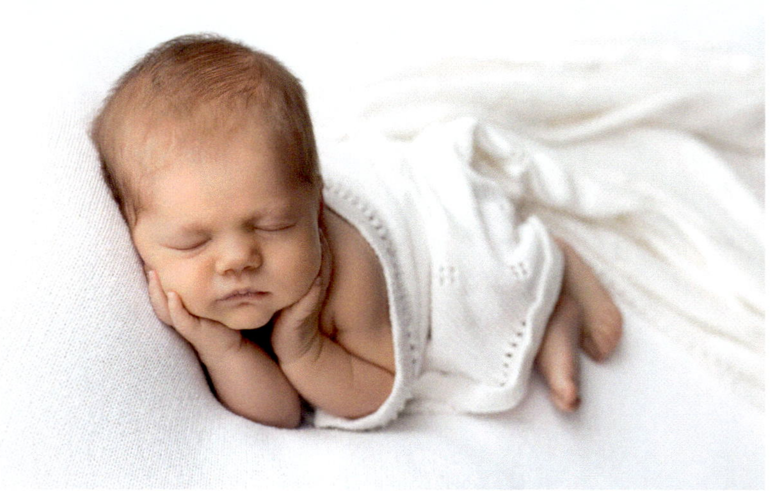

5

SIDE-LYING POSE

In this pose, the baby lies on its side with both hands tucked underneath its cheek. This is another pose that gives you lots of variety.

1. I usually transition baby into this pose from tummy pose (see page 106). Uncross baby's feet and gently turn their bottom and legs towards you, so they are facing forwards.

2. If the legs don't want to stay in place and need extra support, place a rolled-up muslin under your blanket to hold them in place.

3. Lift baby's head and gently pull the arm from the back to the front.

4. Position both arms under the baby's cheek and bring the top part of the baby slightly forwards so the head is closer to you than the bottom. If the baby's head is tucked in, lift it up slightly so the light falls beautifully on the face.

5. For even more variety, I take the top hand and place it on the top cheek, so the baby has a hand on each side of their cheeks. Gently squeeze the baby's wrists so they are together. This hand placement is perfect for close-up shots and also a safe variation for the so-called 'froggy' pose (see page 93).

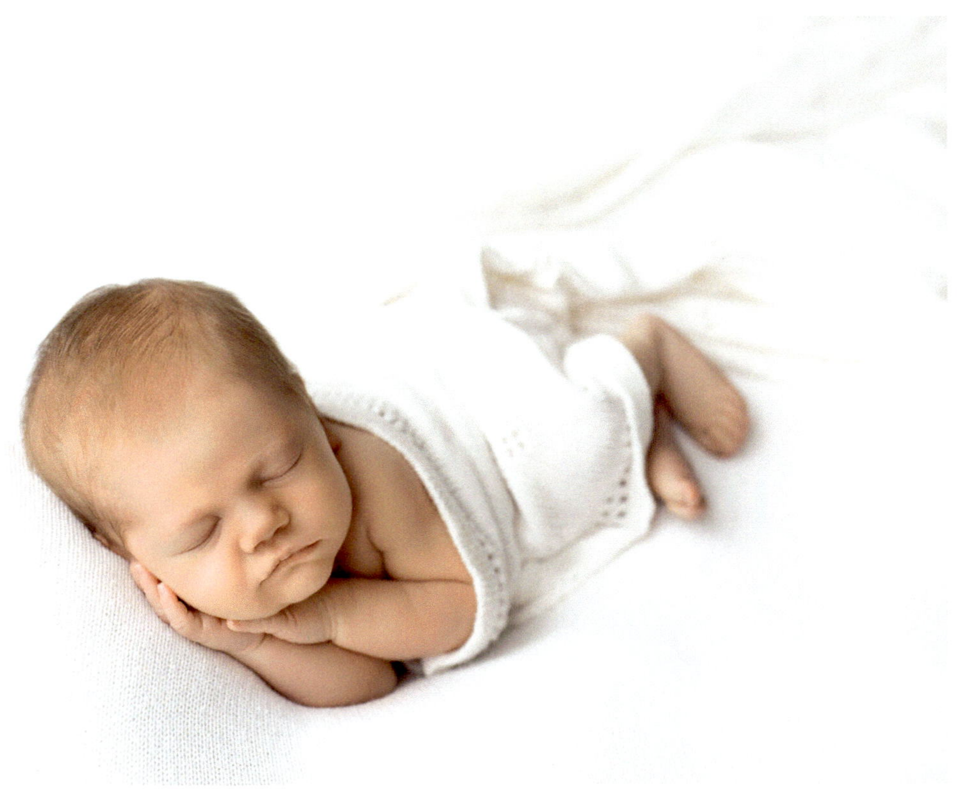

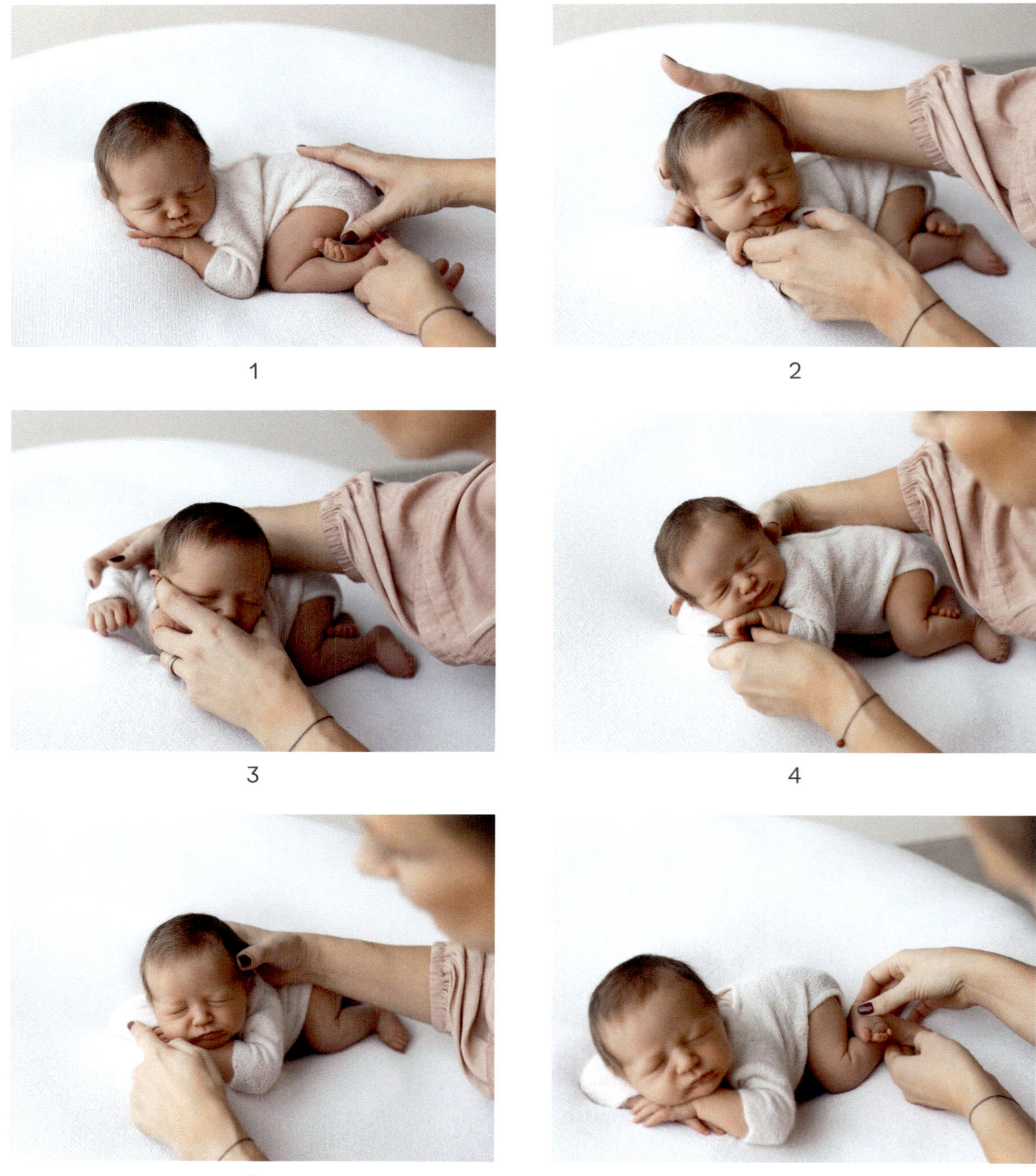

CHIN-ON-HANDS POSE

I love this pose, but it doesn't give you as much variety as those discussed earlier.

1. From tummy pose (see page 106), stretch the leg that is on the blanket.

2. Rotate baby's head to face straight.

3. Bring the arm from the back forwards.

4. Place baby's hands together under the chin.

5. Gently rock the baby to guide him/her into the most natural and comfortable position to them.

6. Adjust the feet. When I pose a baby in this position, I ensure the baby's head is not balanced on the hand but is comfortably resting on his/her hands with the top of the head pointing to the light.

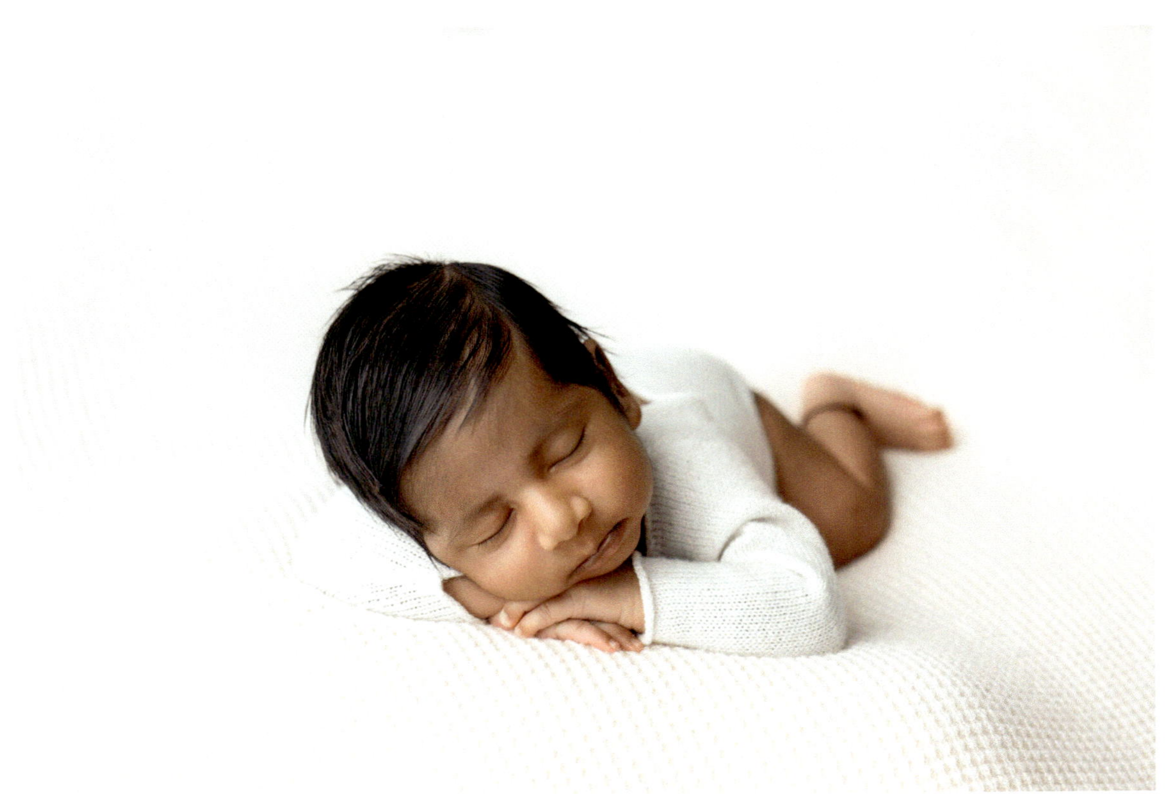

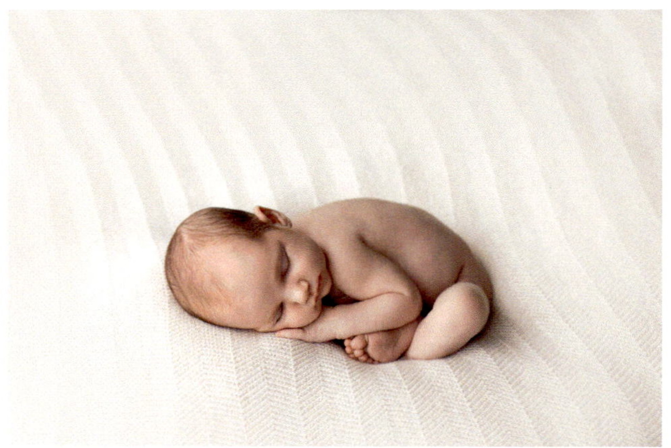

TACO POSE

This pose is somewhat similar to the baby's position inside the womb during pregnancy. Not every baby will be comfortable in this pose, so don't force it if a baby is unhappy. Also, if the baby is slim with long arms and legs, this pose won't be the most flattering for them.

1. The easiest transition into this pose is from a tummy pose (see page 106). Place one hand under the baby's head, holding the hand on the cheek.

2. Use another hand to curl the baby's back by bringing the legs closer to its head.

3. You will need to add extra support under the baby's head. Bring the baby's head and shoulders closer to the camera.

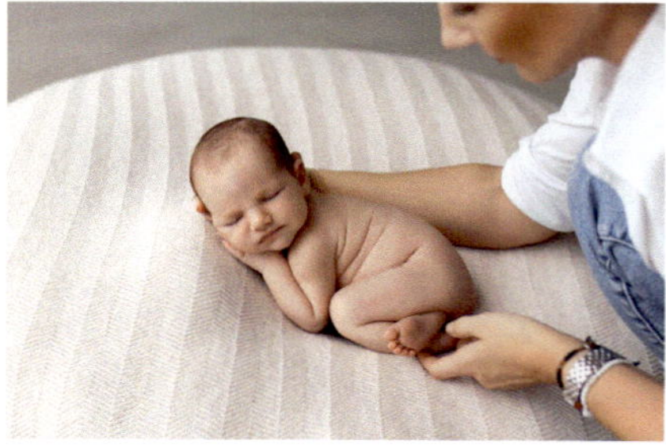

1

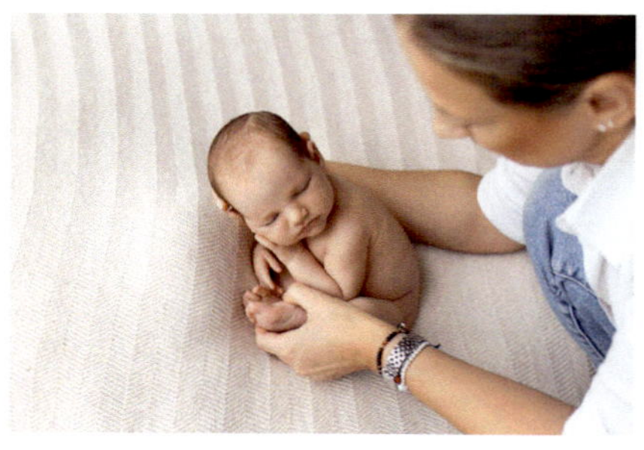

2

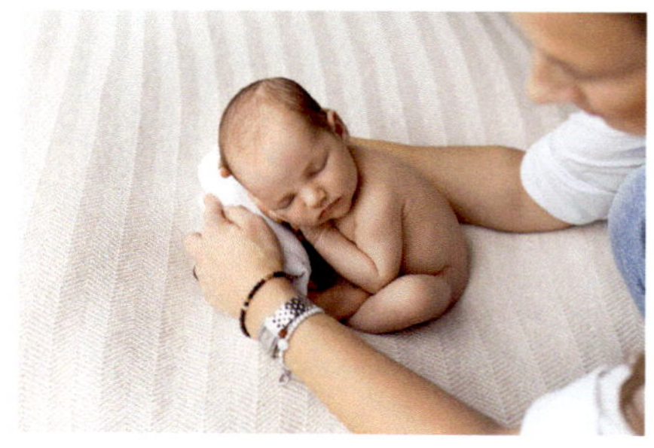

3

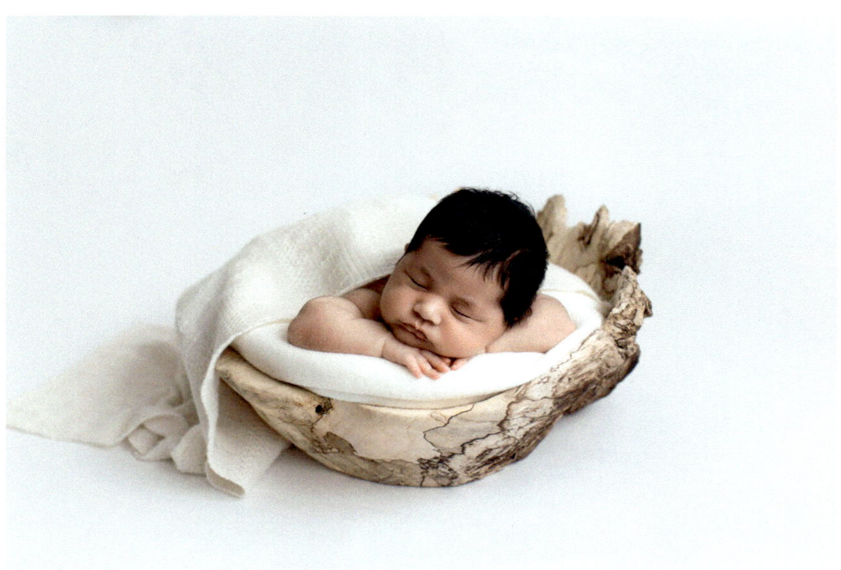

PHOTOGRAPHING BABIES IN PROPS

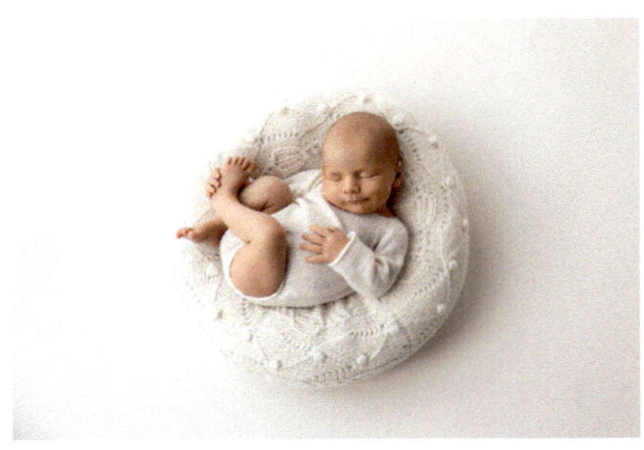

There are many props on the market, not just in specialist newborn photography shops but in home stores and similar, from simple props like pillows and baskets to small beds and strollers. It can be tempting to buy them all, but you may already have something similar. I prefer to focus on the baby, so I don't use many props, but they can add variety and fun to your sessions.

Safety should always be your priority when choosing and photographing babies in props (see page 92). Unless the baby is posed in a prop in a womb pose (see page 104), you must always have someone spotting the baby. If you don't have an assistant, ask one of the parents. Womb pose, chin-on-hands pose (see page 110), and tummy pose (see page 106) are the most commonly used. If you are posing baby on his/her chin, make sure the edges of your prop are padded and soft. Use the same posing methods as you would on a beanbag (see page 110). If you have a baby posed on a beanbag, you can transition to a prop without disturbing him/her much.

You don't want to go to all the trouble of placing the baby in a prop for one image only, so make sure you take a variety of close-up and wider images and shoot from different angles.

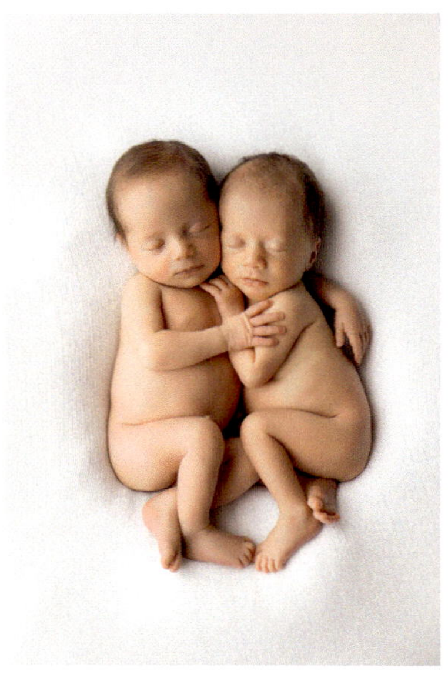

Photographing newborn twins or multiples can be a little more challenging, and a session can take longer than with just one baby. You will have two or more babies to pose and settle, so you will need two sets of hands. I always have an assistant when working with twins. If you don't have anyone to help, ask the mum.

Before the session, I always ask parents if twins or multiples have a routine. Knowing when and how often they feed will make it easier to plan the flow of your session. I also ask parents if one baby is calmer and more settled than another, and usually position the sleepier baby first.

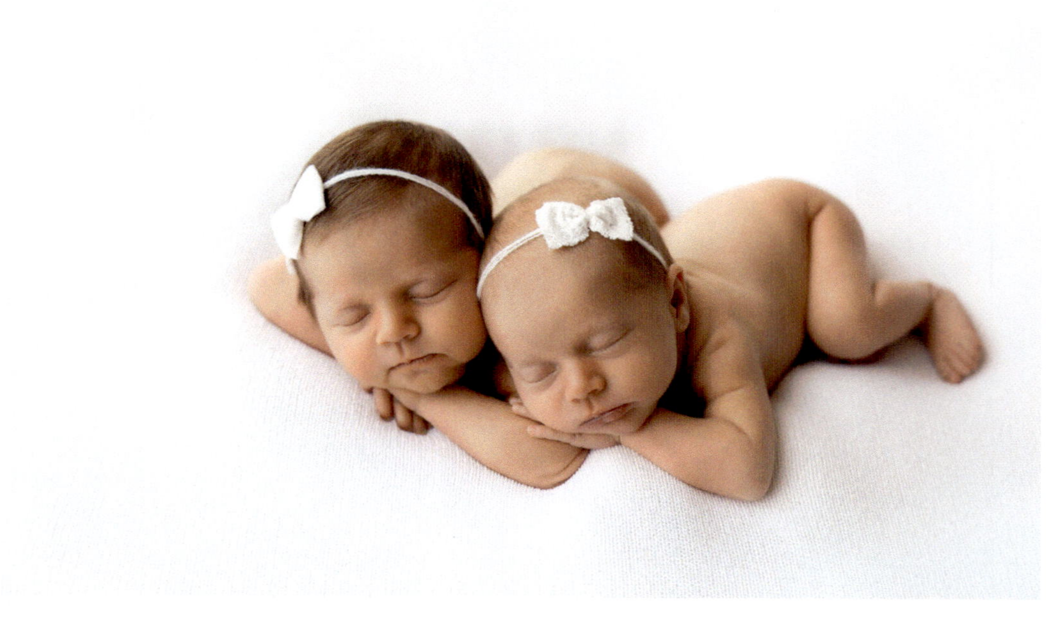

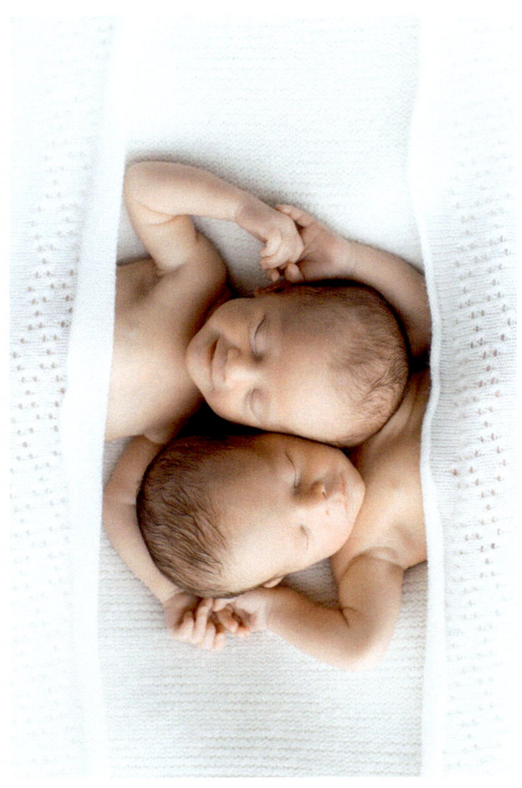

I always start my sessions with babies lying on their backs, swaddled in wraps. Once they have settled and adapted to the environment, I slowly unwrap and pose them, similar to how I would a single baby. I arrange twins's arms in different positions to create variety. For instance, you can wrap their arms around each other. Parents will love images where the babies are cuddling.

Womb pose (see page 104) and chin-on-hands pose (see page 110) are my favourites when photographing multiples. I always have my assistant spotting the babies, regardless of what pose or prop I am using. Not only are her hands there if one of the babies is startled, but she also reads their cues and facial expressions to prevent one twin from disturbing the other.

As with any other session, make sure you explore the angles and take various images from different viewpoints and distances. Bear in mind that if you shoot two or more faces, you might need a slightly narrower aperture, such as f/4 or f/5.6, to ensure both or all babies are in focus.

Full tummies are essential when photographing multiples; the happier the babies are, the easier it will be for you. If one baby gets a little unsettled, they usually disturb the other baby, and you want to avoid that as much as possible.

When photographing twins or multiples, I take images of the babies together and each individually. When babies are calm and sleepy, I photograph them together; when one of them is feeding, I photograph the other and vice versa.

If twins are born early, I arrange a session as soon as they come home from the hospital. If they are born at 37 weeks or later, I schedule the same as any other newborn session.

Stay calm, keep things simple and don't put too much pressure on yourself during these sessions.

Most babies love being swaddled. There are many wrapping techniques and with time, you will find your favourite ones. Swaddling the baby is also a simple way to add texture. I usually use a basic swaddling or wrapping technique. Cocooned baby poses are not my favourites, but I know a lot of people love them.

Don't be surprised if parents tell you that their baby doesn't like being wrapped. I usually just smile and nod, the same way I do when they say that baby doesn't like being naked. Most of the time, parents don't know how to swaddle a baby, and instead of soothing, it stresses the baby even more. I often teach parents how to wrap their baby, so they are nice and snug.

I do almost all my wrapping on my beanbag, as I prefer to handle a baby as little as possible. However, I know a lot of photographers find it more comfortable to wrap a baby on their lap.

I have lots of swaddle blankets and wraps of various stretches, sizes and lengths at the studio. I use them for different types of wrapping. Experiment and find what type of wraps you prefer to work with.

Basic swaddle

1. The basic swaddle is an important technique to master. I do it with the arms down to the side and the legs curled up for a nice, calm swaddled baby. If the baby is in a deep sleep, you can leave arms or fingers out. However, if the baby is a little unsettled, place the arms by the side of the body.

2. Place the wrap across your beanbag and lay the baby on top. The top of the wrap should end at the baby's neck. Place one arm down, cross the swaddle blanket or wrap over to the other side, place the second arm down and cross the wrap to the opposite side, tucking it behind the baby's back. The wrap needs to be snug around the baby. Curl the legs up and tuck them in too.

3. You can either twist the blanket to secure it or tuck it under the baby. The wrap has to be tight but not too tight, as this can restrict airways and put too much pressure on bones and joints.

BASIC SWADDLE

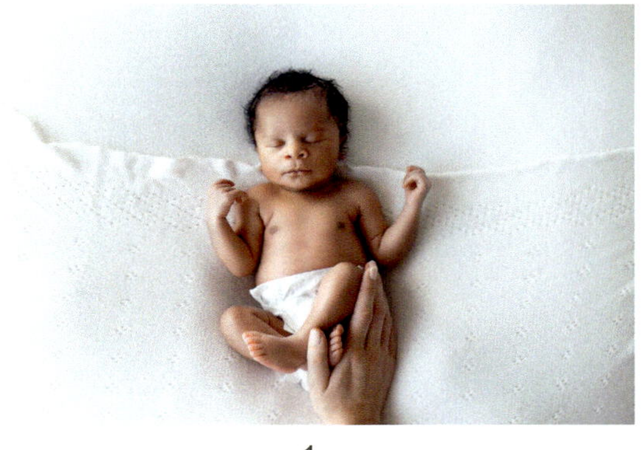

1

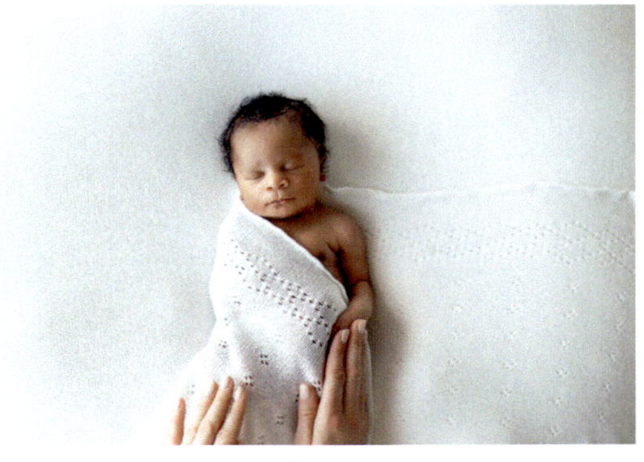

2

3

On-the-back or womb-pose wrapping

You have various options for styling the wrap here, but below are the two that I use most.

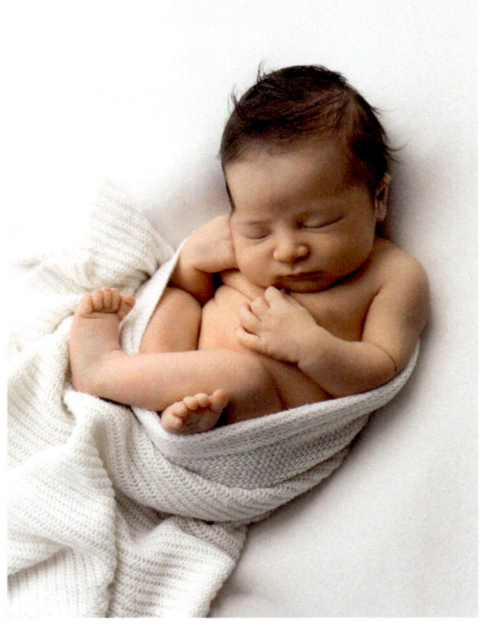

Option one

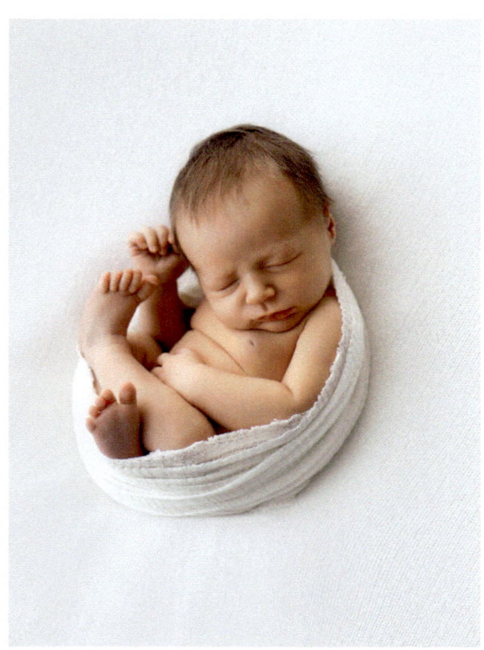

Option two

OPTION ONE

1. Unwrap baby from a basic swaddle; keep hold of baby's legs to ensure he/she feels secure. The wrap from the light side wraps around the side of the baby's body and is tucked under the baby's bottom on the opposite side.

2. Repeat the same thing on the other side. If you have a thin and short wrap, you can tuck all of it under baby's back or wrap around and tuck the edges in. Make sure the wrap isn't bulky. I usually use a bigger swaddle blanket for this, and instead of tucking it under the baby, I arrange it nicely to the side or around the baby.

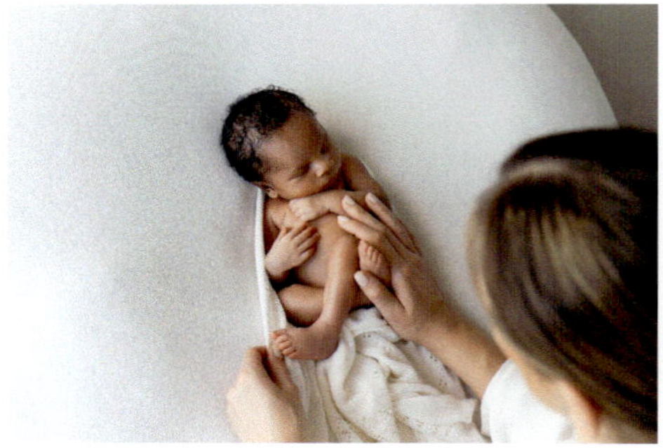

1

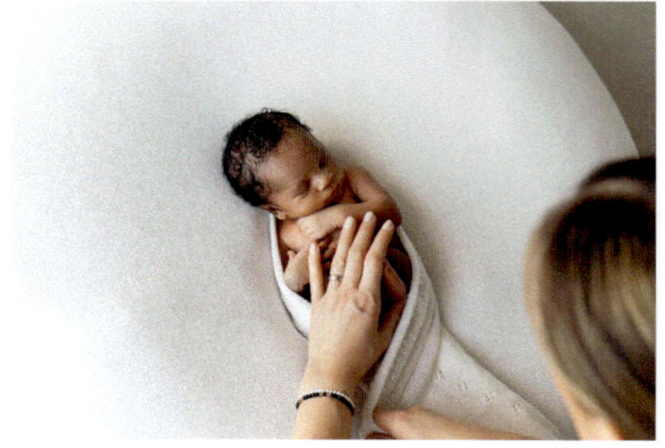

2

OPTION TWO

1. Place your wrap on a beanbag (or your lap). Leave one side of the wrap a lot longer than the other. Lay baby on the beanbag and arrange into a womb pose on it.

2. Wrap the shorter side of the wrap down around the baby's bottom and tuck it under on the opposite side.

3. Fold the remaining wrap around the baby going to the opposite side and tuck the edge under the baby or style it to the side.

4. You can fold the wrap around the baby's head or shoulders, whichever you prefer.

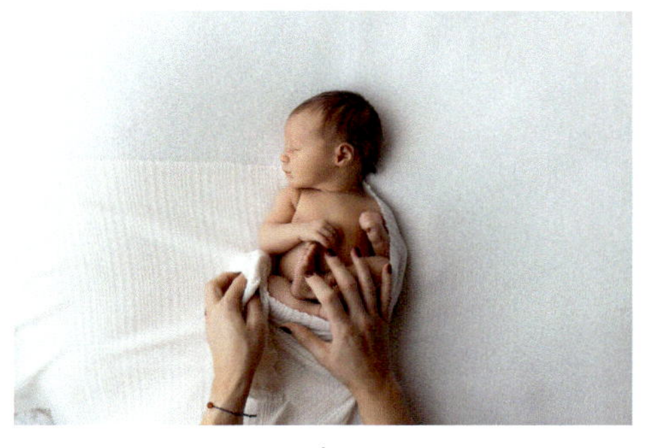

1

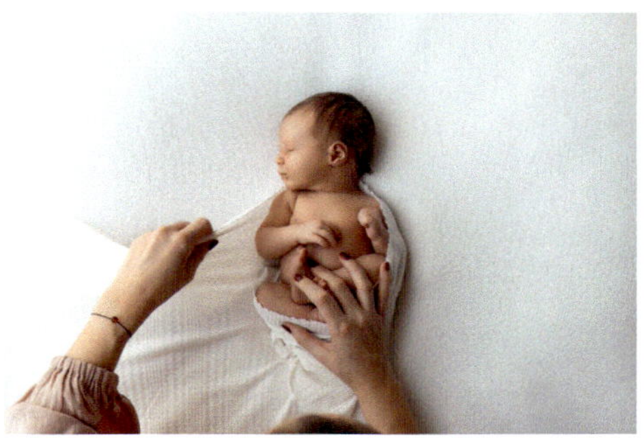

2

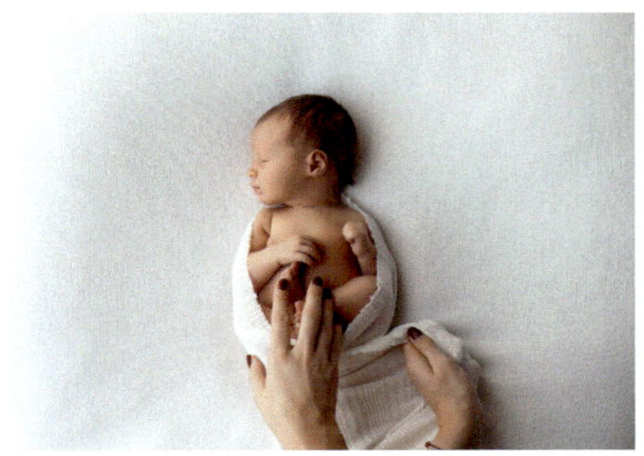

3

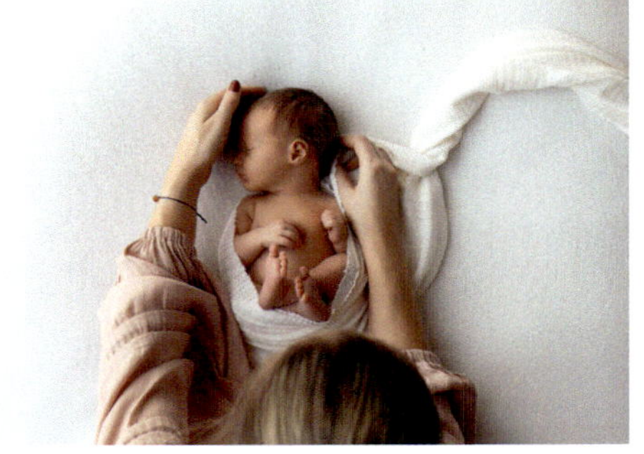

4

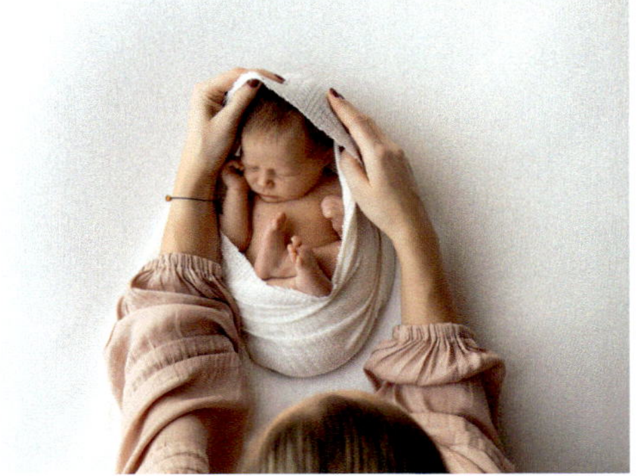

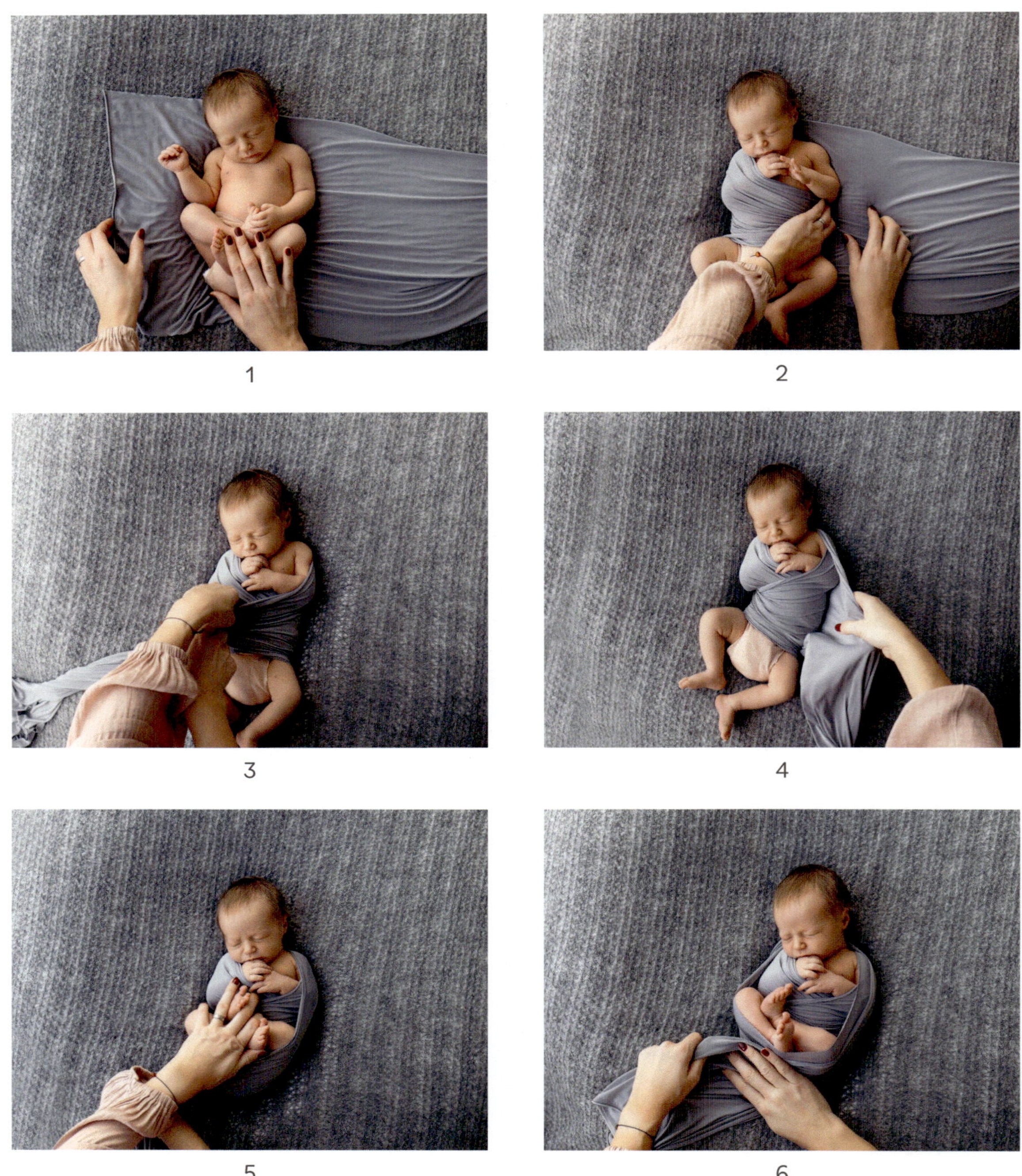

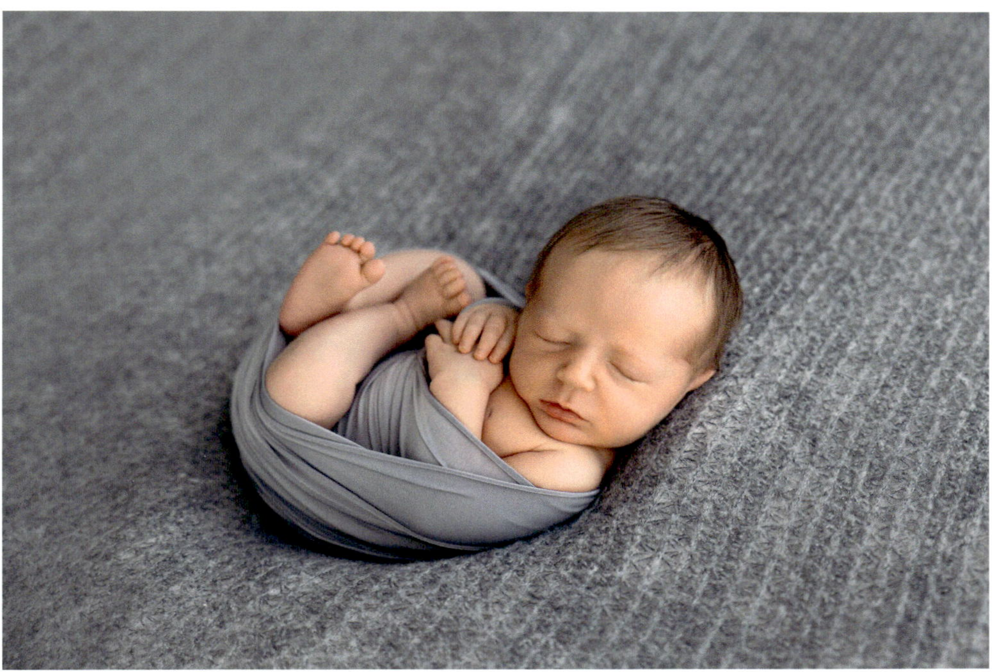

Creative wrapping

You will need a long wrap for 'creative' wrapping. I suggest starting with a 175cm (5ft 9in) long wrap and see if you prefer it shorter or longer.

1. Place your wrap on a beanbag (or your lap). Leave one side of the wrap approximately 30cm (1ft) long only.

2. Cover baby's chest and belly with the shorter side; you can leave arms out or tuck them in, leaving just hands out. Tuck the wrap under the baby's back.

3. Take the long end of the wrap and wrap it twice around the chest for extra support. Make sure the wrap isn't too tight and doesn't restrict breathing.

4. Bring the wrap from the back nice and high, covering the baby's shoulder.

5. Bend baby's legs up and bring your wrap from across the shoulder down to the bottom and wrap around, tucking the excess underneath the baby.

6. If you have a long wrap, you can wrap it around the baby twice or style the remaining wrap on the beanbag.

There are so many different ways to wrap a baby, so keep practising and experimenting to find what you love most.

Composition refers to where objects are placed in a photograph. I always aim to make the baby the main point of focus. Although there are some traditional 'rules' for composition, photography is a creative art, and there are no right or wrong ways of framing your images as long as it pleases your clients. I compose in various ways.

The rule of thirds is the easiest technique to follow when composing your images. Place the main focal point on one of the horizontal grid lines (below left) or where the lines intersect. If placing your subject on the left or the right side of the frame, it is best to have negative space on the side where the light is (below right). If I photograph a baby lying on its back or belly, I place my subject in the bottom two-thirds of the frame. Depending on the pose and angle, you can also place the baby in the centre of the frame.

When I photograph, I pull back for a wider view, and come in close, sometimes filling the frame with my subject. I crop parts of the baby's body (like the top of the head) to draw the viewer's attention to all the little details that wouldn't be visible if photographed from further away.

Variety in newborn photography has a lot to do with simply changing your camera angle. I always explore my angles to create a cohesive collection of images that works well in both albums and on walls. I love that a single pose can be used to create multiple images that flow beautifully together (opposite).

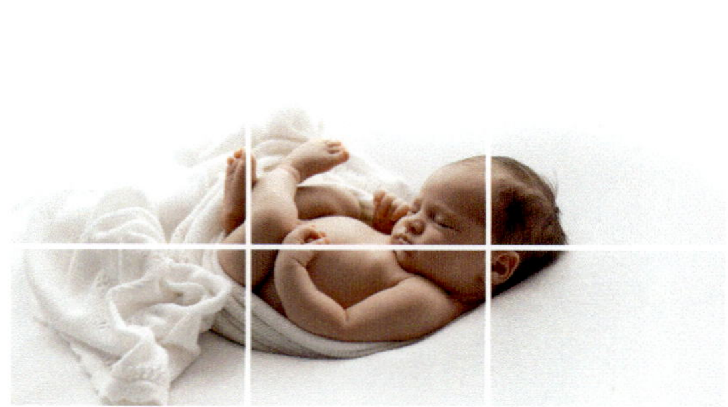

The subject is positioned on the lower horizontal rule-of-thirds grid line.

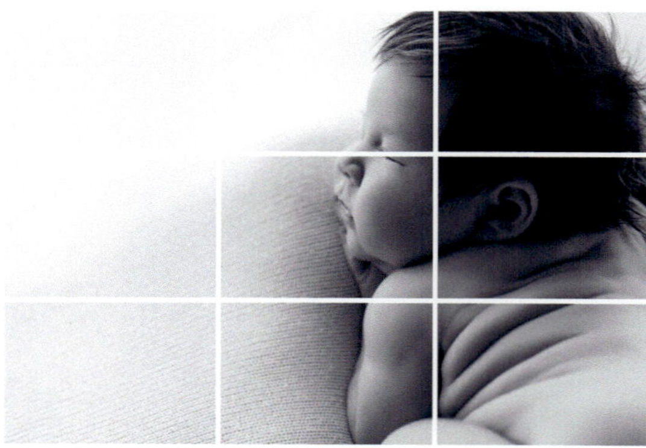

The subject is positioned on the right side of the frame, with negative space on the left-hand side.

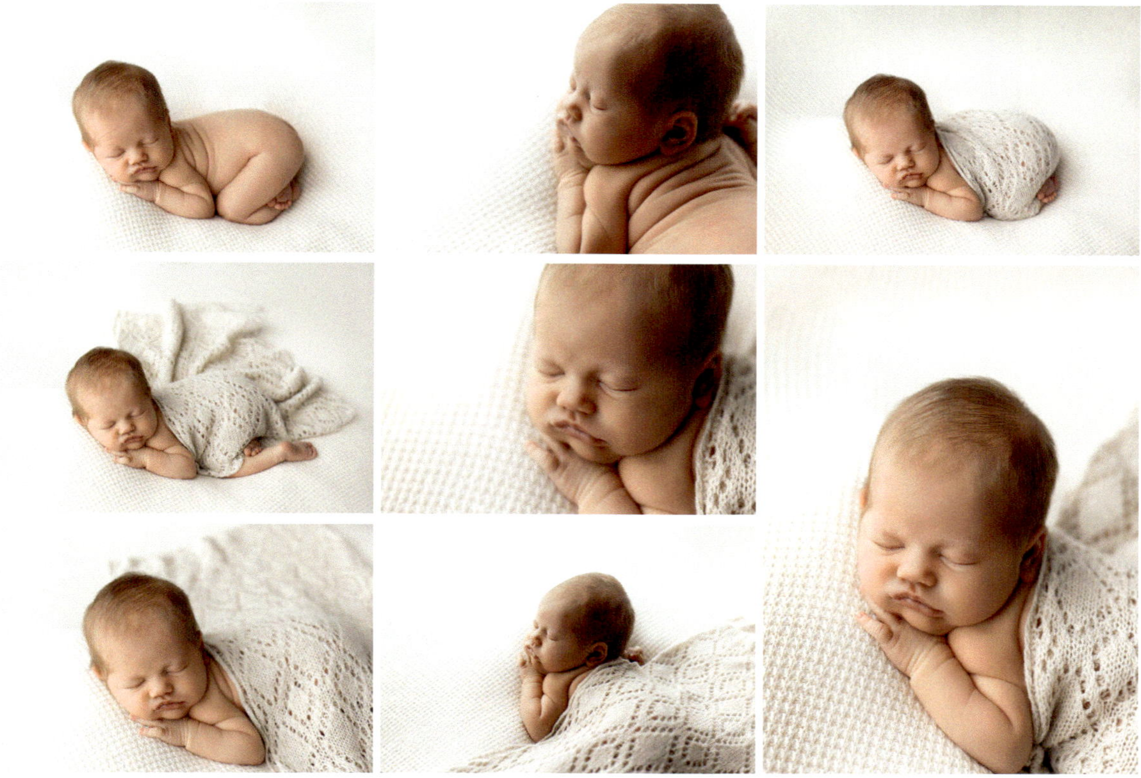

All these images were taken without moving the babies. I added variety by shooting from different angles and distances and by adding accessories.

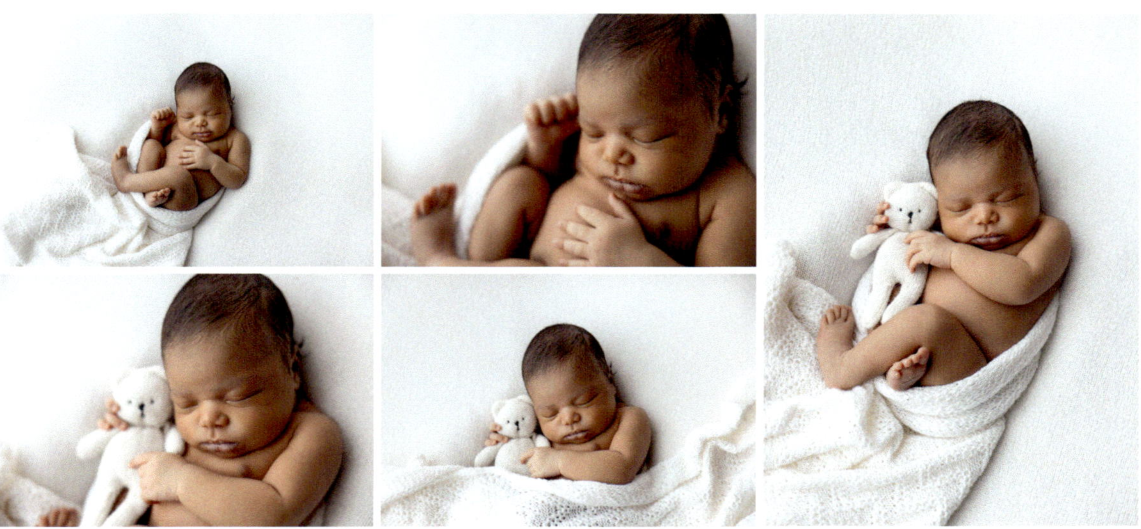

This is something I do in every session, but I find it especially important with a fussy baby, as you never know when you will shoot your last frame. However, angles can be challenging to master when starting out as a newborn photographer.

Don't be afraid to move around and tilt your camera not just up and down, but also left and right. Try to create at least four or five images for each pose before moving on. Eventually, you will instinctively know which way to turn your camera, and which angles you and your clients love most.

Many photographers use props to create variety, but you will often need to pick the baby up and move it to another prop, which might wake him/her up. Being very deliberate and making sure you get the most from each pose minimizes handling, so the baby stays nice and sleepy.

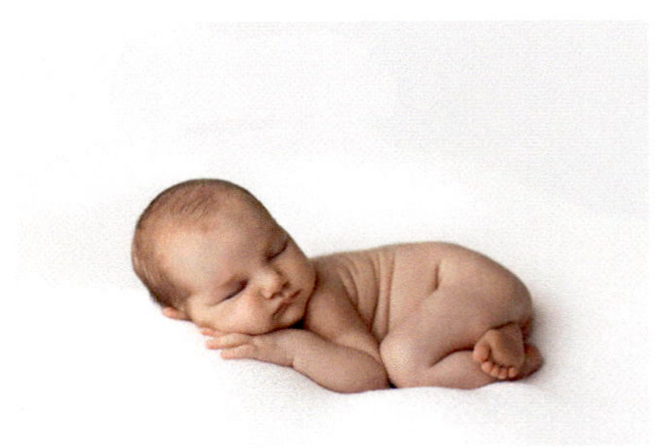

TIP

Avoid shooting from below (like in the image above) and up the baby's nose, as this is a very unflattering angle. If you can see up the baby's nostrils, you are too low, so try to photograph either at eye level or from a slightly elevated position.

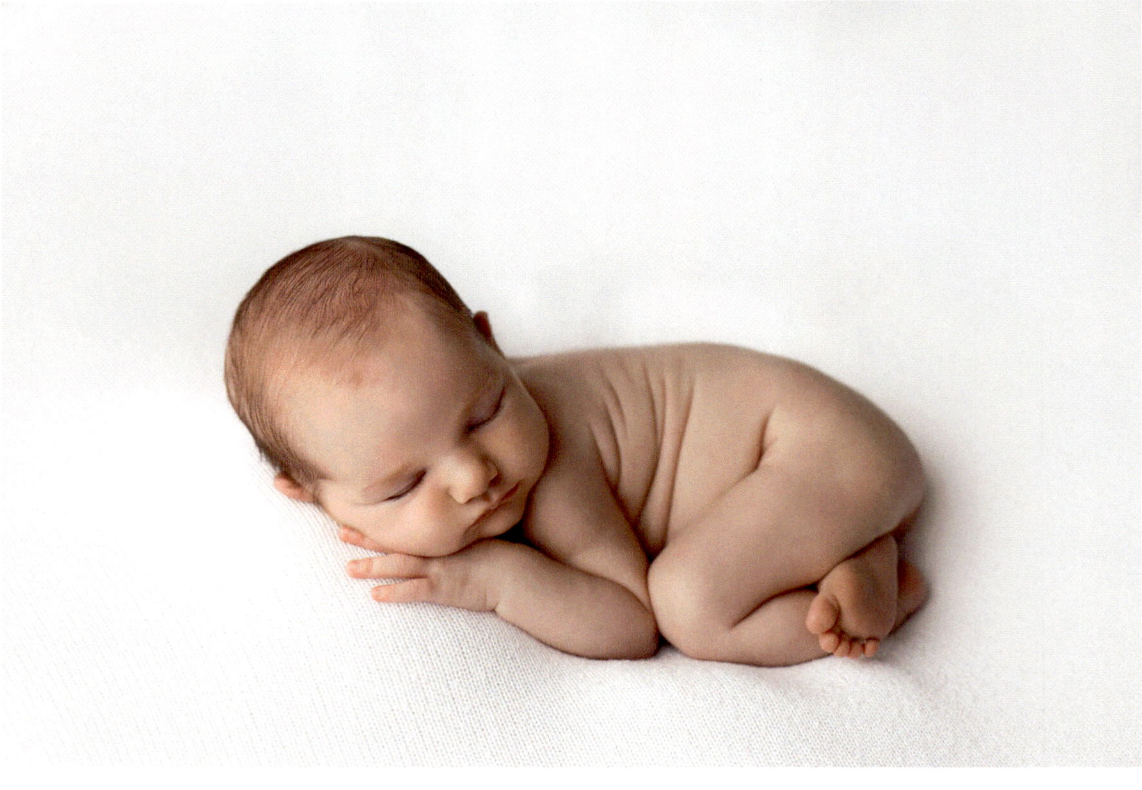

Macro photography isn't just about capturing small details, but also about preserving delicate features, and emphasizing the littleness of newborn toes and fingers by adding parents' hands to the images. Zoom in to capture tiny eyelashes, ears, hair, fingers, toes and belly buttons. These shots can add some creative variety to your gallery.

To showcase the texture of delicate skin, you need to make sure there are highlights and shadows in your images. Just remember that flat light will 'erase' the shadows and all the details with it. You can use black backdrop fabric to make macro images more dramatic. I take most of my macro shots when the baby is lying on his/her back.

If you want to focus on scale, ask a parent to hold the baby's hands or feet. Having an adult's thumb placed on the sole of a newborn baby's foot will exaggerate how tiny those toes are. A macro lens will allow you to get close and magnify these special details.

If you don't have a dedicated macro lens, you can still shoot close-up images with the long end of a telephoto lens. You won't be able to get so close, but you can always apply a tighter crop in post-production. Explore every angle and composition when you shoot close-up images, and don't be afraid to experiment.

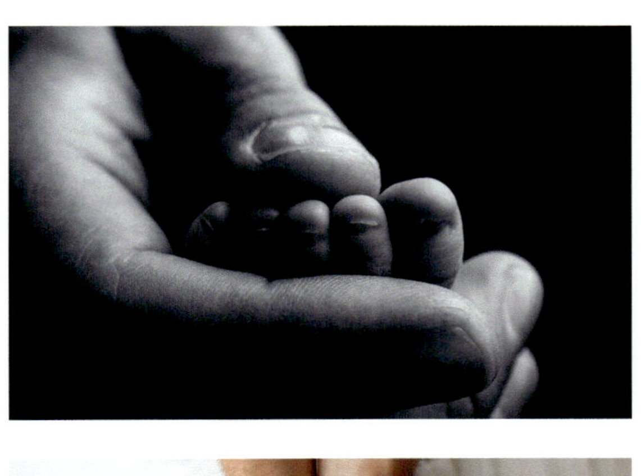
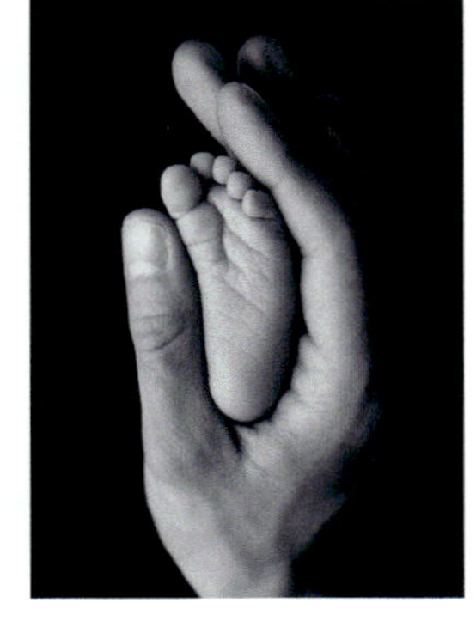
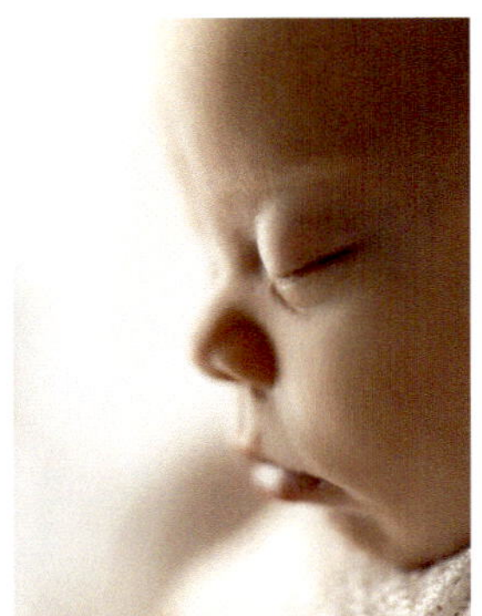
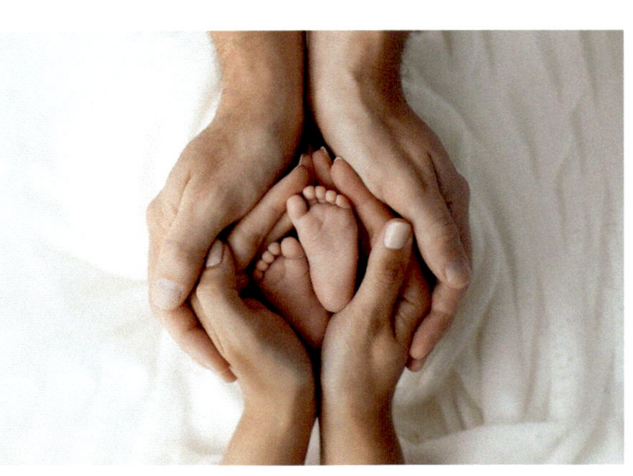
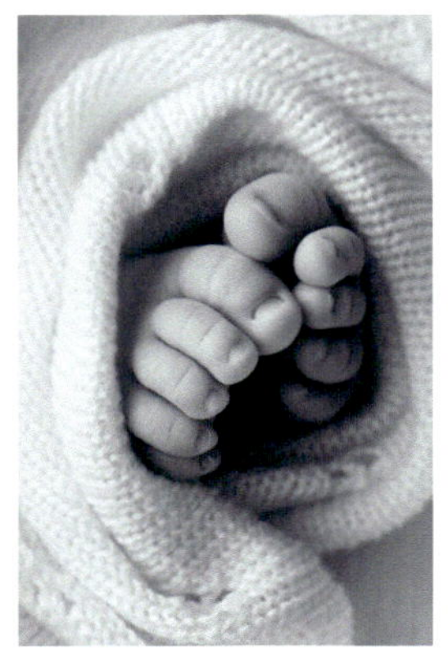
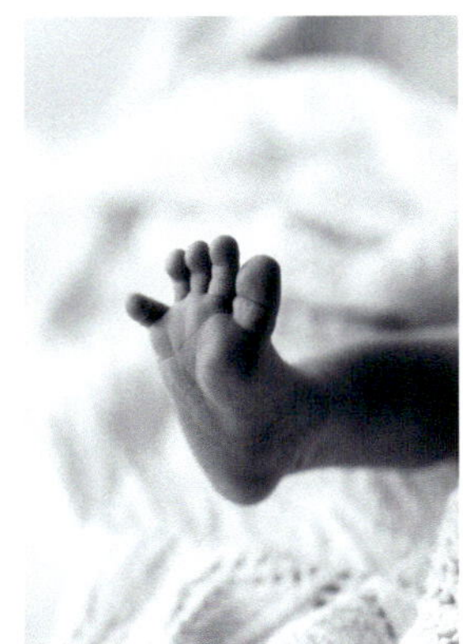

CREATING AN ILLUSION

Not all newborn photographs are what they seem. My clients often request an image in which it looks as though the baby is being cradled by a parent's hands and arms. They are often surprised when I tell them that the baby is safely and comfortably lying on a beanbag.

Many other kinds of images are also created using a beanbag, or they may be composites. Don't attempt replicating an image if you are unsure how it was originally created.

Below is a selection of images that are safe and easy to create using a beanbag. Black fabric hides shadows, which helps to create the illusion and adds a fine-art feel to the end result.

Be aware that some parents are not very flexible and might struggle to keep their hands in this position. You want to make sure that all your clients are as comfortable as possible.

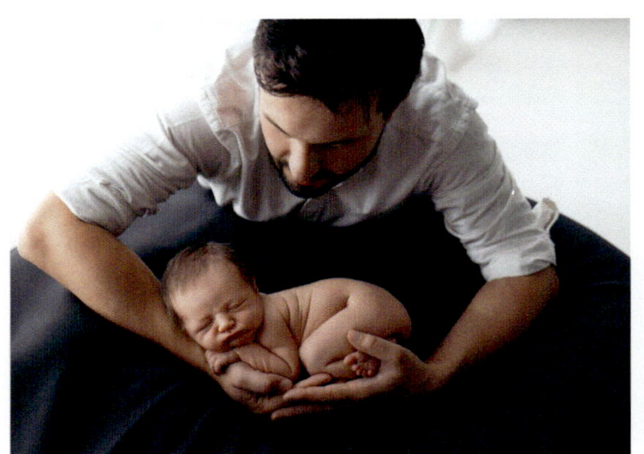

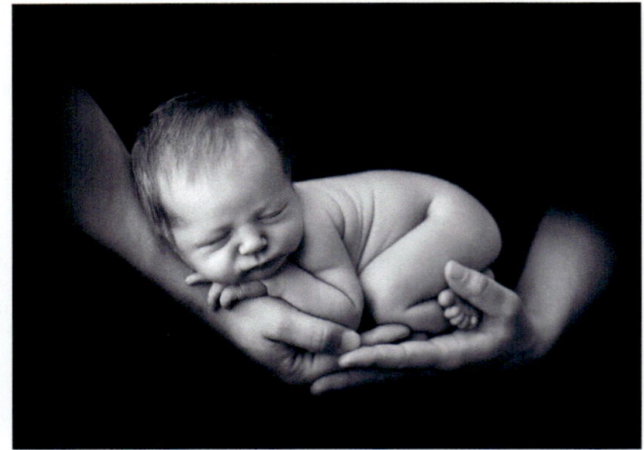

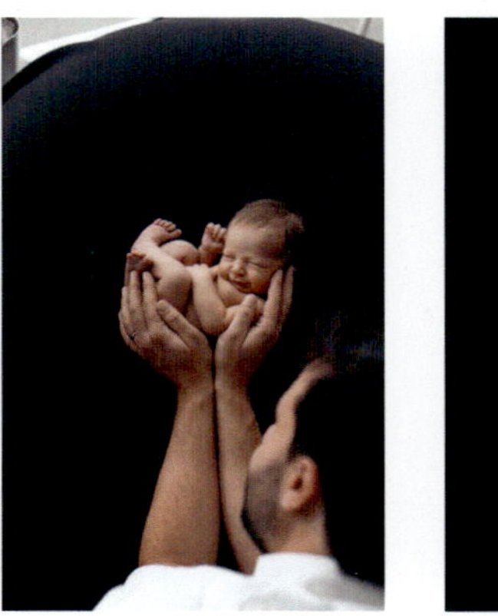

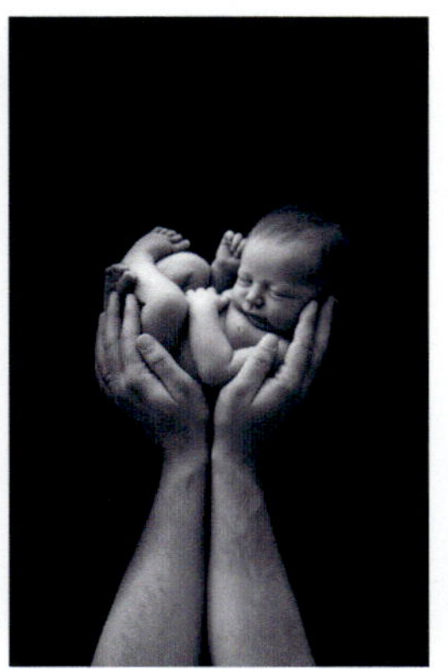

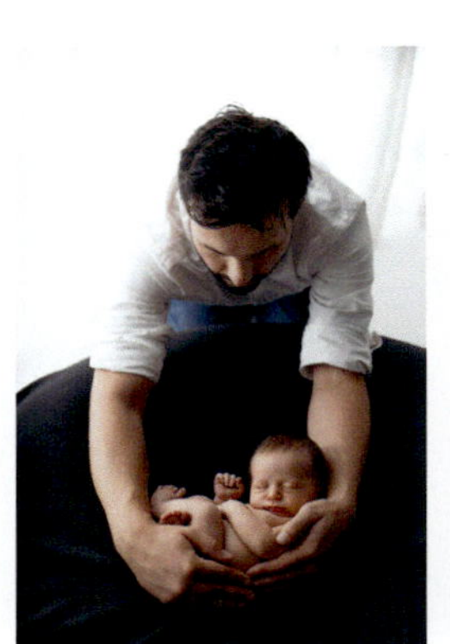

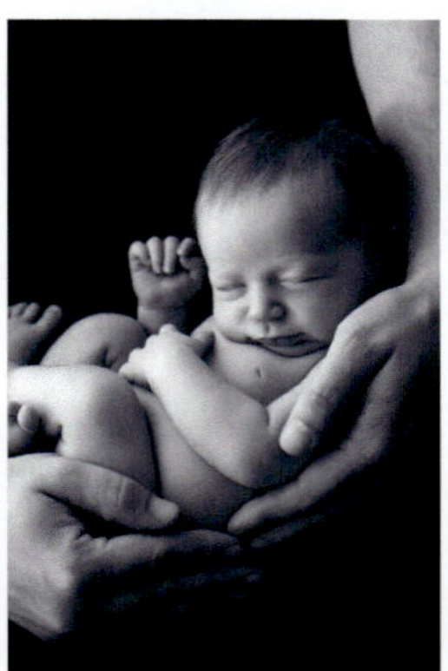

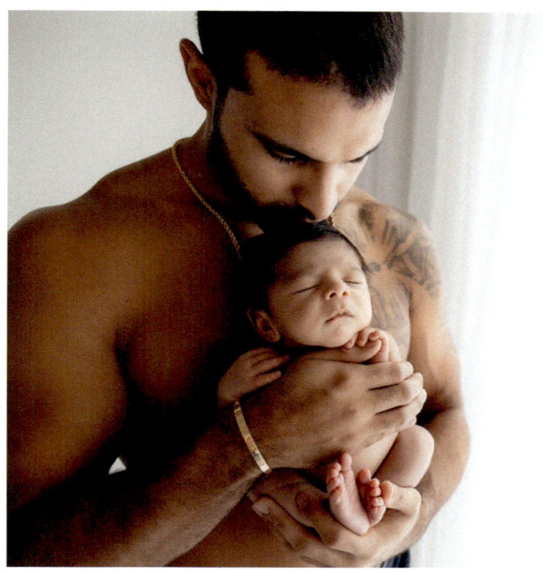

FAMILY POSING

Family images are my favourite; I love creating intimate portraits and capturing the connection. My final gallery of images is usually a 50/50 split between images of the baby on his/her own and portraits with parents or siblings.

Some parents are reluctant to participate in the portrait sessions, but I always encourage it. There is always a heart-warming connection between the parents and their newborn babies. I always tell the parents they can leave the images behind if they don't like them, but there is the chance of regret if these fleeting moments are not captured. Family portraits are often my clients' favourites.

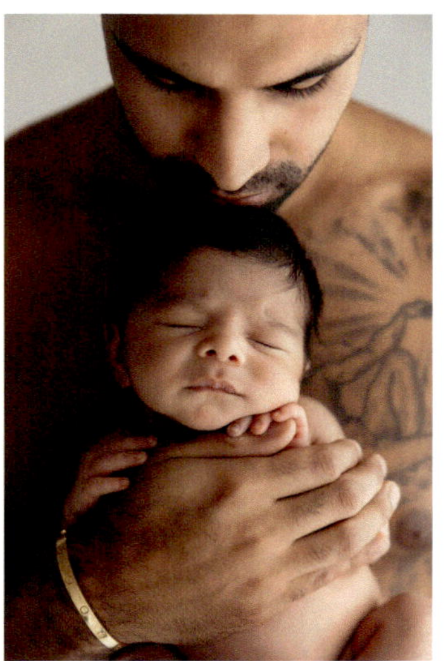

For family images, I always ask if parents prefer their baby to be naked, wrapped in a blanket or dressed. Some photographers like to photograph parents topless, but I like my clients to be dressed. The only time I photograph my clients topless is when a dad is very muscular and wants to showcase his masculine strength and the delicateness of his newborn baby. I love the physical strength and the tender love that these images portray.

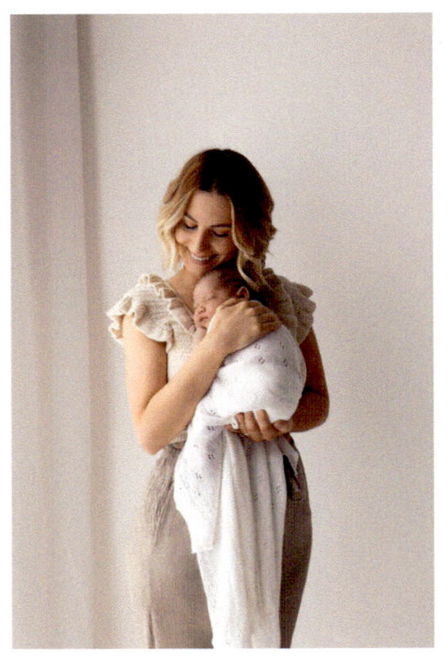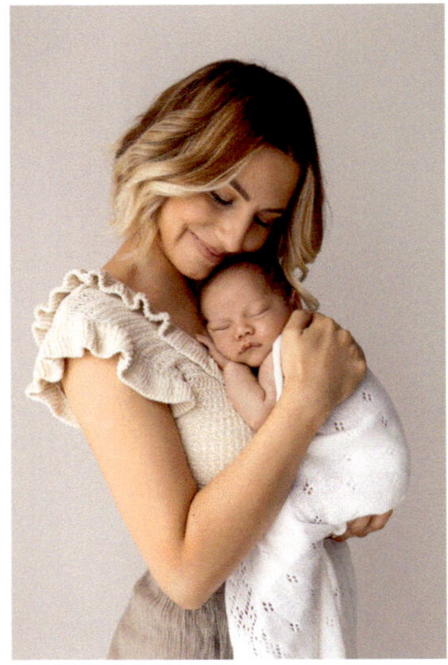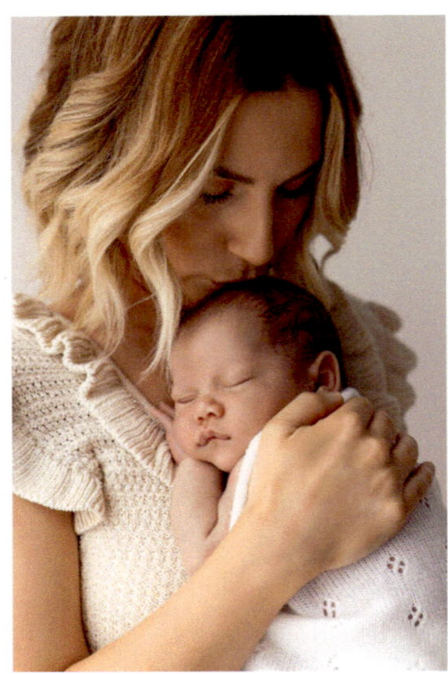

When I pose a newborn with a parent, I first explain what I will do and emphasize that I will not let my hands go until the parent is comfortable and the baby is safe. Parents will often hold their baby in a way that doesn't feel very natural. If they are tense, it will show in their expression, and they might look stiff and uncomfortable.

I never ask my parents to pick the baby up themselves. I position the baby myself and place him/her into the parent's arms with clear instructions on where to put hands, or I demonstrate the pose myself before I place the baby in their arms. I constantly ask if mum or dad feels comfortable, as I do not want them to feel as if they are about to drop the baby or feel too awkward if the baby decides to move or wiggle.

Parents are very different – some are very comfortable handling and holding their baby, while some feel less comfortable. If parents are not very confident in holding the baby, I always have the baby pressed right up against the parent. This way, the baby is supported by their hands and body, which adds an extra layer of comfort and assurance to both parents and the baby. It also allows me to capture the closeness, comfort and safety the parents provide.

Ask questions about the baby – about how this was just a dream only a few weeks ago – and talk to them about the love they are experiencing. This might encourage parents to show pure emotions, which can be quite moving. These are intimate conversations, so ensure they are genuine, and that your clients are happy to discuss.

I don't always feel comfortable talking about intimate feelings with my clients, so I don't force myself or try to pretend. I would rather step back and let them interact while quietly capturing it all. I simply direct them, tell them where to look and ask them to close their eyes or to giggle.

When I take images with parents, my workflow is usually very simple. I pose a baby with a mum, take a few shots, then add dad and take a few more shots. If there are siblings, I add dad and siblings. I ask them to look at me, the baby and each other, and then repeat with the other parent.

I photograph parents from a slightly elevated viewpoint, using a step just to be a little higher.

There are endless variations when it comes to parent posing, so don't be afraid to experiment.

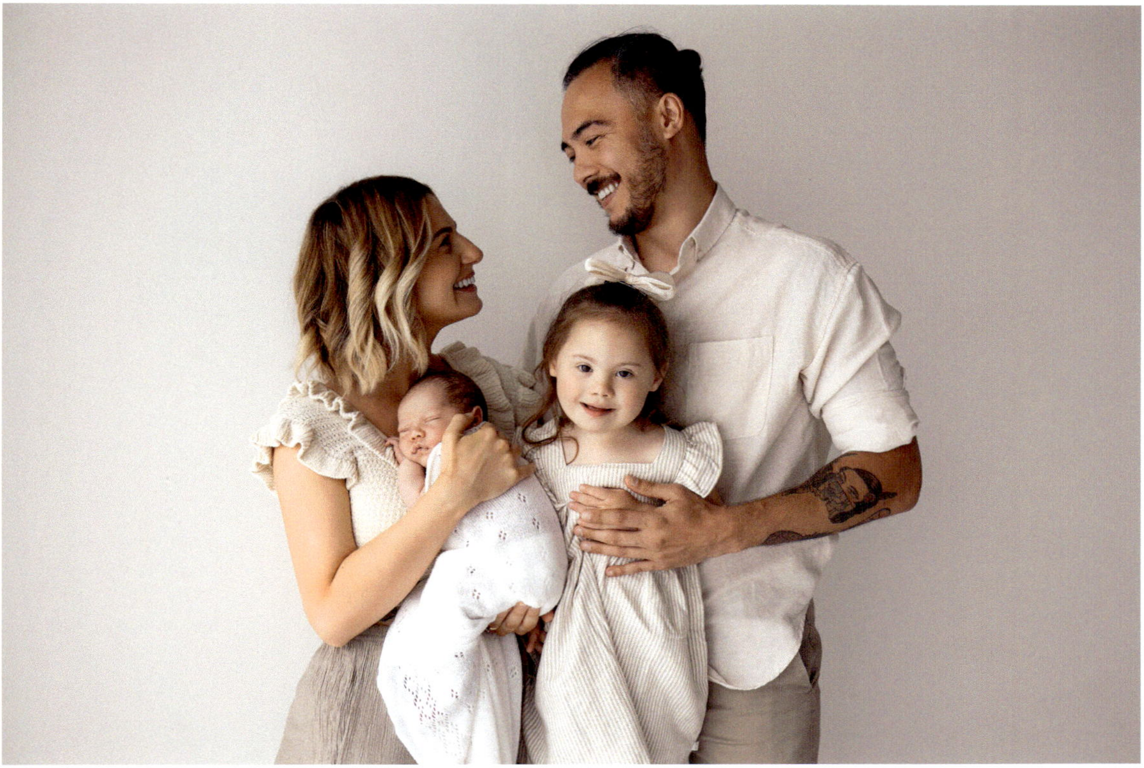

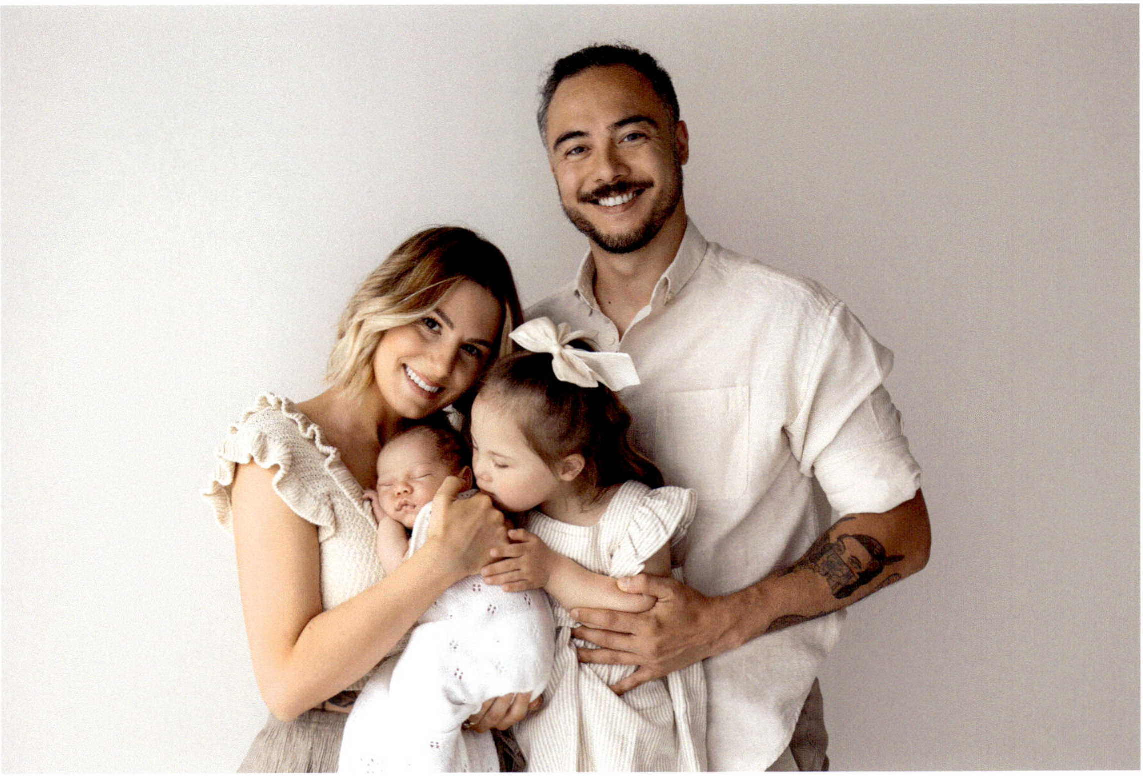

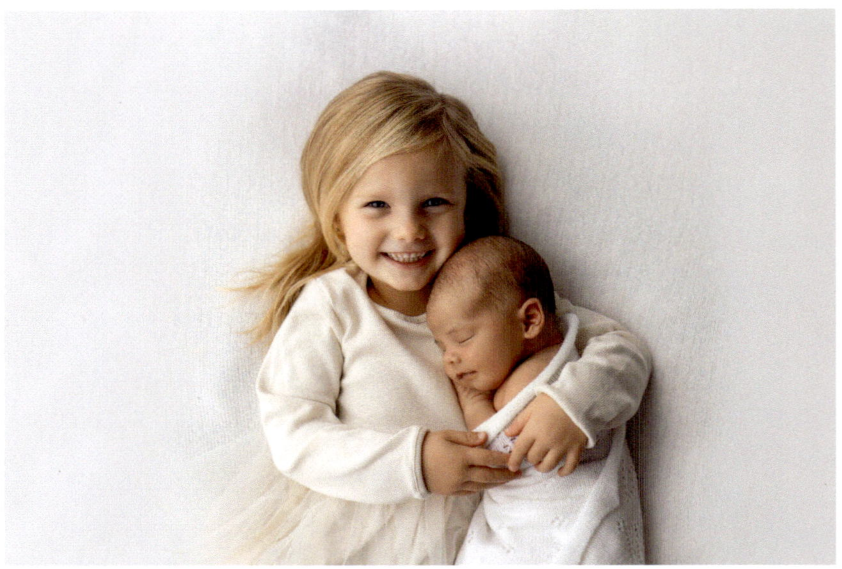

SIBLING POSING

There is never a set plan when a toddler is involved. If the siblings are older children and can take directions, I take time explaining what we will do and photograph in a similar way as I would with parents. However, most of the time, the older brother or sister is still very little.

When they have posed for their images, young children have a tendency to push the baby to one side and walk away, not caring about the baby's safety. Whatever the sibling's age, I always ask parents to stay close by, watch for sudden movements and ensure the baby is safe.

If siblings are young, I lay them down on my beanbag and place the baby next to them. I usually have the baby swaddled to prevent startling, making it easier for the sibling to hold the baby. If a sibling doesn't want to lie down, I lay the baby on its back and ask a toddler to look at him/her, stroke the baby's hair or kiss the his/her head.

Capturing a perfect image of a newborn and his/her sibling can sometimes be impossible. Sometimes, a mum comes to the studio bragging about how much the older sibling loves the baby, and the toddler quickly proves otherwise. Other times, parents are surprised that an older sibling wants to be involved. Toddlers are predictably unpredictable and are rarely shy when letting you know their feelings. If a toddler isn't keen on having his/her pictures taken, these tips might help:

- Build a relationship with a toddler, but do not become their best friend. You want to be an authority figure, almost like a teacher. If you get too friendly, they may not listen to you.
- Talk with the toddler about being a helper and ask them if they have yet to hold the baby. Let them feel and touch the beanbag. Suggest they check how soft it is.
- Don't ask and ask parents to stop asking too. Avoid questions like, 'Would you like to have your picture taken?' or 'Would you like to

hold the baby?'. The answer will most likely be 'no'. Instead, say, 'Let's do it', 'Come and hold the baby' or 'Come to look at the baby'. I also ask the parents not to talk much about the actual photography. If they keep talking about cameras and pictures, toddlers might have an adverse reaction and think being photographed is bad and unpleasant.

- Don't force it. If you force a toddler to lie down, he/she may never trust you again. A few squirms are fine, and you can try to distract them quickly, but if they are trying to escape, let them escape. Do not upset them.
- Distract them. You can use toys, sing or play a peekaboo game. Use a snack or a sticker. Depending on how you have positioned the baby, place the snack on the baby's head or belly or hide it behind the shoulder or arm. I then capture the toddler looking at the baby.

- Praise, clap or give a treat if the toddler cooperates. I have a box with little items like stickers and small toys at the studio – I reward them and let them take one once the session ends. This works especially well with siblings older than two or three years.

If a sibling isn't keen on posing for family images, I often get the parents in place first and quickly 'fly' the sibling into position. I usually use a toy to distract them and rapidly take a photograph. Parents love images of their children together, and I always do my best to create at least a few sibling and family portraits. I know they will make my clients happy and will be treasured for a lifetime.

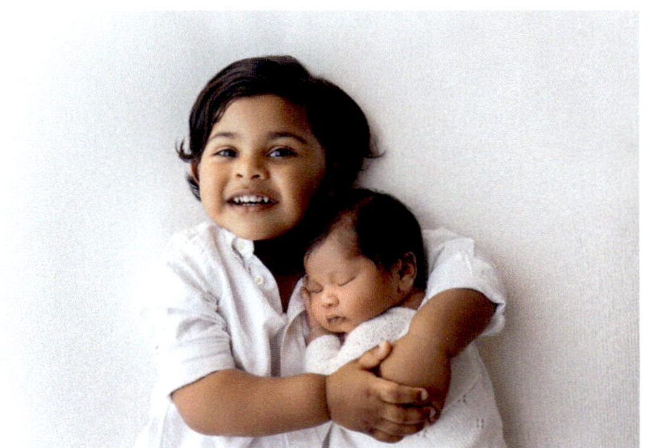

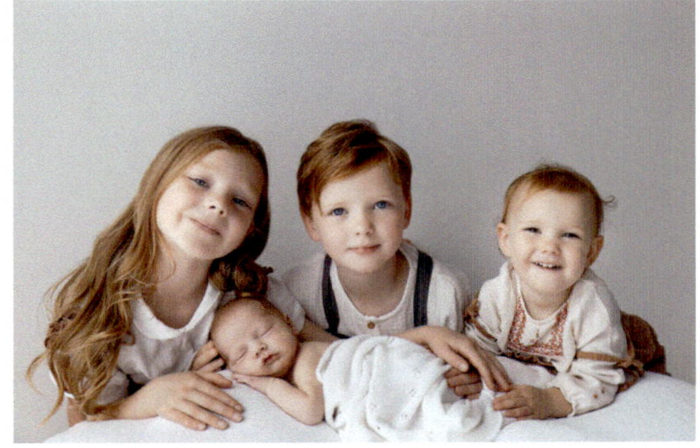

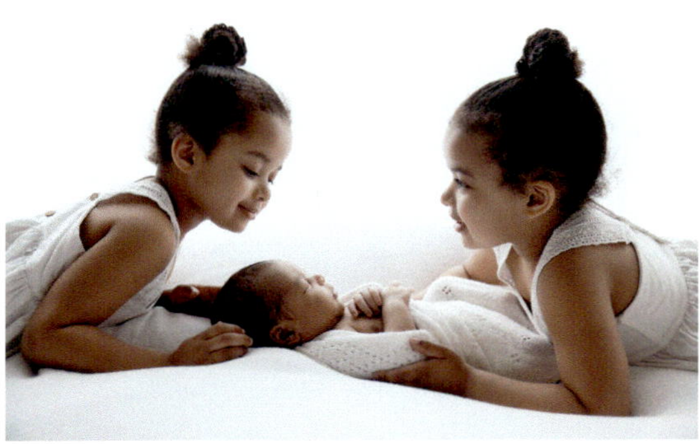

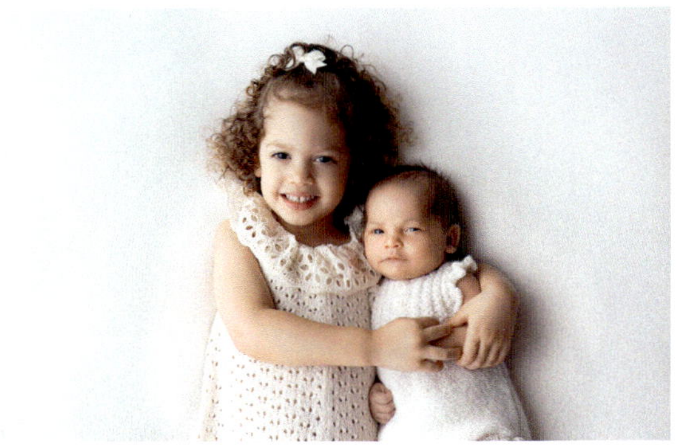

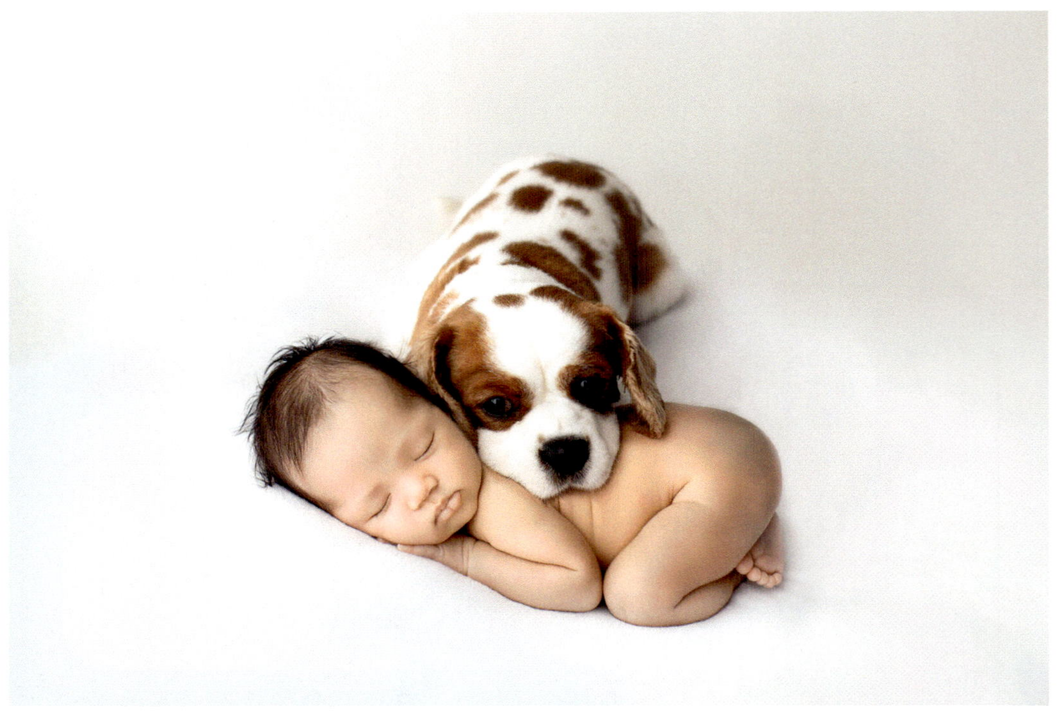

PETS IN NEWBORN SESSIONS

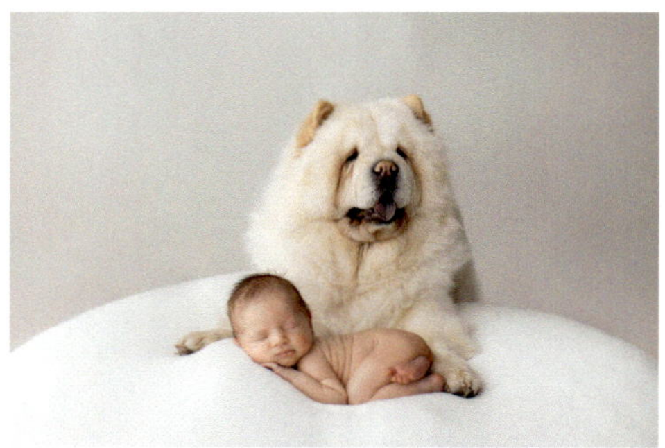

From time to time, a client will ask if they can bring their pet, usually a dog, to their newborn session. Newborn and dog sessions can be a lot of fun and my clients usually adore the images. If a client is thinking about bringing a furry friend to the session, I always like to talk to them about the dog. Not every dog will be happy and comfortable during the shoot. Some are a lot livelier than others, and some are a lot better trained. After all, the baby's safety is our utmost priority. If a dog is calm and well-trained, I love creating baby and pet and family portraits. These images often require a lot of patience, and a lot of the time, they are composites. Only attempt newborn and pet portraits when you are experienced enough and can create them safely.

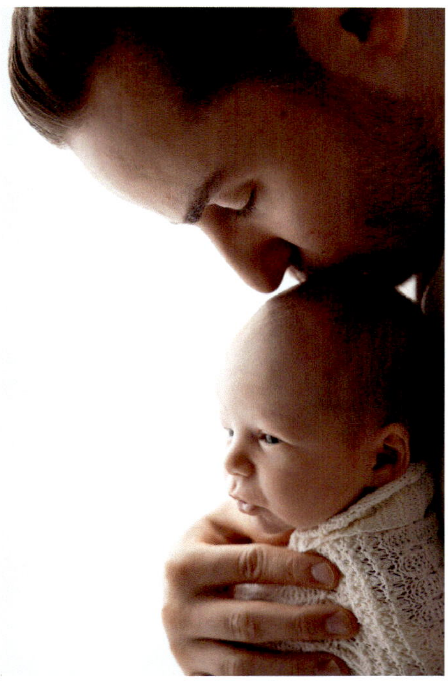

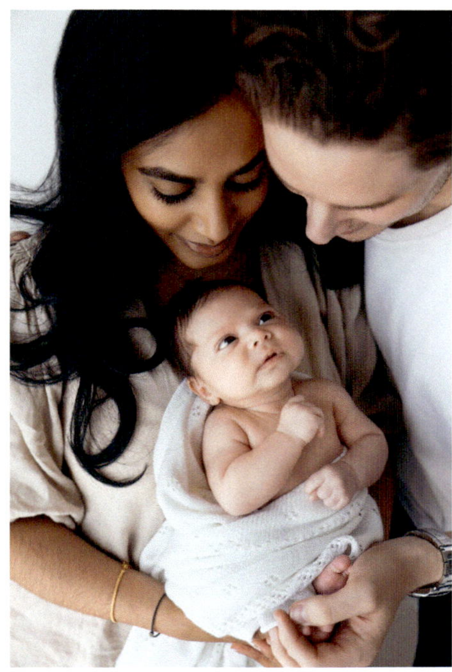

Some photographers panic when babies are awake. Personally, I don't mind an awake baby. However, there is a big difference between an awake baby and an upset baby. If the baby is crying, then soothing it is the first thing I do. However, if the baby is happy or just a little fussy, I keep photographing. The main thing to remember is that if the baby is awake, it is not the time for highly posed images.

You don't always need a sleepy baby to create beautiful images. Yes, sleeping newborns make the job easier, but you can photograph a calm, awake baby too. Don't waste time trying to rock the baby to sleep. Take images of the newborn on its own and then photograph the baby with parents. Babies don't stay awake forever. I never had a newborn session where a baby didn't sleep for at least 20 minutes. The most important thing is to change your mindset and not stress. In my experience, parents absolutely love awake shots. If the baby is fussing, bring parents closer to your light source, give them a swaddled baby and ask them to comfort and soothe the baby. You will capture an incredible sense of love and connection. In moments like this, you will find so much authenticity.

When I arrive at the studio, I prepare my beanbag and some wraps, so I am ready when the baby arrives. My clients usually arrive at 9.30 a.m., and I greet them at the door with a big smile, congratulate them on their arrival and walk them to the seating/shooting area.

I get the baby out of the car seat or pram and talk to the parents while reading the baby's body language and letting the baby get used to me. I find out when the baby was fed, how often the baby usually feeds, what images parents like most and so on. I offer them hot drinks and water and instruct them to sit on a sofa and relax while I photograph and take care of their baby.

I ask parents to dress the baby in a front-opening baby grow, so that I don't disturb the baby while undressing. I turn my fan heater on and slowly undress the baby. I swaddle him/her in a blanket and start photographing. If the baby needs to be fed on arrival, I swaddle the baby in a blanket, and if mum is breastfeeding, I pass the baby to mum to feed. If the baby is formula-fed, I feed the baby myself and chat with the parents while they enjoy their hot drinks. When feeding time is over, I wind the baby and start photographing. I divide my sessions into two parts: I start by taking images of the baby on its own, and then take images with siblings and parents. The first part usually takes about 30–40 minutes; the second part might take a little longer, especially if there is a young sibling.

I always start my sessions with the baby lying on its back swaddled, then move onto the 'baby on its back' pose (see page 104). From there, I smoothly transition to the tummy pose (see page 106), then to either side (see page 108) or chin-on-hands pose (see page 110), and if the baby is happy, I end with the taco pose (see page 112). I don't aim to achieve a certain number of poses – if the baby is sleepier and is full for longer, I shoot more; if the

baby is a little restless or eats more, I try to move him/her less. Once I am done photographing the baby on its own, I usually shoot two set-ups with mum and two with dad, and four family set-ups in between, adding dad to the images when mum is holding the baby and vice versa. Because of my shooting style, I usually produce large galleries of at least 40 images. That said, my clients love albums, and I feel that I need 40 images to create a cohesive, nicely flowing and interesting album.

While shooting, I am always thinking about baby comfort, hand/foot placement, light and camera angles. I want to make sure I create a variety of images for the clients to choose from. My ultimate goal is not to create as many set-ups and pose combos as possible but to create a beautiful, fluid and cohesive grouping of images that tell a story, document the beauty of the family's connection and create a memorable experience for my clients.

At some point during the session or at the end of it, we discuss what happens after the session. We also talk about the products I offer so they can start thinking about how they will display their baby and family images.

After the session, I dress the baby, and if it needs feeding, I give the baby to mum to feed or feed it myself if the baby is bottle-fed. If the baby doesn't need feeding, I place it in the car seat or pram myself. I want to take care of my clients as much as possible and make sure they have the best time while they are with me.

Meet Salor and her family. This is the gallery that I presented to the family; you can see how I transition from pose to pose, and how I pose parents and create variety using angles, crops and gaze.

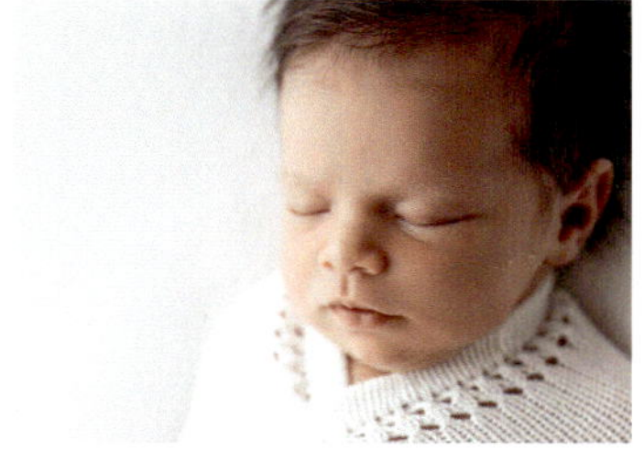
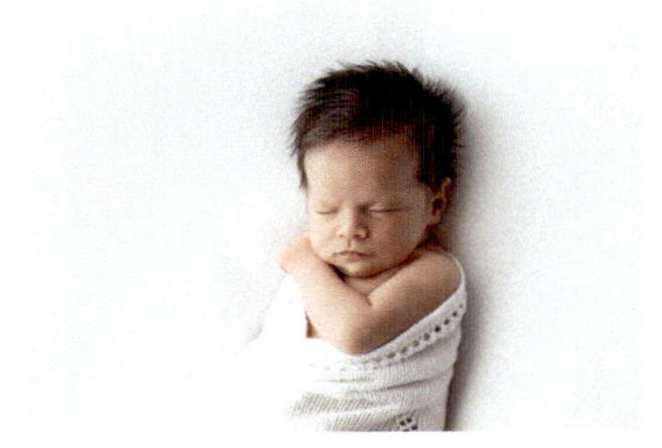
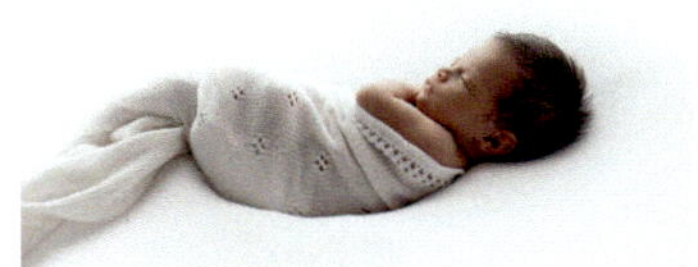
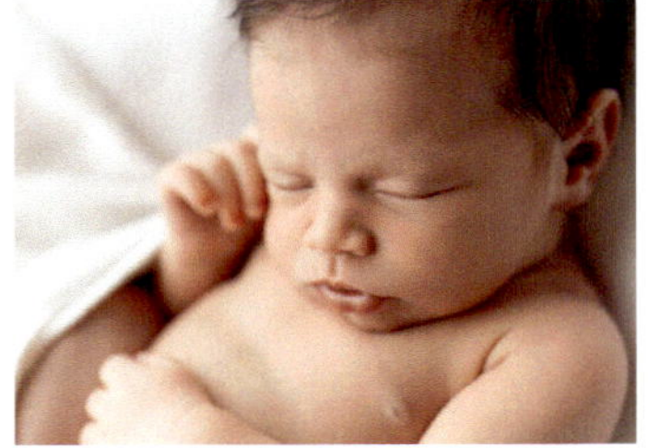
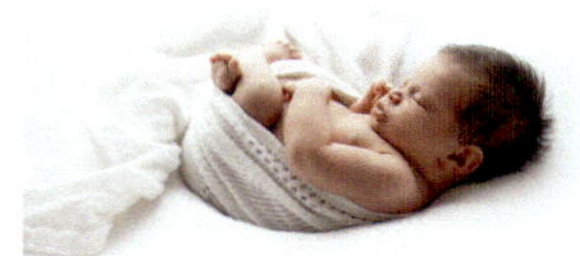
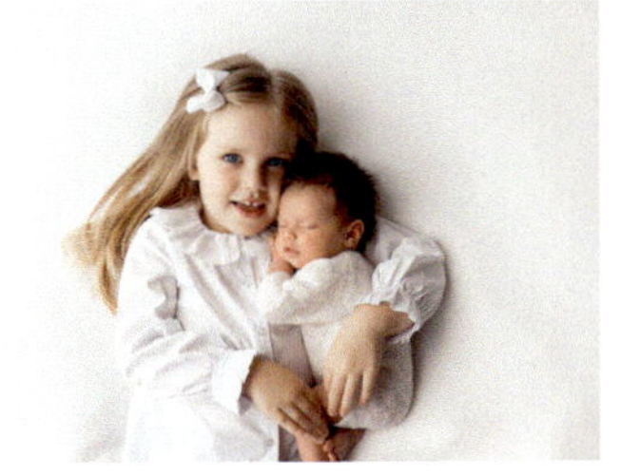
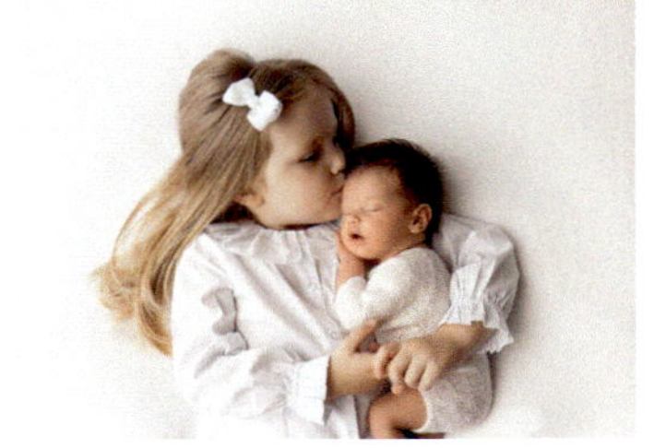
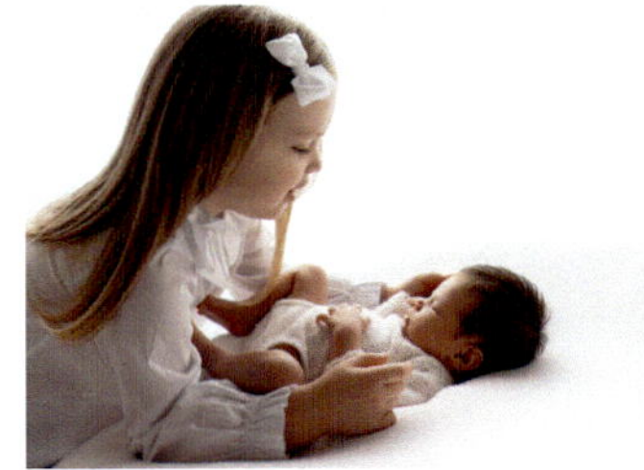
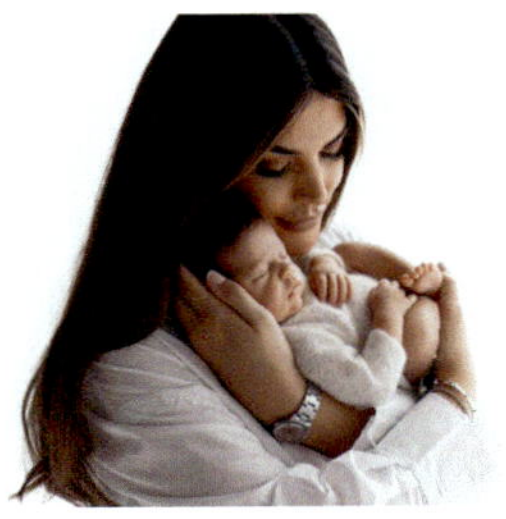
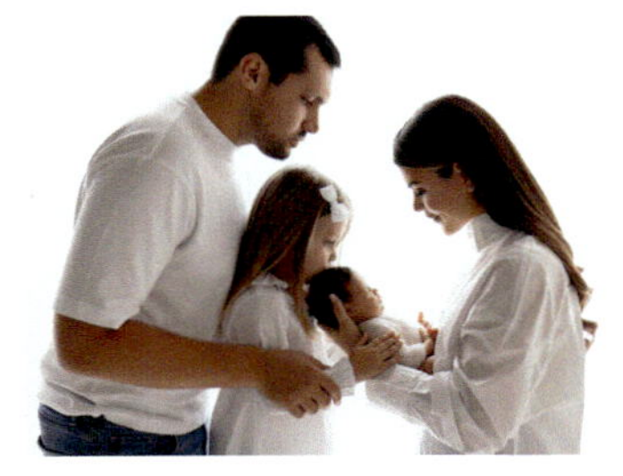
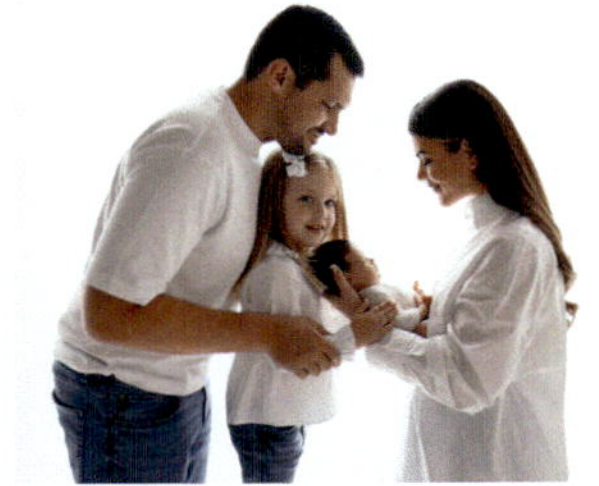
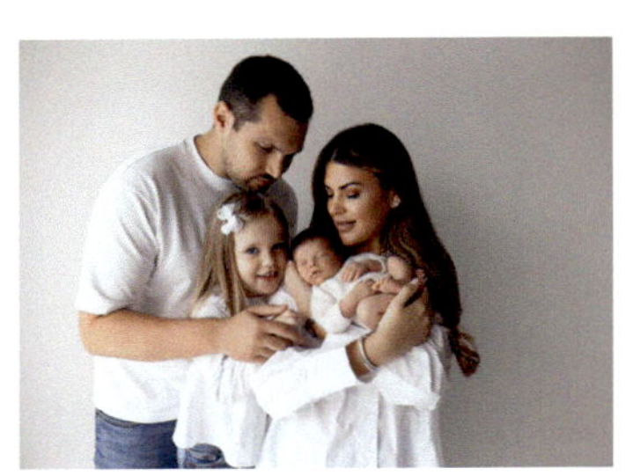
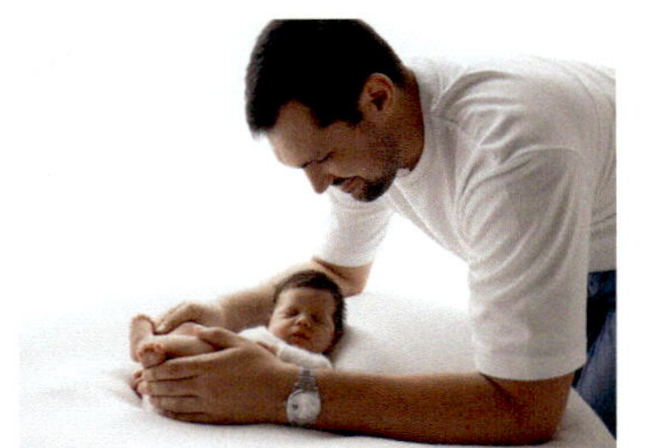
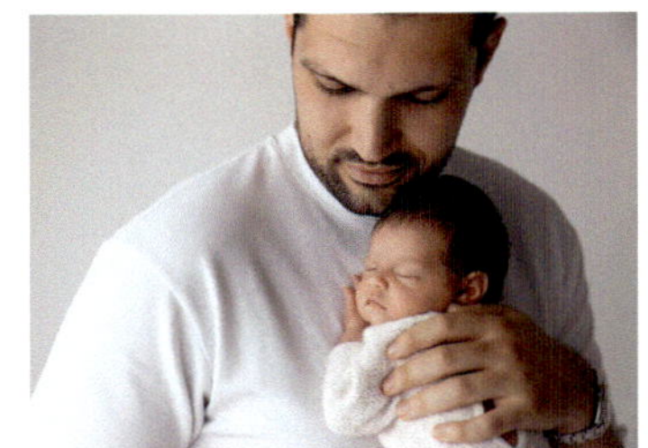

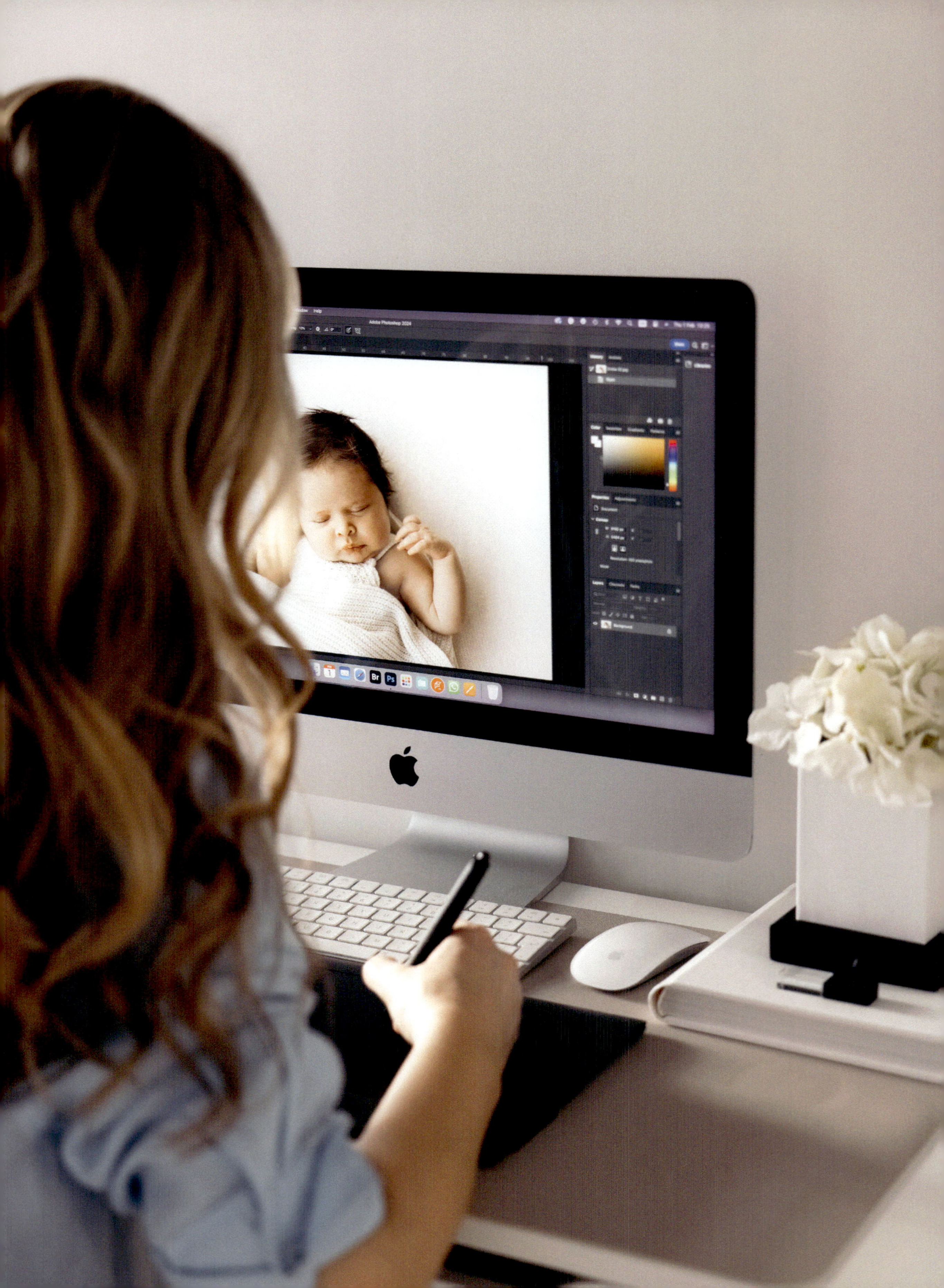

POST-PRODUCTION

In this chapter, we will look at my post-production workflow. This certainly isn't the only way of editing and retouching your images; there are many different ways to achieve the same thing. Also, there are many photography styles, just as there are many post-processing styles. Editing is an important part of the artistic process; it will make your images look professional and, once you find your editing style, will help your work stand out.

I won't teach you basic or advanced editing, but I will show you my way of post-processing maternity and newborn images.

I don't usually use editing to rescue my images, as I like to get my images as perfect as possible in camera to minimize post-production time. Of course, mistakes happen, and just because you haven't got a perfect image straight out of the camera, it doesn't mean you have to bin it. It is good practise to learn how to take images as close to your desired look in camera as possible; post-processing can take a very long time and might be somewhat overwhelming. Image retouching was the first thing that I outsourced in my business. I cull galleries and colour-correct the images to my liking and style myself, but I outsource the final skin retouching. Retouching is very time-consuming, and I'd rather do something else than spend endless hours at a computer screen.

I'm often asked what presets I use and what my SOOC (straight out of the camera) images look like, and my answer often disappoints: my unedited images are very similar to the final images. I keep my editing simple; I like my images clean and natural-looking, and I don't follow any retouching trends. My retouching style is like my photography style: less is more. However, as I have said throughout this book, we are all different, and you should find a post-production workflow that works best for you.

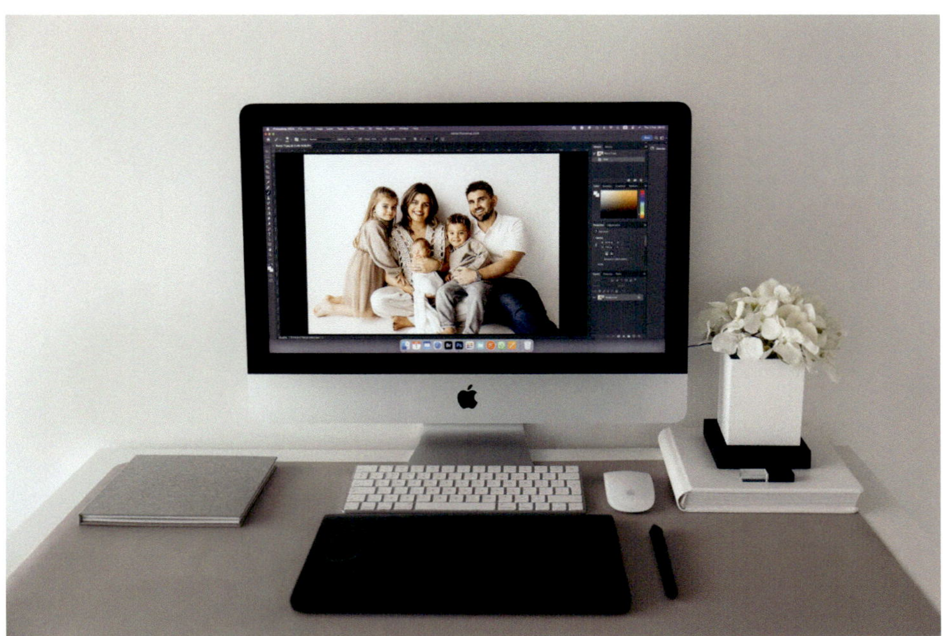

EDITING: GETTING STARTED

In terms of file type, I always shoot Raw. These unprocessed files have so much data and give you maximum control over your images. There are many different editing programs to choose from, but the most popular are Adobe Lightroom, Camera Raw and Photoshop. Capture One is also widely used by portrait photographers.

I use Adobe Bridge, Camera Raw and Photoshop. If you are relatively new to the photography industry, you will most likely use Lightroom, which includes both Bridge and Camera Raw. These programs have some differences, but their core functionalities are the same.

Your first priority is to keep your files organized. As a photographer, you will produce tens of thousands of files, so it's important to create a system that allows you to easily find what you are looking for.

I organize my files in folders by year and which post-production stage the images are at. Every folder within this system is named after the client and the date of their shoot. Create a system that works best for you.

Image selection

I use Adobe Bridge to cull – or thin out – my images. I start by star-rating the images I want to select. In the first pass, I select quickly. In the second pass, I look for duplicates, better expressions, blinks, etc. I also discard any images that are out of focus. If I need to do any head swaps, I give those images a two-star rating.

Basic corrections

Once I have selected my favourites, I open them in Camera Raw. This is where I make most of my corrections. If the light didn't change throughout the shoot, I can usually batch edit the entire gallery. If not, I look for images with the same light settings and try to batch them to save time.

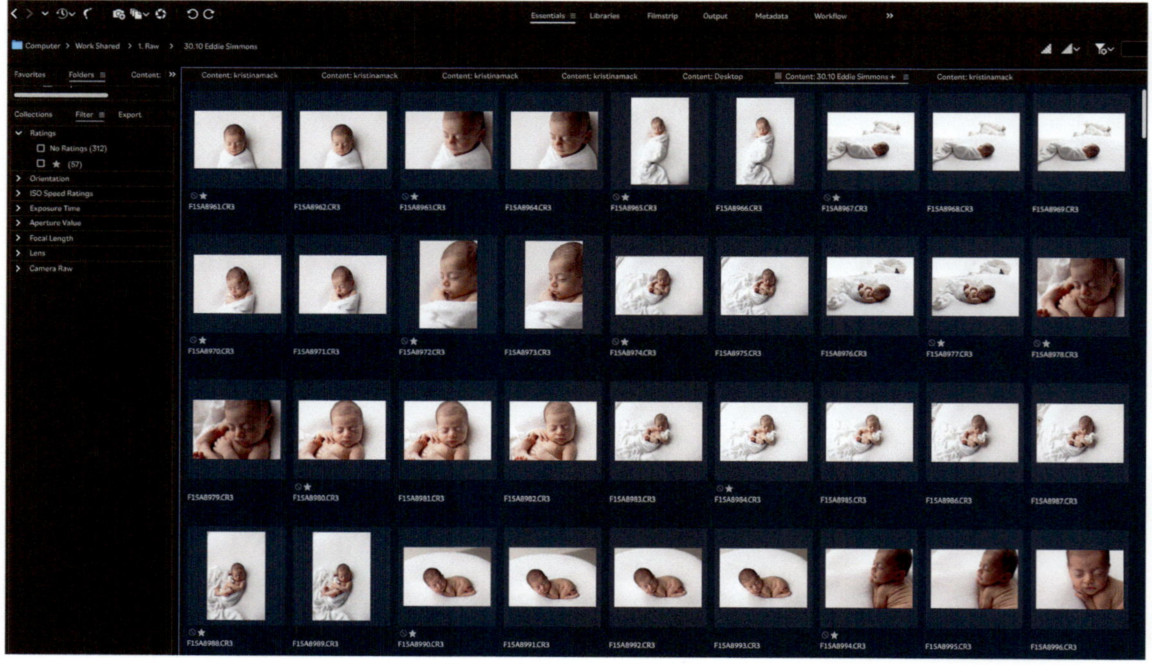

Images from a newborn session opened in Adobe Bridge.
The starred images are the ones I'm keeping for the final selection.

MY CAMERA RAW WORKFLOW

1. **Exposure**. I always start by adjusting the exposure. It is hard to see colours if an image is over- or underexposed.

2. **White balance**. White balance is adjusted using the Temperature slider. If images are too cold, warm them up and vice versa.

3. **Highlights and shadows**. I very seldom adjust any of these. If the light is very contrasty and I have lots of shadows in my images, I might brighten the shadows, but it isn't something I do regularly.

4. **Detail**. If I have used a high ISO during a session, then I increase Luminance and Colour (noise) a little.

5. **Crop tool**. I try to get my crops right in my camera, but if I need to crop my images, I prefer to do that in Photoshop. Crop is another tool that you will find very helpful.

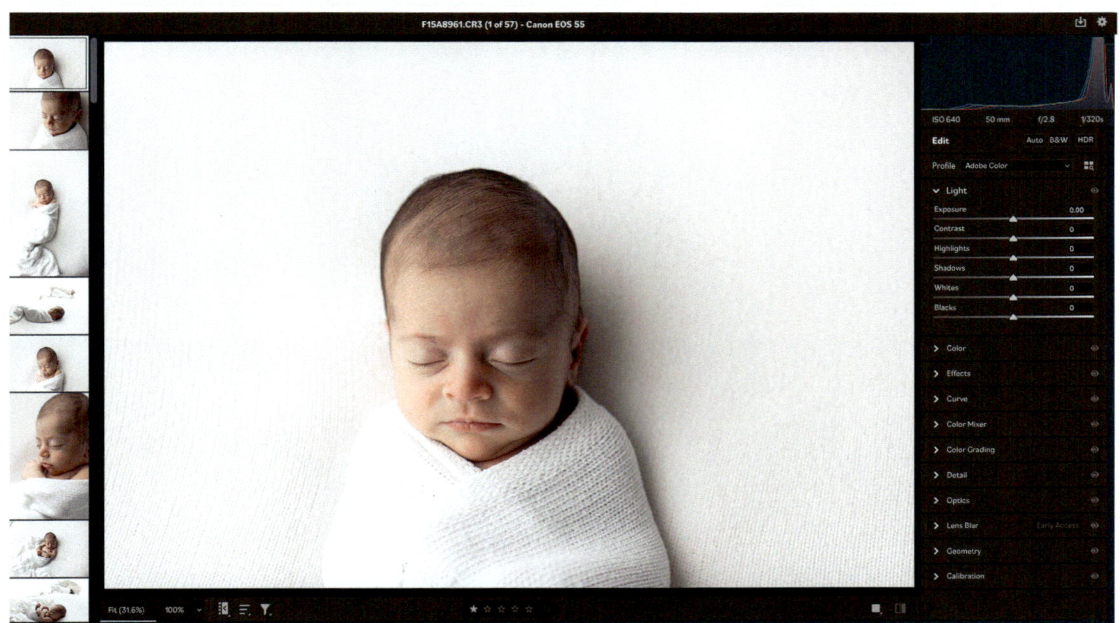

This is a perfectly exposed image, but it is slightly too cold,
so I moved the Temperature slider a little to the right to warm it up.

SKIN TONES

I use the Color Mixer panel in Camera Raw to correct the colour and tone of a baby's skin. Here, you can select and adjust individual colours either manually or using the Targeted Adjustment tool. Simply click on the colour you want to adjust and drag the sliders until you achieve the desired outcome. How you adjust the sliders will depend not only on the baby's skin tone and colour, but also on your personal preference and style.

Masking with the Adjustment Brush tool is another great way to apply local adjustments, particularly if there is more than one person in an image. I fine tune the effects sliders (Tint, Exposure, Contrast, etc.) and specify brush options (Size, Feather, Flow, etc.) for a particular person and use the same brush to quickly edit all the images featuring that person, then reset the brush for another person and so on. Correcting skin tones in Camera Raw or Lightroom will save you a lot of time.

These are the tools that I use on a daily basis. Depending on the baby's skin tone, the quality of light and the accessories I used, I might also increase contrast, increase or decrease saturation and sometimes use the Curve panel. However, I always aim to keep my retouching to a minimum.

Once I've made my tonal adjustments, I save the images as JPEG files and switch to Photoshop for my finer retouching.

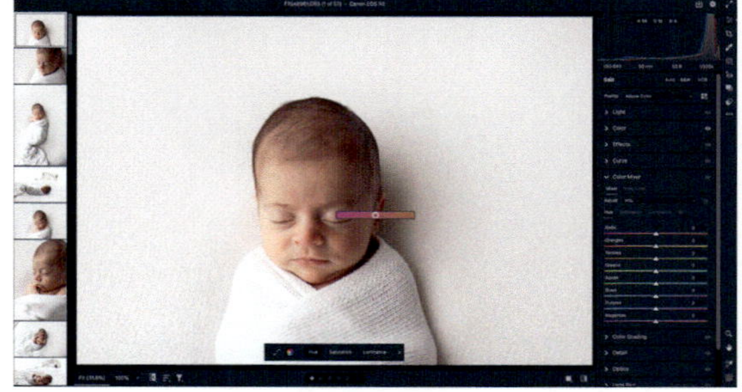

The Targeted Adjustment Tool slider.

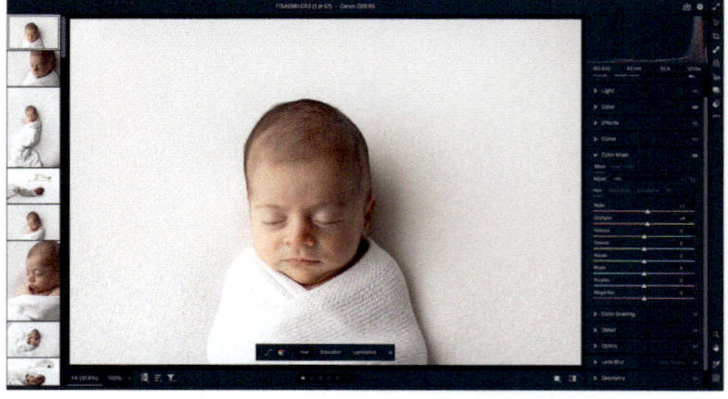

The adjustments I made to achieve beautiful skin colour.

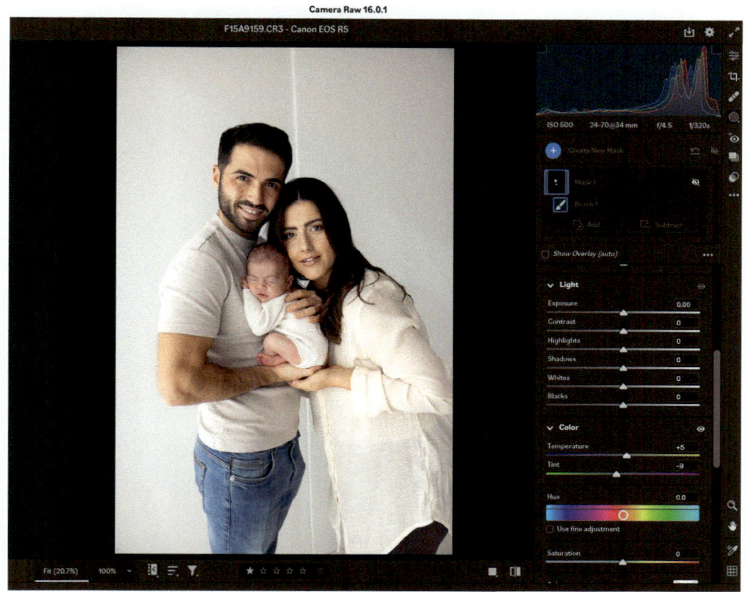

The baby's skin has a slightly magenta tone
in comparison to the parents.

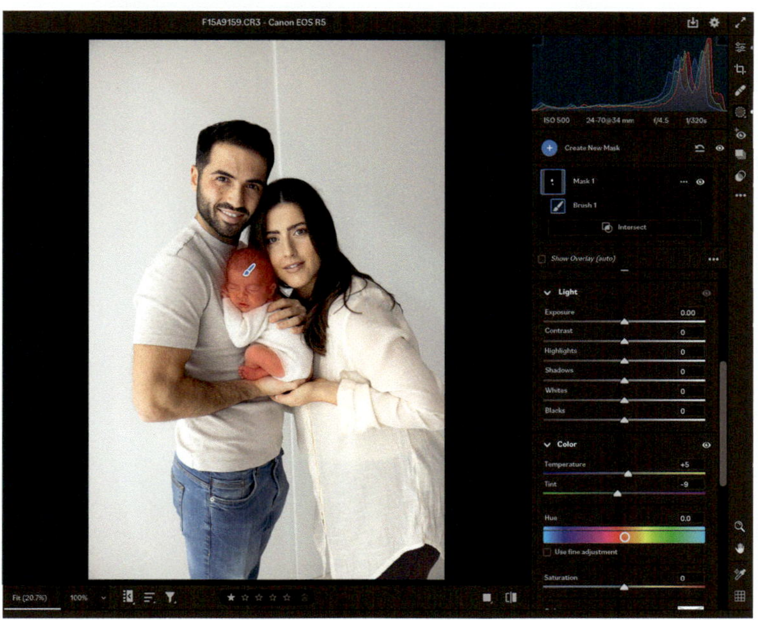

I painted over the baby's skin with the Adjustment Brush
and adjusted Temperature and Tint.

Once the basic corrections have been applied in Camera Raw or Lightroom, I use Photoshop to retouch finer details. This powerful image-editing software allows you to manipulate, refine and polish your images to a professional standard.

Camera Raw and Lightroom both feature Healing tools, but they are not ideal for fine skin retouching. Your edits might look acceptable on screen, but poor retouching is a lot more visible on a print. Using Photoshop for skin retouching is quicker and allows for more accurate edits. I don't like overly retouched images – I still want to see skin texture and facial hair.

The Clone Stamp and Healing Brush are the two tools I use most in Photoshop. The Clone Stamp allows me to fill missing parts of a blanket or background, while the Healing Brush allows me to retouch skin, remove stray hair and clean up backgrounds and clothing, etc.

Photoshop allows you to create 'actions'. Actions are sets of recorded tasks; they are a great way to save time by automating tasks you perform regularly. The Signature Newborn Photoshop Action Suite by Lauren Bennett at LSP Actions is a great set of actions to help you retouch maternity and especially newborn images.

Liquify

Liquify is a powerful tool, but use it with restraint, as it is very easy to get carried away. I use Liquify to make subtle changes. If I 'slim' someone, I slim them slightly from the back. I also use it to 'tuck' chins if needed, and sometimes to perfect the hair. I use this tool so subtly that I have never had a client notice that anything had been done to their images. One thing I never do is change the shape of pregnant bellies, as this defeats the point of photographing them in the first place.

Before retouching images, I always ask my clients if there is anything they would like to keep or remove, and I always retouch images to my clients' tastes. If they ask for something that I don't agree with, like changing belly shape, I gently talk them out of it.

Perfecting images in post-production takes a lot of time, so do your best to capture your images correctly in camera and to batch edit in Camera Raw or Lightroom. As I mentioned earlier, I seldom do my own retouching, and unless you absolutely love it, I recommend outsourcing it as soon as you can.

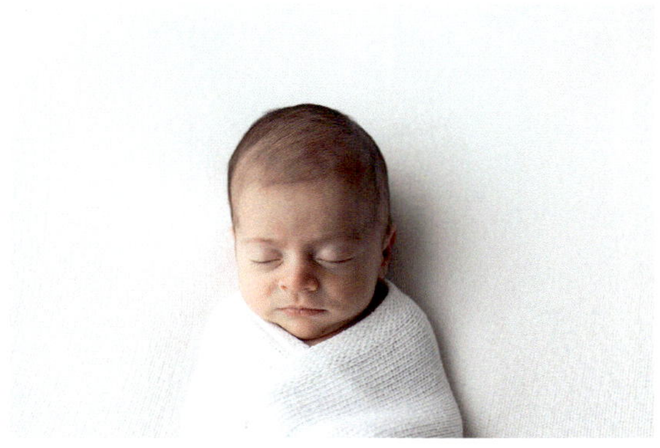

Raw image 1

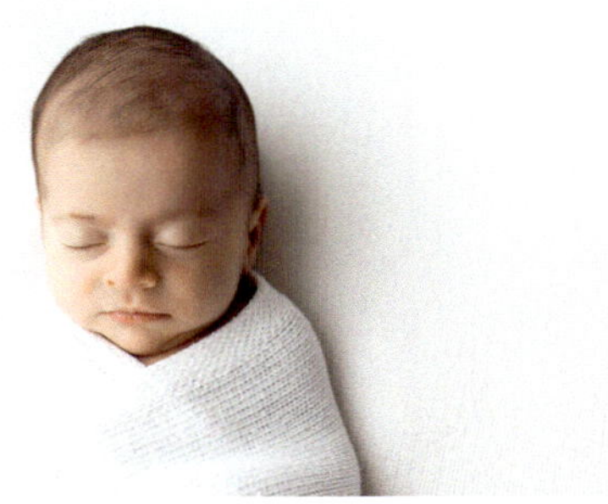

Final image 1

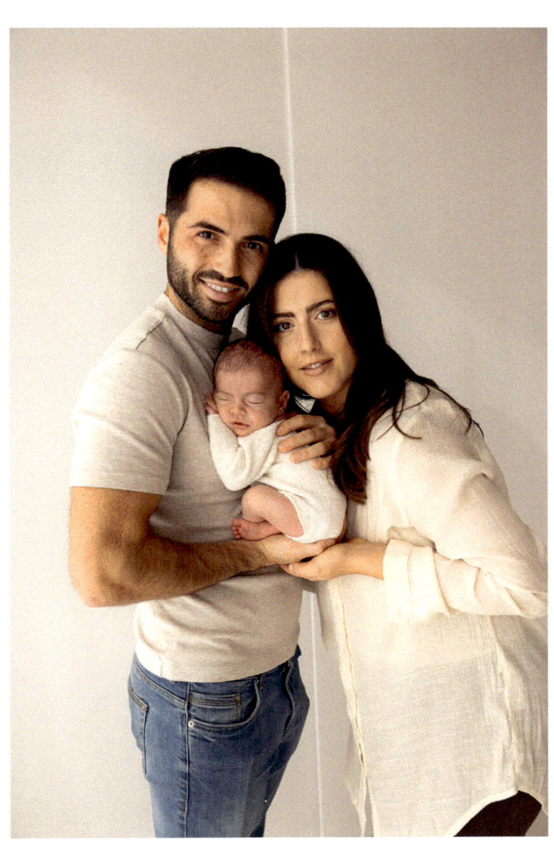

Raw image 2

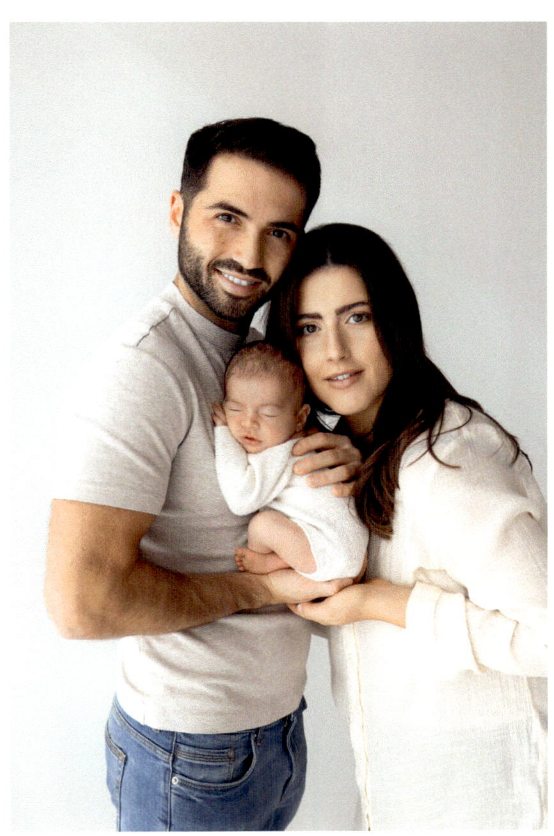

Final image 2

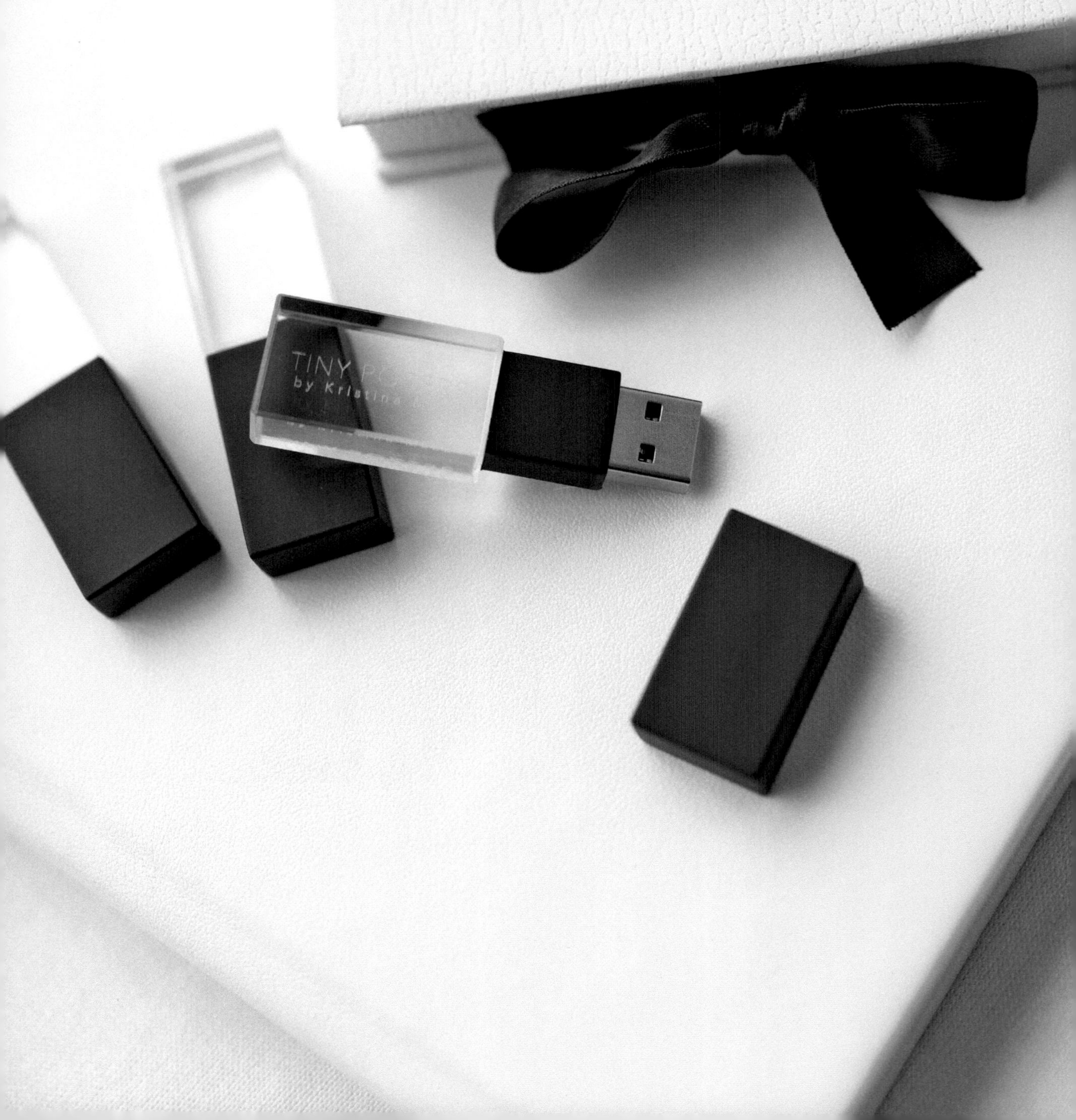
TINY POSERS
newborns by Kristina Mack
TINY POSERS
by Kristina Mack

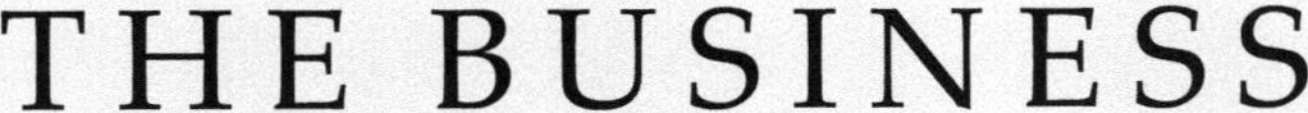

THE BUSINESS

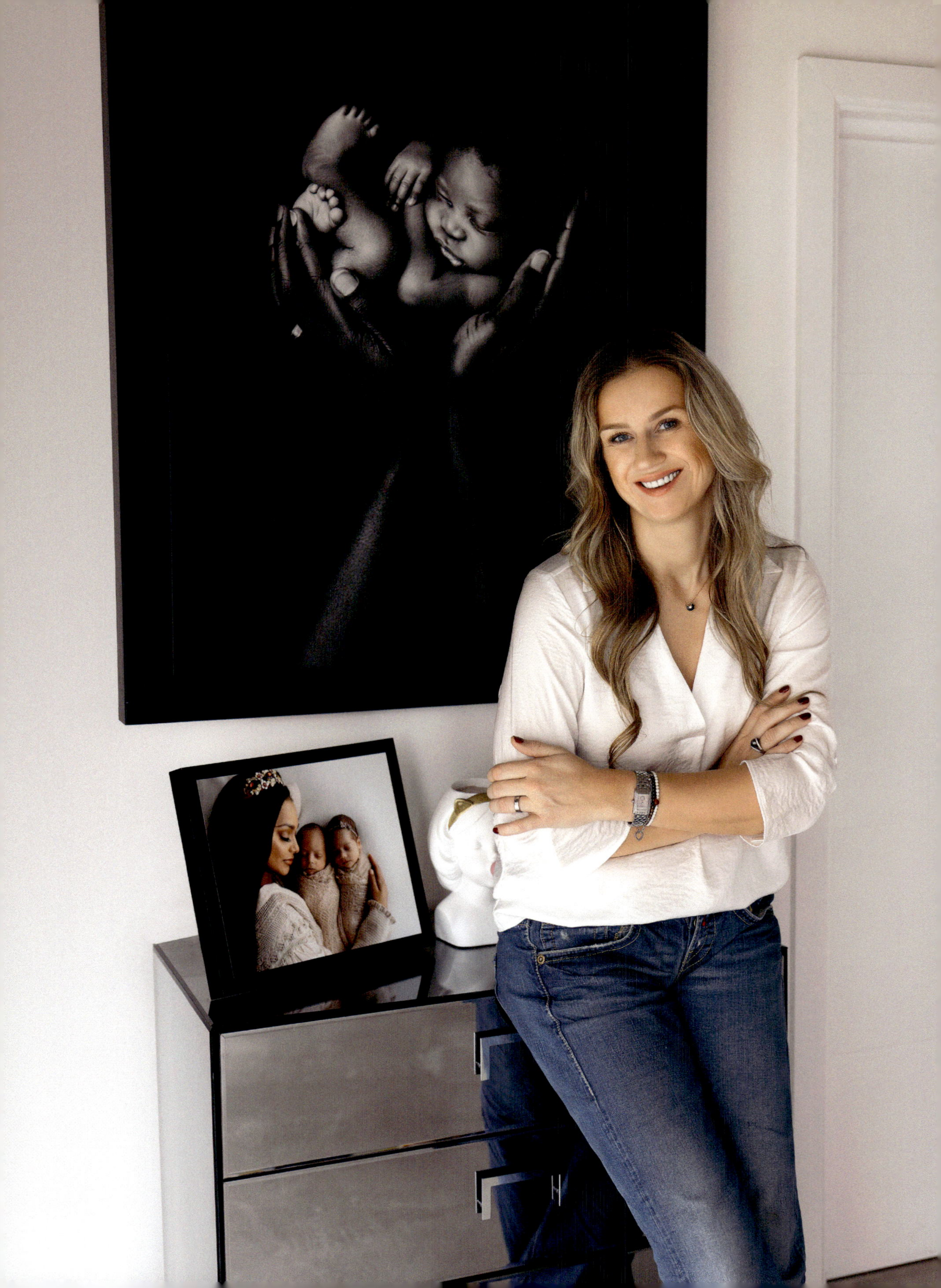

*'To have a successful and profitable career in photography,
you have to take care of every aspect of the business.'*

THERE IS NO SECRET

When I started my career as a newborn photographer, I had a completely different mindset than I have now. Firstly, I didn't look at this venture as a business. Secondly, I thought that if you take great pictures, 'business' will automatically happen. Looking back, I want to cry and laugh at how naive I was. I still see so many photographers thinking the same way; even with all the information and free educational resources on the internet, so many photographers still think that great photographs is all it takes. Yes, you need to master your craft, but that alone is not enough – you also must master the business side of it, otherwise you will just have a hobby.

When it comes to marketing your business, I always use a car as a comparison. Your ability to take photographs and run your business is the chassis and body, but marketing is your wheels. If your wheels are spinning, but your engine is faulty, you won't get very far. To have a successful and profitable career in photography, you have to take care of every aspect of the business. Despite many people thinking the opposite, there are no secrets or shortcuts when it comes to running a business and filling your calendar with bookings – just hard work.

In this chapter, I want to share the essential components of a successful photography business and encourage you to start from the very beginning, not the middle.

ART & BUSINESS

Long gone are the days of the starving artist.
People often don't look seriously at those working
in the creative arts industry. I admit I was and
partially still am the same. We all believe that
doctors, lawyers, bankers and other professionals
earn more and enjoy a better standard of
living than everyday musicians, painters and
photographers. However, this isn't necessarily
true. Yes, it is hard to earn a comfortable living
working as an artist, but that doesn't mean that
you can't do it. A lot of people in the creative
industries may treat their jobs as hobbies or have
a 'my talent will get me bookings' mindset and
never manage to live from their craft, however, I
know a lot of photographers who run successful
businesses. Is it easy to succeed in the creative
industry? I'd say yes – if you put in the work.

There is logic in every artistic brain. If you don't
believe this, you must change your mindset. It's
unlikely you will succeed without business skills.
Even average artists can succeed if their business
skills are amazing. If your work is exceptional but
you are not business savvy, it will be very hard to
make photography your full-time job.

What's the recipe for success? Excellent technical
and creative skills, business knowledge and
implementation, and a positive mindset.

Money is not a dirty word

How much money have you spent on cameras, lenses, props, workshops and software already? You have all the kit and all the information, but your business is still stagnant. You haven't yet moved forwards. If anything, you are just a little more in debt.

You and I both know it doesn't take a certain lens or camera to succeed; it takes business knowledge, a ton of marketing and a particular mindset.

Money is not a dirty word – it is something we must talk about. Imagine how much easier it would be to sell your products and raise your prices if you knew your value and were confident talking about money. Imagine how much your business would change if you started saying no to discounts, charged what you believe you are worth and, most importantly, believe that there is always plenty more business there.

We all need money, but desperation does not bring it to us. Money is simply something you get in exchange for your talent and hard work. It does not describe your worth, your characteristics or personality traits. You are doing a job and you need to be paid for it.

Discounts scream desperation. Imagine there are two shops selling similar products: one has a queue outside, the other has sales assistants offering passers-by 'buy one get one free' deals. Most people will happily queue for a desirable product but will do anything to avoid being accosted in the street. Why is that? It is because we presume the product must be inferior or not worth what the seller is asking for, and we fear being conned or cheated. Don't be that desperate salesperson.

Believing in yourself and having a positive money mindset is part of a successful business. You need to believe that you are worthy and know that there is plenty of money to go around. If you have a positive money mindset, you will be more inclined and willing to take action, learn new skills and grow as a person. You are a unique and valuable person, and you are worth every penny you decide to charge. If it helps, keep notes, read books or write a journal; whatever it takes to foster a good relationship with money and your personal value.

Whether you are starting from scratch or have been running a photography business for a while, it is important that you start with the basics and build from there. It's a bit like a house – you must start with the foundations. The sooner you have a clear picture of your dream business and goals, the sooner you will create the business that makes you happy.

Setting yourself apart

You have announced to the world that you are a photographer. What happens next? You get asked to photograph kids' birthday parties, some family images, a new baby or siblings, a dog, a wedding and so on. You are happy and take every opportunity, hoping one job will lead to another. You photograph things you love and things that just came your way and you didn't want to or couldn't say 'no' to. However, soon you will become a photographer of everything while specializing in nothing, or you will slowly lose your passion for photography. Clearly defining your niche will not only set you apart and make your clients see you as an expert in your field, but it will also help you work in a genre of photography, style and price range you love most.

The Oxford Dictionary defines 'niche' as 'a small section of the market for a particular kind of product or service'. Even the dictionary uses 'small' in its definition. However, I would say 'targeted' defines a niche a lot better.

A business niche is choosing to service a specific area/client in the marketplace. This can be by location, audience type, demand, financial situation or some other narrowing criteria. Simply put, your niche is the group of people for whom your products and services have been created.

Having a niche truly matters. When starting out, photographers often think that selecting a niche will reduce opportunities for potential work. However, do not make this mistake. The niche is more about being targeted and relevant. By choosing your niche, you get to clearly understand your audience's specific needs and support those needs through a well-targeted service or product. Once you know the why (they will buy) and the what (they will receive from you), you can better define how to plan, market, sell, service, price and achieve recognition for your work.

I know the thought of limiting your target market can be scary, particularly if you're starting out or are not yet making much money from your craft. But while it might sound counter-intuitive, the benefits of having a niche might just be the secret to your success.

What is the benefit of having a niche? A niche is something that can be used to differentiate your business from others in your industry and give you a unique edge over your competitors. Instead of promoting yourself just as a photographer, you could get more specific and market yourself as a maternity and newborn photographer.

From a marketing perspective, having a niche also lets you be clear about how you serve your audience. You would market to brides in one way, and market to new mums in a very different way. Let's take a personal trainer as an example. A man who is looking to build muscles will be attracted to a completely different message than a new mum who is looking to strengthen her body after pregnancy.

Another benefit is that you will be competing with fewer businesses. You're no longer 'a personal trainer' or 'a photographer' competing with many PTs and photographers. Instead, you're fulfilling a specific need; you are a maternity and newborn photography expert. You'll give yourself the opportunity to become the go-to business for whatever products or services you offer.

The more targeted your niche is, the more likely you will attract your ideal audience or client. And this doesn't just apply to the genre of photography – it applies to the price of your services too.

I often hear photographers saying that they like photographing everything – a little bit of family, a little bit of weddings, a little bit of branding. However, the danger with failing to niche down is that you market yourself so broadly that it dilutes your message. This will result in you attracting fewer ideal clients, and fewer people will be interested in buying from you because they won't be sure of what exactly you photograph and if you're the right person to help them.

If you love maternity and newborn photography, focus your attention on these niches in order to help you create a really strong brand message that attracts ideal clients to your business. At the end of the day, most customers aren't just looking for any photographer, they are looking for the best option to suit their style and budget.

'Clearly defining your niche will not only set you apart and make your clients see you as an expert, but it will also help you work in a genre of photography, style and price range you love most.'

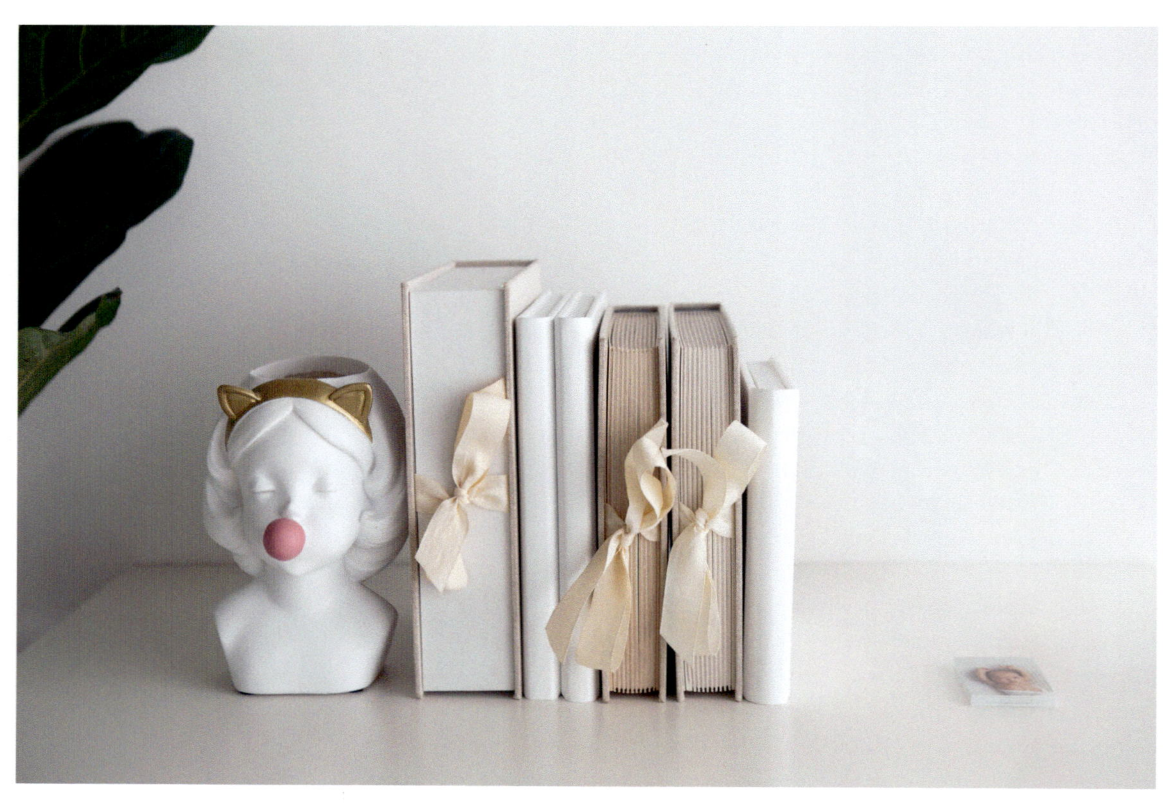

Fitness trainer Ren Jones said, 'Marketing is the equivalent of asking someone on a date. Branding is the reason they say yes.' This is the easiest way to understand what branding is and why it is essential. If you market your business, but the people you are marketing to are not connecting with your brand, they will not book you.

The first step in your journey as a maternity and newborn photographer is to decide what you want your message and style to be. Refining these two things is going to set you apart from other maternity and newborn photographers, and it's also going to make your marketing so much easier. When you have a clear brand identity, clients who resonate with your message will book you and value your work and experience so much more.

So, how do you establish your brand identity? The easiest way to start is with your aesthetic style, message and mission statement.

When identifying your brand, consider:
• Your personal style
• Your personality
• Session styling
• Lighting style
• The products you offer
• Your message

For example, I wear very neutral, functional clothing, seldom anything trendy. I like simple, carefree outfits and minimal make-up. I want to look as though I haven't tried too hard to look a certain way. I like clean lines, minimalist styling and solid colours. I am not a loud person, but I love to talk a lot to my clients. I want to hear their stories and share mine. I like to build an intimate, close relationship with them. I use soft, natural light, and seldom shoot high-contrast or vibrant colour images. I like to provide full service to my clients; they return to my studio to view their

images and place an order – most of my clients like to order framed wall art and albums.

My message and mission statement is that, above all, I strive to deliver a remarkable experience to my clients. A lot of my clients are new parents and are often very emotional, sleep-deprived and anxious. I don't just want to take beautiful images for them; I also want to take care of them, so they have a relaxing time with me.

Your mission statement might be completely different. You might prefer a styled shoot or want to provide a full makeover and large tulle or boho-style gowns to your clients. You might be loud or, the opposite, an introvert. There is a demographic for that too. This is why it is important to figure out your style.

What lighting and editing style are you drawn to? What space do you shoot in? Do you travel to clients' homes? What products would you like to offer? Are you happy with selling just digital images via a download link, or would you like to sell framed images and albums? Do you sell via online galleries or do your clients come back for their viewing and sales appointments?

Your message and mission statement are as important as your personal style. When you know what message you want your work to convey, you will keep it in mind every time you create something for your business.

Consistency is critical when it comes to branding. The brand must be consistent to not only develop trust but also to be recognizable.

Remember, branding is not just a visual thing. It's personality and promise driven. It must be consistent, and that consistency in your brand is paramount to its success.

Ideal client

Now that you are clear on your brand message and style, you'll need to figure out who you're talking to. Knowing who your ideal client is will help you with marketing your business and reaching the client that suits your business best. Getting specific about your audience isolates your market and increases the effectiveness of your message. Remember, nailing down an ultra-specific target demographic doesn't mean you will never photograph anyone outside of those parameters, but what it does mean is that your job will get a lot easier when it comes to filling your calendar with clients that align and resonate with your brand and you personally.

To establish who your ideal client is, think about who will be drawn to your brand message and style. Describe who you would like your typical client to be. Is it a mum or a dad that you are going to target? And what is your business model? Are you high volume, low price, or boutique? Where are you going to find your clients? What are their interests? Your ideal client will likely be a new mum; what are her fears, her objections, her needs, her wants? Does she value photography? Does she like to display images on her walls or just share a few images on social media? The answers to these questions will help you to create a marketing message using language that is going to resonate. She's going to feel like you are talking directly to her; she's going to feel like your business is just what she is looking for.

Building business foundations

The business plan often scares photographers. However, instead of thinking about a complicated document, treat your business plan as a road map. There are so many things to do and set up when you are running a business; a business plan will let you stay on track and map out the next steps.

The process of creating a business plan can be a long one, especially if you are new to photography or have never built a business before. Creating your business plan should take weeks, if not months of work while you add new ideas, explore new aspects of your business and give thought to areas you've never considered before. Be sure to keep a journal or notebook handy to jot down ideas and features to add to your business plan over time. You may also find setting aside dedicated time each week for business-planning activities helpful. I usually dedicate Friday afternoons to business tasks; I check my calendar for booked sessions and appointments, create my to-do lists, plan my working hours and more.

Once completed, your business plan will remain forever in a state of change and growth; business plans are known as an 'evergreen' document, meaning they are constantly updated and adjusted. I dedicate the first two days of the new quarter to revisiting, reviewing and revising my business plan. I check if I am on track and what needs to be done, examine what worked, and focus on my marketing, business and financial plans. Many of us immediately jump into trying to price our products and services. After acquiring the camera and props, pricing is the next logical step, right? In reality, a solid business plan should come first.

How to write a business plan

When creating a business plan, your goal is to create a map to navigate your business with. This goal may appear simple when written in black and white, but in reality, this is often a monumental and overwhelming task for most creatives. Many of us prefer to be inspired and go wherever creativity takes us, and sitting down to make a plan for how we'll be inspired seems counter-intuitive. However, business requires a more structured approach.

By having a plan to refer to, we can compare and assess new opportunities that come our way, evaluate our progress, refine the experience we offer our clients and build a foundation for our marketing efforts.

Here is a list of what you need to include in your business plan:

- Table of contents, so you can easily find whatever you are looking for.
- Your brand identity, vision, values, message and mission statement.
- Market analysis. Who are the photographers that are working in the same geographical area? What services do they provide, and what clients do they serve? Do you have a potential market in your area? How many nurseries and schools are there? This is your chance to do some detective work and learn more about your local area from a business perspective.

- Marketing plan. This can be as detailed as you want it to be and should at least include a description of who your ideal client is, how they get information and where you can reach them. A more detailed plan may include a calendar of activities that you will implement each week. Think about your marketing budget – do you have it or will you rely on free marketing for now?
- Financial plan. This section of your business plan is more than just your price menus, products and services; it should also include more of the bigger picture too. What does success mean to you? What are your overall financial goals for your business? This section of your business plan should include:
  * An overview of your financial goals.
  * Profit and loss calculations, balance sheets.
  * A detailed description of your products, their source, your supplier and how you order them.
  * Your product pricing worksheets and menu.
  * A detailed outline of how you get your products from your camera to your client, the delivery timelines, when you need to place your orders and the usual workflow from camera to the final product.
  * Your sales methods e.g. online or in person.
- Training. Do you need to improve your skills? Is there a workshop or a conference that you would like to attend?
- An action plan. Probably the most important part, because without an action plan, all will remain just a dream. I recommend breaking your action plan into smaller sections and writing it in a format that allows you to tick off and track tasks, like a planner or a calendar, but make sure to link it to your overall business plan, so you don't lose track of the big picture while you're busy with daily operations like responding to emails and editing. Give your tasks a time limit, otherwise they will be left and never completed. It is important to keep moving forwards.

Systems and workflows are essential to your business plan's success; they are almost an extension of it. Systems create a consistent customer experience and produce reliable results. Once put in place, they will save you so much time and ensure that nothing falls through the cracks. Building the systems and workflows takes time, but it will be a lifesaver once you've done it.

To help keep track of your business, you should have a system for every part of your business and every session you offer.

So, how do you create the systems? Simply put, systems and workflows are detailed step-by-step guides and lists of tasks that you repeatedly do – or should do – for your business to succeed. Although you became an artist because you wanted to take photographs and be creative, you will spend more time on all the other tasks involved in running a business.

There are so many parts to the business: branding, marketing, booking, shooting, editing, selling, ordering and delivering, scheduling and management, to list a few. And every single one has smaller parts within. It will take time to create your business, and it will feel overwhelming, especially if you are a newcomer. Start with the basics and build up as time goes on. I have broken the systems and workflows down into the primary and smaller parts.

Studio management software & automation

If you want to run a successful photography business, I recommend getting studio management software as soon as possible. This type of software is often called client relationship management, or CRM. It will save you a lot of time, keep you organized and help you provide a fantastic client experience. CRM will help you with business admin tasks and help you manage shoots, clients and finances. It can store your client's details, and you can use it to collect payments and get clients to sign their contracts. It can also send automated emails and text messages. If set up correctly, it will be the biggest time-saver. I use Light Blue software, and I couldn't run my business without it. There are lots of software options available – some only manage client communication, scheduling and data, while others will allow contract signing, take payments and even provide financial data.

To set up your CRM software correctly, you must have every step of your workflow written down. Make sure you have clear and thorough workflows for every part of your business to make the most of the software and provide a professional experience for your customers.

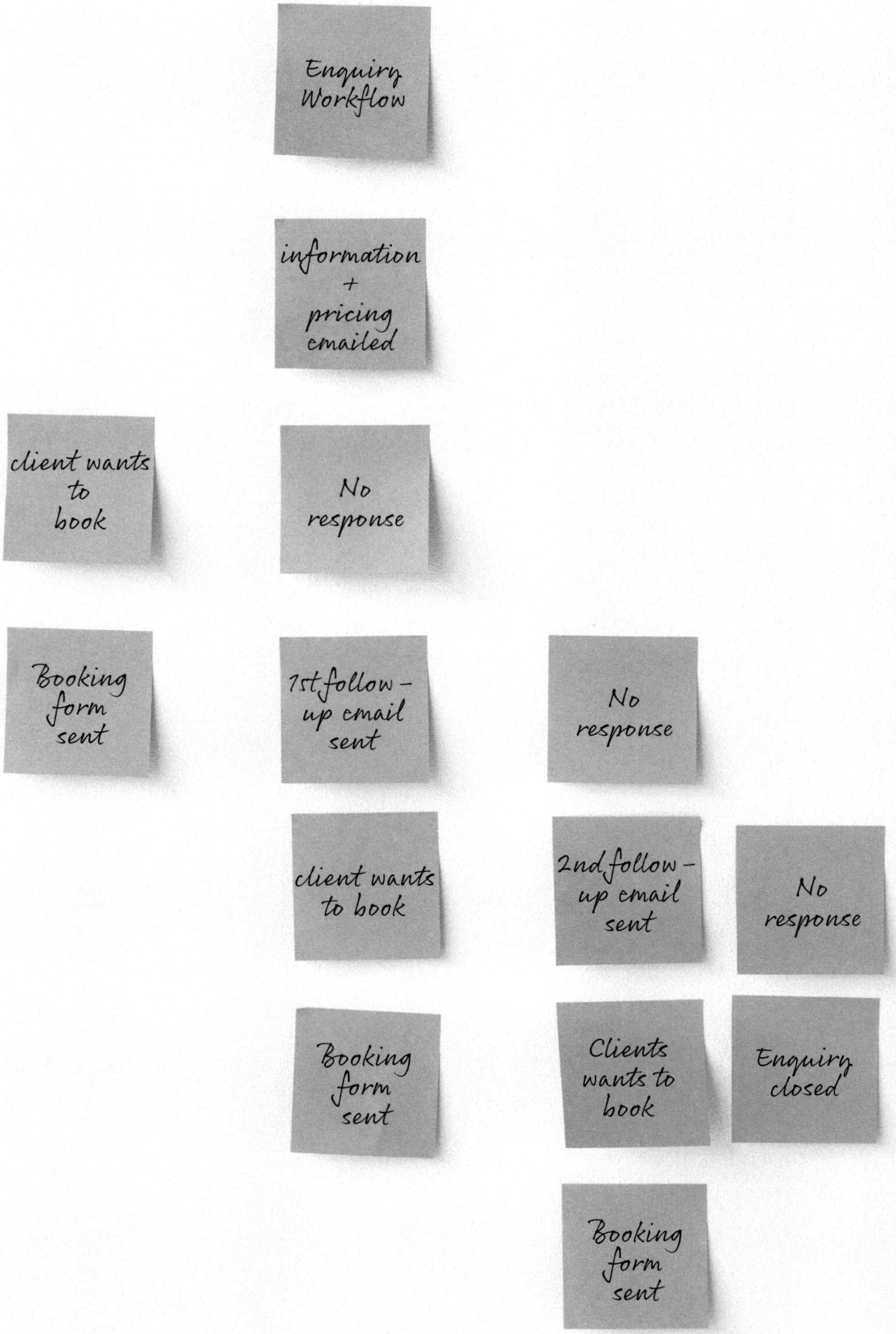

Enquiry
Workflow

information
+
pricing
emailed

client wants
to
book

No
response

Booking
form
sent

1st follow-
up email
sent

No
response

client wants
to book

2nd follow-
up email
sent

No
response

Booking
form
sent

Clients
wants to
book

Enquiry
closed

Booking
form
sent

1. **Photography session systems.**
   What are your go-to poses? Do you have a session flow that you always follow?

2. **The studio, whether it is home or commercial.**
   If you photograph in clients' homes or on location, you still need a system. Your shooting space, equipment and prop storage and organization and office space.

3. **Image workflow: from camera to client.**
   This is a very important system. Being disorganized with your files might cause you a lot of problems; the last thing you want is to lose the images that you have taken. Think about where you will store the files, how you will name them, and how you will file and archive them.

4. **Post-processing systems.**
   What software do you use? Do you apply the same editing techniques to every image? Can you batch-process some of your images? Do you retouch yourself, or do you decide to outsource?

5. **Back-up and archiving systems.**
   Where and how do you back up your files? Do you use an external hard drive or cloud storage? What happens to the images once the order is complete?

BOOKING, SALES & ORDERING
WORKFLOW SYSTEMS

1. **Enquiries**.
    How do potential clients get in touch with you? How do you respond? Do you call or do you email? Where do you collect client data?

2. **Booking systems**.
    What is your booking system? How do you keep track of your clients? Do you document everything on paper or use client management software?

3. **Emails**.
    Do you write the same emails all the time? Do you have templates? Where do you store them and are they easy to find?

4. **Client workflow tracking**.
    How do you keep track of your tasks? Do you have it all on paper or use an online task management system?

5. **Products**.
    What do you offer? How long is the production time? What is the cost?

6. **Sales session**.
    How do you sell your images? Do your clients pay for a package in advance? Do you sell via online galleries? Do you invite clients back for in-person sales appointments?

7. **Sales objections**.
    How do you respond? Think about statements and questions like 'I can't pay now, can I pay later?', 'Can I pay in instalments?', 'We are moving house, I don't know what I want at the moment' and 'Can I take products out of your packages?' Be prepared to respond to every objection.

8. **Legal systems, policies and contracts**.
    What policies do you have? How do your clients sign their contracts?

9. **Tracking and packing**.
    How do you track, package and deliver your orders?

PRICING & FINANCIAL SYSTEMS

1. **Financial tracking.**
   - How many sessions do you shoot monthly?
   - How many do you need to shoot?
   - What is your sales average?
   - What is your profit?
   - Have you paid yourself a salary?

2. **Pricing and products.**
   - What is your perceived value?
   - What is your cost of doing business?
   - What products do you sell?
   - How much for?
   - Do you have packages?
   - How do you create them?
   - What products do your clients want most?
   - What can you add to your offerings?

MARKETING & BRANDING SYSTEMS

1. **Brand systems.**
   Remember, a brand is not just your logo and colour scheme, it is the client experience.

2. **Living your brand.**
   Do you, your space, the products and the service you offer align with your brand?

3. **Marketing Systems.**
   - How do you market your business?
   - Do you have a marketing calendar?
   - Do you partner with other businesses?
   - What social media platforms do you use?
   - How often do you post?
   - Do you schedule your content?
   - Do you have a referral system?
   - What are your marketing goals?

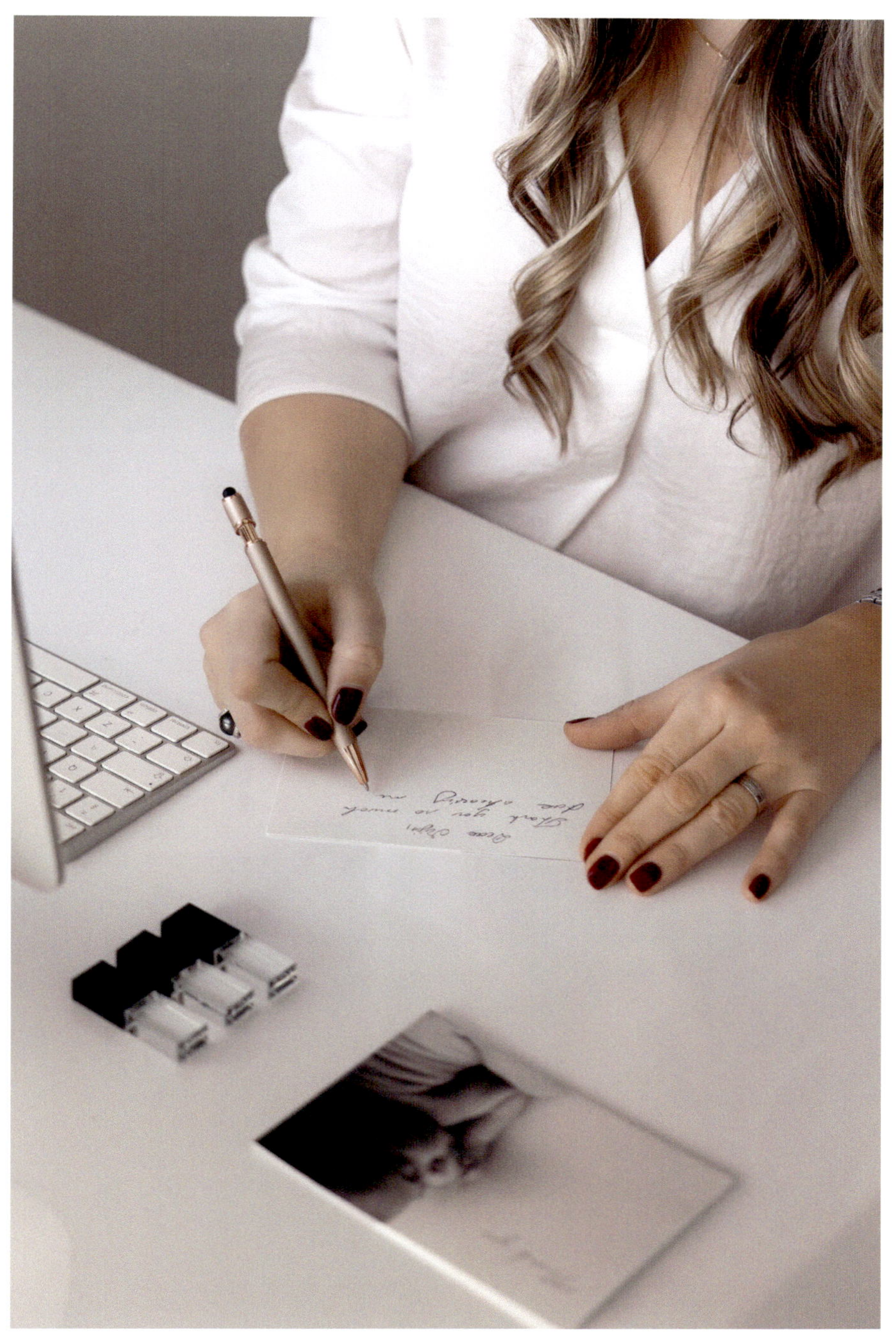

Creating an unforgettable client experience is crucial to running a successful business. I always do my best to exceed clients' expectations and do everything I can to ensure they have the best time with me. Clients book you to capture that special time in their lives and to create memories. However, you also need to provide them with a fantastic experience, not just beautiful images.

Communication and client education play a big part in creating client experience. Start with an easy-to-navigate website with all the information that clients might need. The FAQs section is very important, and so is the prep guide. The more your clients are prepared, the smoother your session will go and the more beautiful the images will be.

Be sure to cover everything in your pre-session communication. If you don't have on-site parking, list the nearest car parks – you don't want your client stressing about trying to find a parking spot. Anything that you can tell your client before their session will benefit both of you during the session. Make sure you know the type of images a client loves most and what they expect. If it is a maternity session, does mum want images with fabric? Does she want nudes? What style does she prefer? If it is a newborn session, do the parents want the baby dressed, wrapped up in a blanket or naked? Do they like props and accessories? You need to know it all so that you can create a bespoke session.

Prep them for every step of the process. I send many emails to my clients explaining and reminding them. Sometimes, this feels like overkill. However, my clients often comment about how clear my emails were and how easy it was to prepare for their session and to find me.

After the session, I send an email thanking the client for the experience and their trust in me, and include a link to my online calendar so they can book an appointment to return for their ordering appointment. I clearly explain every step of my client's journey, using saved templates and emails sent via CRM software. I communicate and answer their questions before they even ask them, which contributes to a very positive client experience.

I want the client to feel special, welcome, comfortable and important. Once they are at the studio, I carry their clothes or bags, I dress and undress the baby, change him/her and feed the baby if bottle-fed. I offer my clients hot or cold drinks and snacks and let them relax. I make sure my studio is clean and smells nice. I always have candles burning in my studio, and when people walk in, they often comment on how nice the studio smells and how welcoming the space is.

To create an unforgettable client experience, take care of the tiniest details. Explain that you will look after them while they are with you and that they can relax and trust your expertise. I don't expect my clients to know how to pose or position the baby, so I guide them through the entire shoot without them having to worry about where to look or where to place their hands. I instigate conversations with them and build rapport, which makes them more comfortable.

Do everything in your power to ensure that your clients enjoy the best possible experience. Clients who are happy will tell their friends about you and sing your praises, and what can be better marketing than that?

Getting booked

So, you've mastered the craft of newborn and maternity photography, you know your brand identity and demographics, and you have created workflows and systems. Now, how do you get paying clients through the door?

Finding clients and turning enquiries into bookings is one of the biggest challenges for new photographers. More experienced professionals who have been in business for some time, but haven't built a solid client base, must also evaluate their skills and business.

Photographers often complain about saturated markets, competitors charging very little for their work or social media algorithms. Yes, external factors can sometimes influence your enquiries, but most of the time, it is because your skills are not there yet, or your marketing is lacking.

If you have perfected your craft but haven't worked on your business, then you are the world's best-kept secret. For people to enquire about your service, they need to know that you exist.

The first thing you need to do is build your audience. Not everyone you reach will need to book you right now, but they will keep you in mind for when the time comes. For those who are ready and enquire, not everyone will book. So, the more people know about you, the more enquiries you will get. The more enquiries you get, the more sessions you will book. We can split marketing into two parts: audience building and generating bookings from your existing audience (see page 172).

Audience building

There are so many different ways to build an audience. We look at these on the following pages. Select a few and work on them and remember that things take time – do not expect results overnight. Your website is the first and most important tool, as it is your brand's and business's online home.

If you don't have a website with a blog, build one as soon as possible. Your website will be the fastest way for your potential clients to find you. Even if someone hears about you via word of mouth or social media, they will most likely go and check your website first. Make sure the first impression is a good one and your website is aligned with your brand and services.

Your potential clients will make the decision to stay or leave your website in seconds. There could be a few reasons for this. The first is they don't like what they see. They might think that your work is not of the quality they are looking for, or they don't like your style, or they are not keen on the overall look of your website. If your website looks professional and represents your brand, know that you are not for everyone, and that is absolutely fine. However, if your website is not aesthetically pleasing, update it as soon as possible.

The second reason is that your offerings aren't clear, and your potential client does not get a clear message of what you do and where you are based.

Search engines

Search engine optimization, or SEO, is also very important. You can either learn about SEO yourself or hire someone to help you with it. If your SEO is poor, search engines won't find your website. Blogs are great for SEO, as you can write articles about subjects that your ideal clients are interested in and include many relevant keywords in the text. For example, your client might search for information about preparing for birth and what to pack in their hospital bag.

Focus not just on the text you write but also optimize your images so that the images come up in searches. To help search engines find your images, name your images with descriptive keywords and add alternative text, known as 'alt text' or 'alt tag'. Alternative text is a written description of an image; it describes what is in the image. Make sure to create useful, specific and accurate descriptions, using your keywords, when adding alt text to your images. However, avoid filling your image descriptions with lots and lots of keywords; excessive use of keywords might make search engines think that your website is spam.

To determine which keywords to use, consider what your potential client might be typing to search for a maternity or newborn photographer. Often, clients will type the genre of photography, style and location, for example 'styled maternity photo shoot London'. Write a list of relevant keywords and use them in your website and blog. Don't be scared of SEO – it might sound complicated, but it is actually not that difficult.

FOLLOW THIS CHECKLIST WHEN BUILDING A WEBSITE

1. Is it aesthetically pleasing and does it represent your brand?

2. Does it clearly say what you are offering and where you are geographically located?

3. Does it say how you can serve your client and solve their problem?

4. Is your portfolio up to date? Only showcase your best work. It is better to have a small portfolio of a few great images than an extensive portfolio of mediocre images.

5. Do you have a frequently asked questions (FAQ) section? Your website should answer your clients' questions.

6. Is it easy to navigate?

7. Does it have a clear call to action on every page? A call to action could be 'Click to get in touch', 'Click to book' or 'Enquire here'.

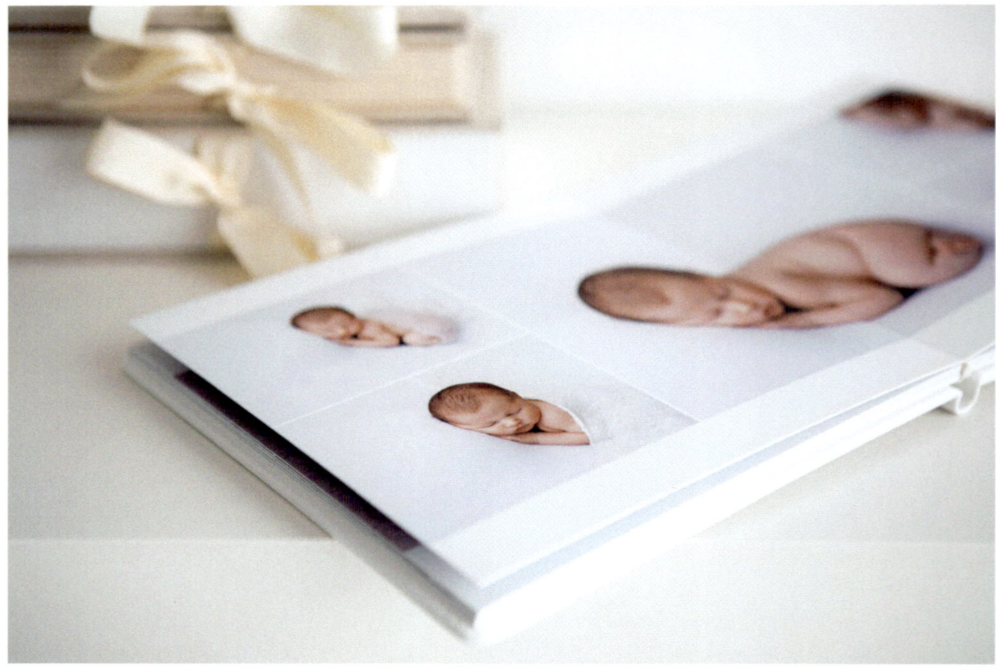

SOCIAL MEDIA

If you don't have a social media account, you must create one. The number of platforms can be overwhelming, so choose a couple and concentrate on them. When choosing a platform, consider which one you like most and which your clients will likely be on. You must enjoy the platforms you choose at least a little bit, otherwise it will be hard to stick to them. And when it comes to social media, consistency is the key.

Link your accounts together. This way, if you don't have much time, you can post on one and automatically share your content on the others. Also, make sure to include links to your social media on your website and email signature.

It is very difficult to grow a social media account organically. You might be tempted to buy followers or likes to make your account look more popular. Don't! There is no point in posting for robots or people who are not interested in your content. A small number of followers or likes might be disappointing, but having real followers will pay off in the long-term.

THINGS THAT WILL DEFINITELY
GIVE YOU MORE EXPOSURE

1. Choose your social media name wisely, and make sure to write a targeted bio, what you do, your style and where you are located.

2. Hashtags and captions. Write extended captions, a bit like a blog post, write about the subject that your client is interested in using keywords, and write about the service you offer. Use relevant hashtags.

3. Use tags. Tag locations, people and brands – anything and anyone that is in the photograph or helped you to create the image. My clients often get their hair and make-up done. If I know who did it, I tag make-up artists and stylists. When you tag others, they will likely share it to their profiles, exposing and promoting you to their audience who might not have known about you before.

4. Ask your clients if they would like to see a sneak peek of their session and if they would like you to tag them. Most clients will share your post with their followers and friends.

5. Find local businesses and ask if they would like to share your page in exchange for you sharing theirs. Like and comment on their posts. Build relationships.

6. Most importantly, be consistent. Social media can take a lot of time, and sometimes it is the easiest thing to drop. I am speaking from my own experience! I use a scheduling platform and always batch my social media posts. I usually spend an hour or two a month scheduling my posts for a month.

Word of mouth

Word of mouth is one of the most powerful tools for audience building and converting enquiries into bookings. Your clients will tell all their friends about you if you create an extraordinary experience for them with customer service, products and professionalism. However, the same is true if you don't – if you don't deliver on your promises, they will tell everyone how dissatisfied they are with your services.

Networking

You don't have to attend a traditional networking event – you can simply meet people face to face or online. Get chatting with people casually in a coffee shop or while queueing in a supermarket and tell them what you do. They might not need a photographer now, but they will remember you when they do. Join local Facebook groups and participate in relevant discussions on there. The more people you chat with, the more people will find out about what you do.

Networking with businesses that have the same target audience

Find local businesses that serve the same ideal client as you but offer different services or products. Email or call them – they might like to work together and promote you in exchange for you promoting them. Consider ways you could collaborate. If the business doesn't want to exchange promotions, ask if you could provide some photography services to them in exchange for them promoting you to their audience.

Paid advertising

If you have an advertising budget, consider buying Google or Facebook/Instagram ads. If you don't know how to set them up, hire a professional. Maybe you could advertise in a local magazine or newspaper.

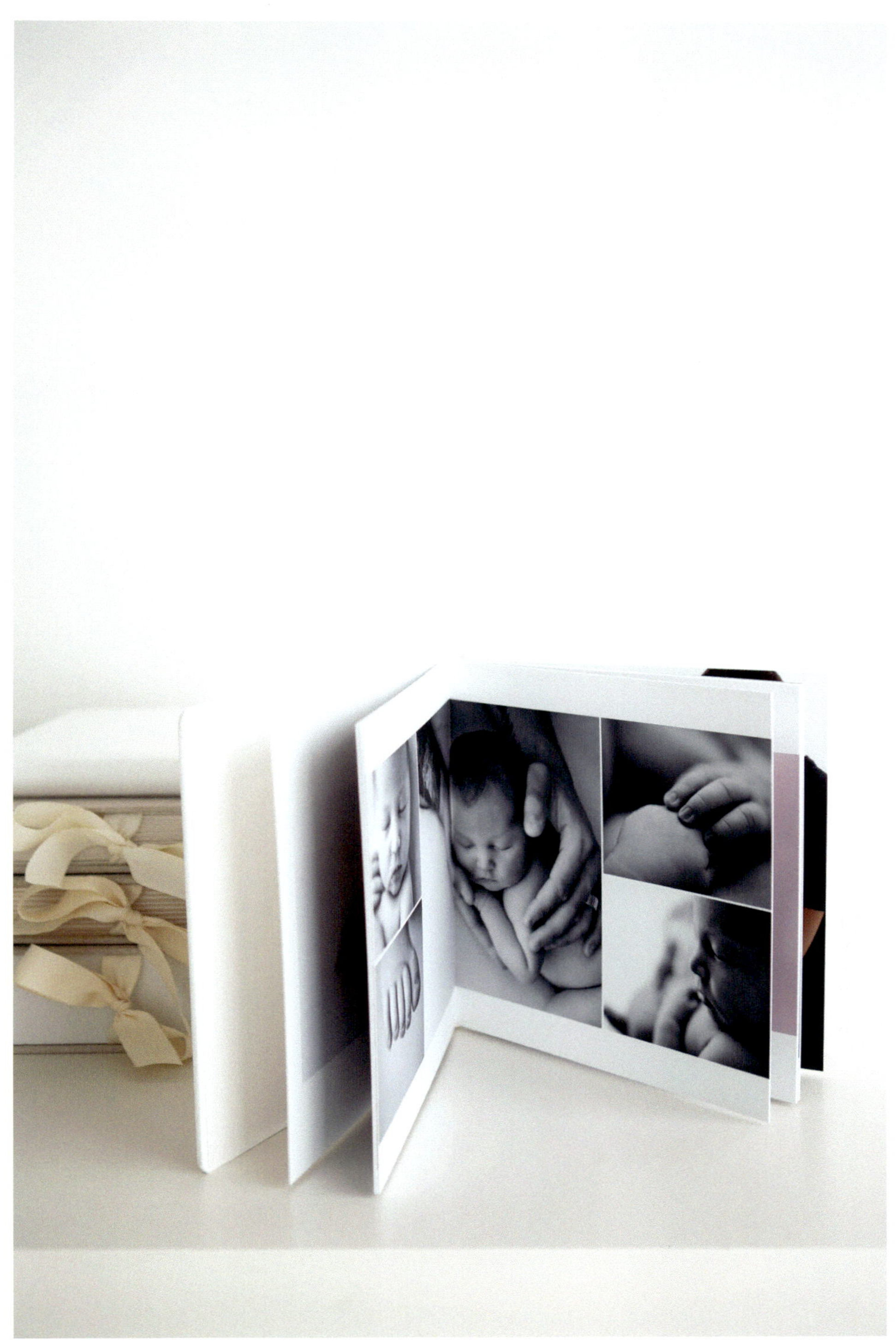

So, you have the audience and need to generate
more enquiries and bookings from them. If you
are a maternity and a newborn photographer,
it might be trickier simply because a potential
client might not be pregnant yet or have a baby.
However, you need to provide them with as many
opportunities as possible to engage more with you
and your business, get to know you better, and like
and trust you more so that they become clients
when the time comes.

You can use the same techniques as you would if
you are building your audience, but you can also
add a few extras.

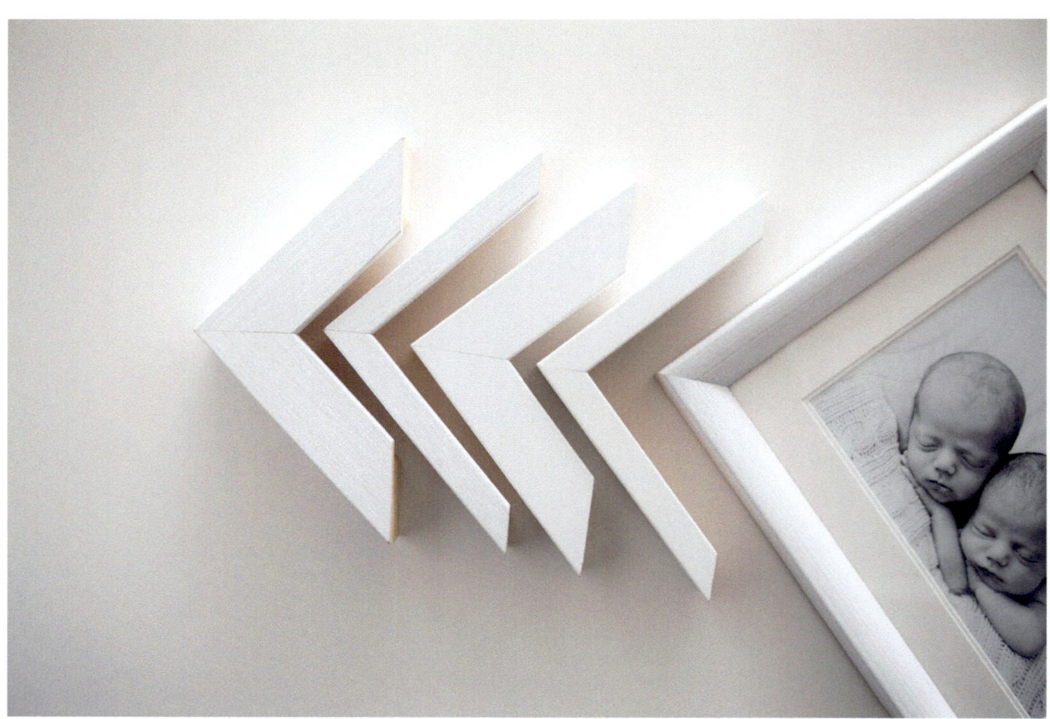

Mailing list

This is one of the best and most effective ways to grow your business. I always try to direct my audience to my mailing list. Why? Because I then own their contact details. Social media can be unpredictable – algorithms change, free platforms become paid for, and accounts can be hacked. If social media is all you have, you could lose it all in an instant. You can create regular content that's useful to your ideal client and send a newsletter every week or month. However, do not spam your audience – you want to build a relationship and get them to trust you, not annoy them by filling their inbox with unnecessary information. Set up an opt-in form on your website and let people know they will receive helpful advice like 'What to wear for your photography session' and 'Most popular baby names and their meanings'.

Market to your past clients

Past clients are people who already trust you and hopefully rave about you and the service you provided. If your client had a maternity session with you but didn't book a newborn with you, email her to check how they are and maybe she will book a newborn session. If the business is quiet and you are desperate for work, offer her a complimentary session or a discount. If your client had a newborn session with you, send them an email when the baby is six or twelve months old, suggesting your clients celebrate these milestones with a photography session. If you are using studio management software, you can set it to do this automatically.

Sell on social media

Let your audience know your availability on social media, encourage them to book, and talk to them about the new products you offer and any promotions or anything else you are planning or running. Avoid constantly selling on social media, but do it from time to time.

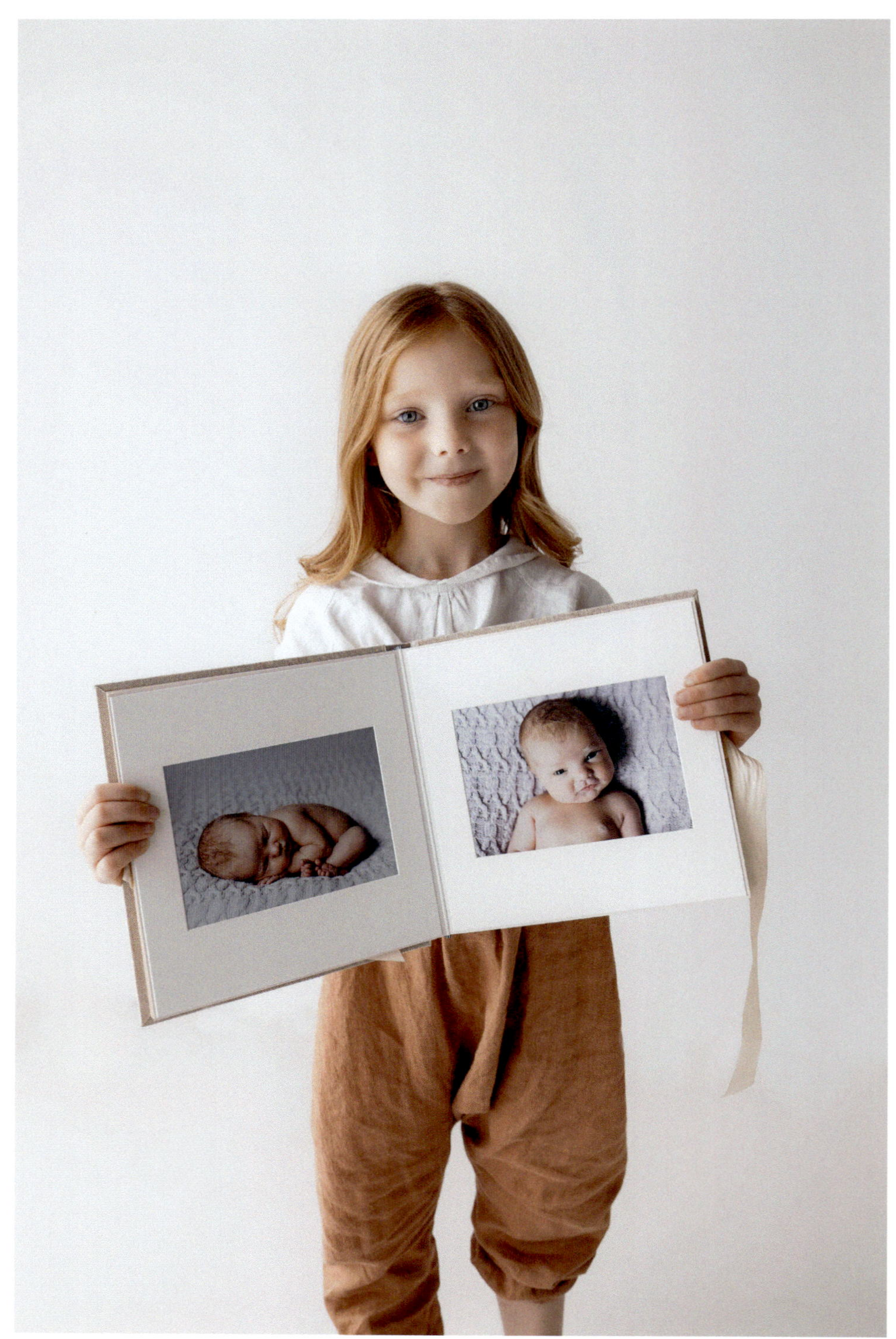

Create a perfect enquiry sequence

I use Light Blue client management software (see page 158) to respond to enquiries automatically, but if you don't have software, you can respond to enquiries manually. Potential clients usually get very excited and can't wait to hear from you, so always respond promptly. Also, people often forget to reply or get sidetracked, so always follow up if you don't hear back.

Mini session

Run a mini session or a promotion. Mini sessions are a great way of generating income. They are a low-cost way for people to try out working with you and can be a fantastic solution for those people who are sitting on the fence about booking you. Always have options to upgrade. Limit the number of mini sessions you offer – too many and you might compromise your main bookings.

Consistency is the key

The first and most important thing that will bring you booking clients is providing spectacular customer service to your existing clients. Word of mouth is the most trustworthy form of advertising.

Bear in mind that even if you go ahead and complete every single marketing activity listed in this book, nothing will happen immediately, but you will build a steady stream of enquiries and bookings over time. Consistency is the key to everything you do, and you must keep doing the same activities repeatedly to have a steady flow of incoming enquiries and bookings.

You might have started photographing to create beautiful images, but unless you start making money, your photography will remain a hobby rather than a business. You must start charging for your work to make a living from your creativity.

It might be tricky to figure out what to charge, especially if you are at the beginning of your journey and have never had your own business before. Most likely, you have emailed a dozen other newborn and maternity photographers trying to find out what they charge.

You might have worked out a pricing structure but are now wondering if you're too cheap or too expensive. Not being confident with your prices makes you vulnerable to everybody else's opinion. Knowing your numbers and understanding your pricing system will make you confident. There are no absolutes when it comes to pricing – you simply need to figure out what works for you and aligns with your lifestyle. How much do you need to earn? How do your clients value your work?

Worth

People will pay what they think you are worth. That expensive iPhone in your client's pocket wasn't essential – they could have bought a much cheaper phone, but it was worth it for them. Your clients choose to value what they are taught to value. You must value your work to teach your clients to value it too.

Price communicates that you believe in the value of your work enough to charge that price for it. Step one of helping clients understand that your work is worth whatever you want to charge for it is knowing your numbers and believing it is worth that much in the first instance. Clearly state the value of your work through the price you place upon it.

'Knowing your numbers and understanding your pricing system will make you confident.'

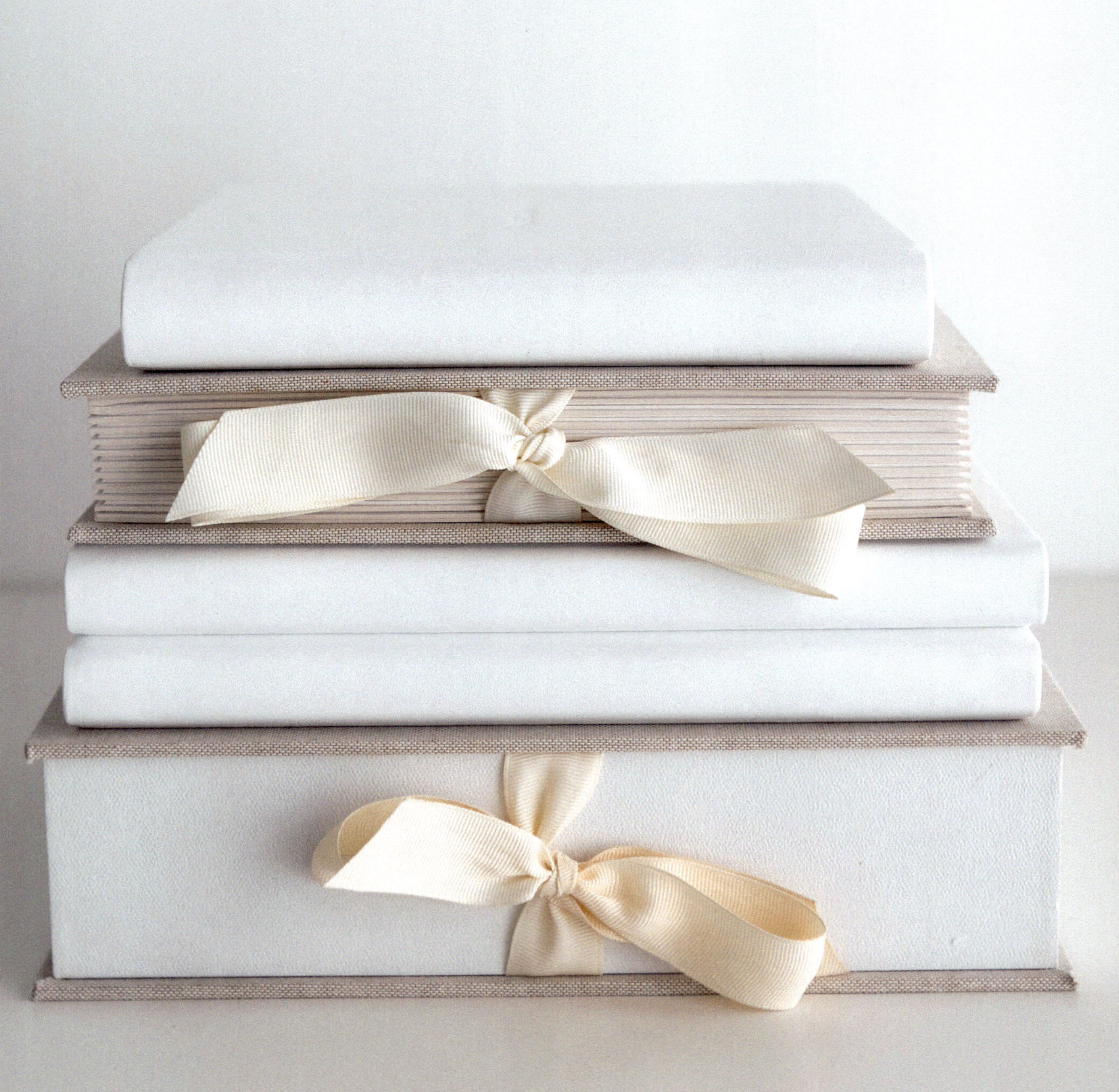

COMMON BUSINESS EXPENSES

Your work space (retail studio, home studio or home office)
- Rent
- Cleaning
- Repairs (interior maintenance, plumbing etc.)
- Security/alarm
- Utility bills (electricity, gas, water)
- Rubbish removal
- Internet
- Furniture
- Beverages and snacks for clients

Business inventory
- Product samples (frames, albums and all other products you offer)
- Printer
- Office supplies (paper, pens, tape, notebooks, sticky notes etc.)

Marketing
- Website
- Graphic design
- Mailing campaigns
- Displays
- Expositions
- Posters, business cards, flyers

Insurance
- Public liability and indemnity
- Equipment
- Property

Equipment
- Computer
- Camera(s)
- Lenses
- Lighting equipment
- Backdrops
- Batteries
- Backups for all equipment
- Softboxes and light modifiers
- Clamps and fasteners
- Camera bags and straps
- Memory cards and portable external drives
- Backup software/services
- Software – Photoshop, Lightroom, CRM or any other photography or business-related programs
- Props – beanbags, blankets, wraps, posing aids and supports, accessories, etc.
- Client wardrobe
- Equipment repairs and maintenance

Training
- Subscriptions
- Workshops
- Mentoring
- Conferences
- Conventions
- Business coaching

Travel
- Car maintenance, fuel
- Travel fare (train or tube)

Expenses & profit

Knowing your numbers is essential. Let's start with what you must charge to cover your costs. What is your cost of doing business, or CODB? It is the total of all your expenses related to running a business. This number will influence all other decisions you make about pricing your work.

Write down every single expense you have in a year. Your expenses will depend on how you run your business and a lot of its specifics. Opposite is a list of things to consider – you might take some out, add some and make it personal. Be as accurate as you can possibly be. If this is your first year in business, fill in everything you know.

Don't forget your business plan. If you plan to have a retail studio or rent an office space, you must add these to your future calculations. The same is true about equipment – you might have an old camera that doesn't cost anything, but if you pursue photography as a career, you will need an upgrade. You might need new lenses or lights.

This exercise in determining your business numbers may seem simplistic on the surface, but these basic calculations are the foundation for your pricing structure, and they are quite logical once you understand how they all fit together. This will not depend on geographical location or your experience.

The total sum of your costs – your CODB – is what you must make to break even, not to make a profit or pay yourself a salary.

Time is money

The next number you need to calculate is time. You might say time is free, but I believe that time is the only thing we don't have an abundance of. You can always make more money, but you can never buy time.

You need to know how much time is invested in a client before figuring out how many clients you can realistically take on in a week or month.

It might not be easy to calculate the time you spend on one client, and we often tend to underestimate how long a particular task will take us. You can use a timer or just try to be honest with yourself.

The amount of time you spend with a client will vary a lot, not only depending on whether you have your own space or travel to the client, what type of session it is and what sales method you use, but also on whether you have your admin automated with the help of CRM software or how much of your work you outsource.

1. Initial contact: emails, admin, scheduling and rescheduling, consultation.

2. Session planning or preparation: cleaning, setting up and then tidying up or location research.

3. Session travel time.

4. Session time.

5. Post-session workflow: downloading, backup, emails, ordering, appointment date set up, prepping files for retouching.

6. Editing: basic editing and fine retouching.

7. Sales or online gallery preparation: file saving, file uploading, slideshow, sample wall display ideas or sample album design.

8. Sales session and invoicing.

9. Final products: image preparation for printing or framing, album design, product ordering, packaging/shipping order, email confirmations.

Most portrait photographers who are working on their own will spend an average of eight to ten hours on one session.

Now that you know how much it costs to run your business and how many hours a week you can work, you can easily calculate the rest.

How much do you want to earn? This can be any number you desire. Whatever that number will be, make sure that you truly believe you are worth it.

Basic pricing calculation formula:

CODB ÷ 12 to work out monthly CODB + the amount of money you desire to make a month (A).

Work out how many sessions you can do a month: available hours to work every month ÷ average number of hours spent per client (B).

A ÷ B will equal the minimum amount of money you must make per session to achieve this.

It might be complicated, but here is an example for you. I used easy numbers to make it easier to comprehend. Do not use these numbers as an indication of what you should charge.

Annual CODB is £24,000; monthly CODB is £24,000 ÷ 12 = £2,000

I want to pay myself £4,000 a month.

£2,000 (CODB) + £4,000 (desired income) = £6,000

I have 120 hours a month that I can work, and I spend 10 hours working on one customer. 120 hours ÷ 10 hours = 12. This means I can book 12 sessions a month.

£6,000 ÷ 12 (sessions) = £500

This means that to cover the cost of doing business and pay myself the desired salary, I need to make at least £500 per session.

Another thing you must consider is experience and investment. You might want to spend some time offering free or cheaper sessions to master your craft faster and then increase your prices to what you believe you are worth. Equally, you can spend years trying to get people to pay the minimum amount you've calculated using the formula above, and it may take you much longer to improve because your client flow will be low. Consider all aspects when pricing your services.

Don't forget that you will have to pay taxes on the amount you make. The taxation system is complicated, so consult your accountant.

BUSINESS MODELS & SALES METHODS

There are various business models and types of sales to choose from. One may work better for you than others depending on numerous factors, including where you are in your career.

You can have a low- or high-volume business model. Low volume is also called a boutique business and focuses on client experience and quality. Prices are usually a lot higher than those of high-volume businesses. The high-volume business focuses on inexpensive experience and a large number of clients. It has dramatically lower prices because it makes up for quality and time by generating a lot of sales. Neither business model is right or wrong, and both models can thrive in the same geographic area. It is entirely up to you which route you want to take. If you need to practise the craft of maternity and newborn photography, a high-volume business will help you to perfect your creative skills a lot faster.

There are a few main types of pricing and sales models for photography businesses: in-person (IPS), shoot and burn, and online. In-person sales have been around since portrait photography began. However, the digital era introduced online sales, significantly changing the industry. It is often said that you can't have a profitable photography business without the IPS method, and I do think there are a lot of advantages to it: you can build great long-term client relationships, and you will definitely have higher sales.

An alternative way of selling is shoot and burn. This method involves taking pictures and loading files onto a USB drive or sending a link for clients to download the images directly to their computers or phones. The advantage to this approach is that you can deliver images quickly. On the flipside, you're potentially leaving a lot of money on the table, and you're not creating the best possible experience for your clients.

Another way to sell your images is via online galleries. You can offer digital-only packages, or you can also sell physical products. A downside of this method is that you will have to retouch all the images that you are showing, as your clients will download them directly as soon as they make a choice. If they only choose a handful of images, many hours spent retouching will be wasted. Contrary to popular belief, online galleries do not save you time. No matter how perfect your process is, it will still involve additional back-and-forth emails, more confirmation and clarification messages, and lots of tracking and reminding. To be profitable using online sales methods, you need to put a lot of thought into your pricing structure and educate your clients before the sale.

No one likes to be sold to, and very few of us are natural salespeople. However, if you educate your clients throughout the process, you won't need to sell. Client education starts before they book and continues during their session and before their in-person appointment or before their online gallery is published.

Selling starts the moment a potential client contacts you, and every interaction you have with your client will impact how much they spend.

Depending on your business model, you might not want to publish your prices on your website. I share my starting and average spending on my website, as I want to avoid potential clients coming to my website and comparing me with other options purely based on price. Once a potential client contacts me, I email them information about a session and include a beautifully presented pricing guide that describes all the products I offer. I always ensure my clients know the prices before they book, as the last thing I want is for them not to be able to afford my prices or to have a bad experience by thinking I lured them into spending more than they would like to spend.

After they have seen your product and pricing brochure, they are mentally prepped and can start thinking about what they would like to have after their session. Keep copies of your pricing brochures at your studio or take them with you if you're an on-location photographer. It's likely they've booked their session some time ago and might have forgotten what you offer, so make sure they see it over and over again, keeping thoughts about your offerings fresh.

I have samples of every product I offer at the studio, framed images are everywhere, and clients usually flip through the albums while waiting for me to photograph their baby or resting during maternity sessions. If you travel to clients' homes, make a product catalogue with lots of images and detailed information about what you offer. This will get them thinking and preparing to invest in tangible products.

After the session, I give my clients a brochure showcasing my products and pricing, as well as advice on what to buy. I also email the pricing and product guide the day before they return to the studio for their IPS appointment. You don't need to be a salesperson; you simply need to educate your clients about what's available.

What and how you sell will depend on the factors discussed earlier. Packages tend to work best for online galleries, while à la carte pricing works better for IPS. You can also mix the two together.

If you offer in-person ordering appointments to your clients, they will feel better served because you will be able to guide them through the process, validate their decisions, give your opinion when they need it, and assist them in getting the products they want. This will lead to more satisfied clients, which means higher sales, more referrals and more profit for you. IPS is by far the best way for you to increase your sales and to provide the best start-to-finish experience to your clients, but if you're not able to offer IPS, you can make online galleries work too.

With so many pricing strategies and methods, I always recommend starting simple and seeing what business model works best for you. Let your pricing and sales methods grow with you. As you gain more experience and become more familiar with the industry and the niche, you can revisit and restructure your pricing and sales methods.

First, learn the craft and build your portfolio. However, do not wait until your work is perfect. We, as artists, often criticize our work too much, have low self-esteem and undervalue ourselves. Remember, just because you are less experienced doesn't mean you are not worthy of getting paid. There is a space in the market for everyone and every skill level. You don't need to start with high-end pricing, but at some point, you need to start getting paid for your time, your gear and your creativity. It is very easy to get stuck in portfolio-building mode and either photograph for free or charge very little. Often, it is very scary when you do start charging, especially if you were in the hobbyist stage for far too long and got yourself a name as a free or affordable photographer. In

earlier chapters, I spoke about branding (see page 155) and shared different marketing strategies (see page 165) that will get your business moving forwards and help you get into a higher price bracket. For now, let's focus on pricing and selling.

Use the pricing calculation formula that I shared earlier (see page 181) and determine your pricing. Find out the bare minimum you need to charge to cover your costs and pay yourself at least a small salary. If you are uncomfortable charging that at the moment, mark it down by 50 percent or whatever you feel comfortable with. Let your client know that as a new business, for a limited period (three months, six months, etc.), you are offering discounted sessions. This way, your clients will know your price and will not be shocked when it doubles in a few months. Also, they won't be telling their friends about free or cheap sessions; they will be recommending you for your work and the experience they had with you and not for the price you charge (or don't charge).

Stick to your word. If you said that you would offer discounted sessions for three months only, make sure you change your pricing after those three months. Not only do you want to build trust, but you also need to keep moving forwards in your business and get out of your comfort zone.

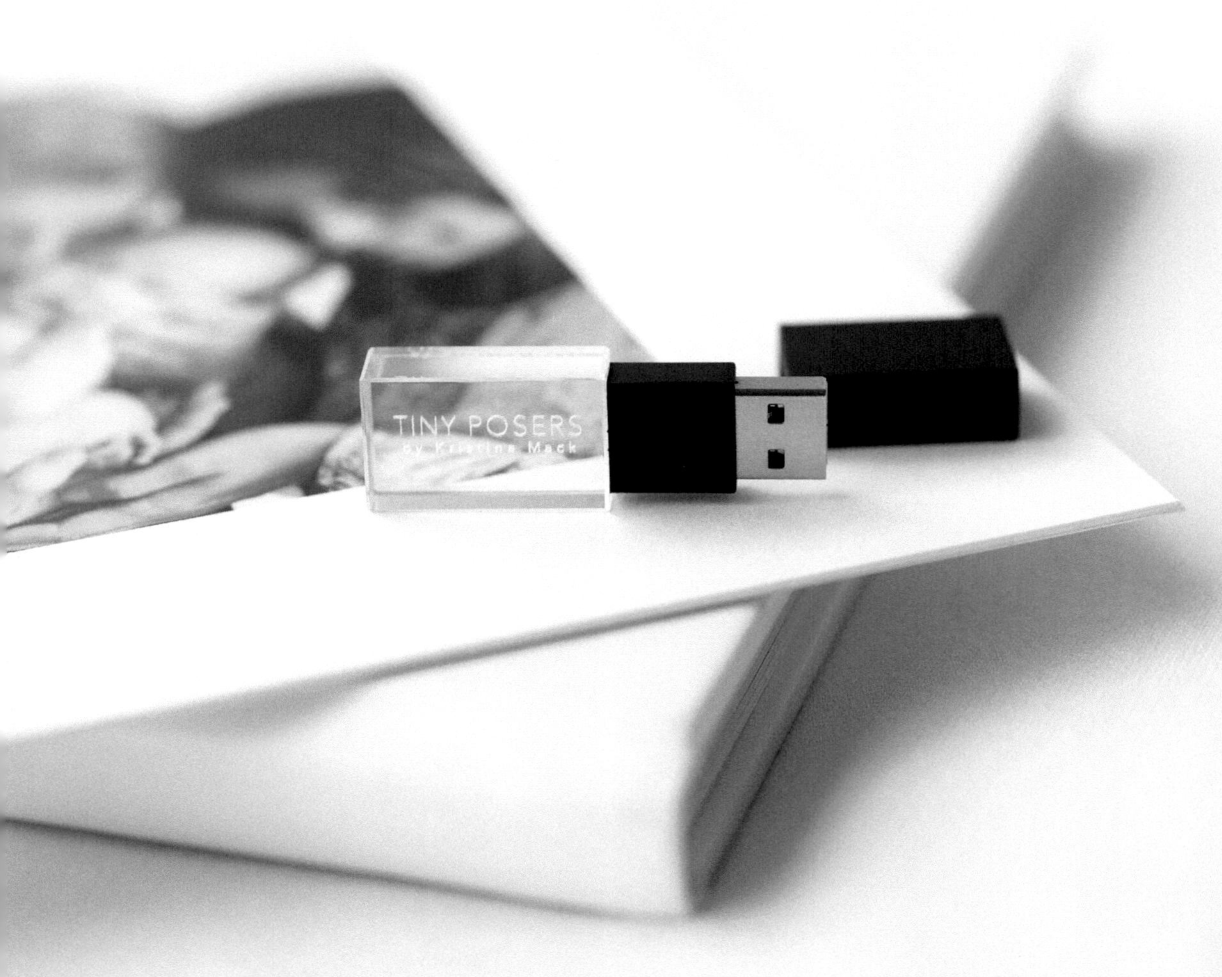

TINY POSERS
by Kristina Mack

Choosing & selling products

There are so many products available on the market, it can be overwhelming, and not only for beginners, to know where to start. Photography products, especially albums and smaller goods, can be made anywhere worldwide. If you want to start selling products, the best thing to do is attend a photography show. You want to see, feel and touch the product. You also want to talk to sales representatives and see if you want to work with them. Choose the products you love – this is so important. If you love a product, you will love selling it. You will be passionate about it, and your clients will feel your excitement and get excited about it themselves. How many products you offer is up to you. To avoid confusing or overwhelming my clients, I limit the number of products I offer, and I only offer the products that I absolutely love. Display the products you offer, as your clients will want to see them before buying them. If you don't have your own space, make smaller samples and create a product catalogue.

Try to find unique products to stand out from a crowd of other photographers.

Only start offering products like albums and framed images once you are more experienced and comfortable with your skills. Digital images are usually the most desirable and easiest to sell.

Packages

Start with offering your clients two or three digital packages, as you want to make it simple for your clients and also manageable for you.

Think about how many images you can comfortably create every session. If it is 20, make this your top package. You can then make your first package five images, your second package ten images and the top package twenty images. Ensure that the price per image decreases with every higher package – you don't want to make the price per image the same in your lowest and highest packages. Also, you don't want your lowest package to sound too attractive.

Think about coffee shops. Small and large coffee prices are very similar, so it is almost a no-brainer to go for a large cup. You want to create the same with your pricing.

Below is an example of three simple packages. Please note the numbers I use do not reflect the actual price nor are they in any currency. They are simply an example of a ratio and something to help you get started.

5 images – 175 (single-image price 35)
10 images – 225 (single-image price 22.5)
20 images – 300 (single-image price 15)

TIPS FOR BETTER ONLINE GALLERY SALES

1. Watermark your images. Most clients will screenshot their gallery – it's simply human nature. Ensure the watermark is large enough and not easy to remove.

2. Set a time frame. Once your clients receive the gallery, they will likely be very excited, scroll through the images and leave it to another day to choose. Don't allow more than a week for your clients to choose their package. If they don't place an order, remind them when their gallery will expire.

3. Have a fee for gallery re-opening or time extension. Ensure your clients know it before they book a shoot with you.

4. Limit the number of packages you offer and make sure that your smallest package covers your CODB and your salary.

5. Create a product catalogue and give it to your clients to take home at the end of their session.

Once you set your packages, think about how you are going to showcase and deliver the images. IPS appointments are great for experienced photographers who offer high-end services but are unnecessary and might be stressful for a beginner. Platforms such as Pixieset and ShootProof allow you to sell your work via simple online galleries that deliver digital images directly to your client via a download link. Try a few different platforms and select your favourite.

When you are ready to take it a step further, start offering a USB stick with your top package, and then add a set of prints. Make it simple for yourself but keep moving forwards. It is easy to get comfortable selling just digital images. However, if you want to have a highly profitable business, you must start introducing products to your business.

Your primary goal at this point in your career as a professional maternity and newborn photographer is to start selling your work, get some paid clients, perfect your customer service and work hard to improve your craft. Just get started, book that first paying client and build your confidence with every single session. Before you know it, not just your photography skills but also your selling skills will improve. You will start feeling more confident in yourself and your work, and you will be ready to earn more.

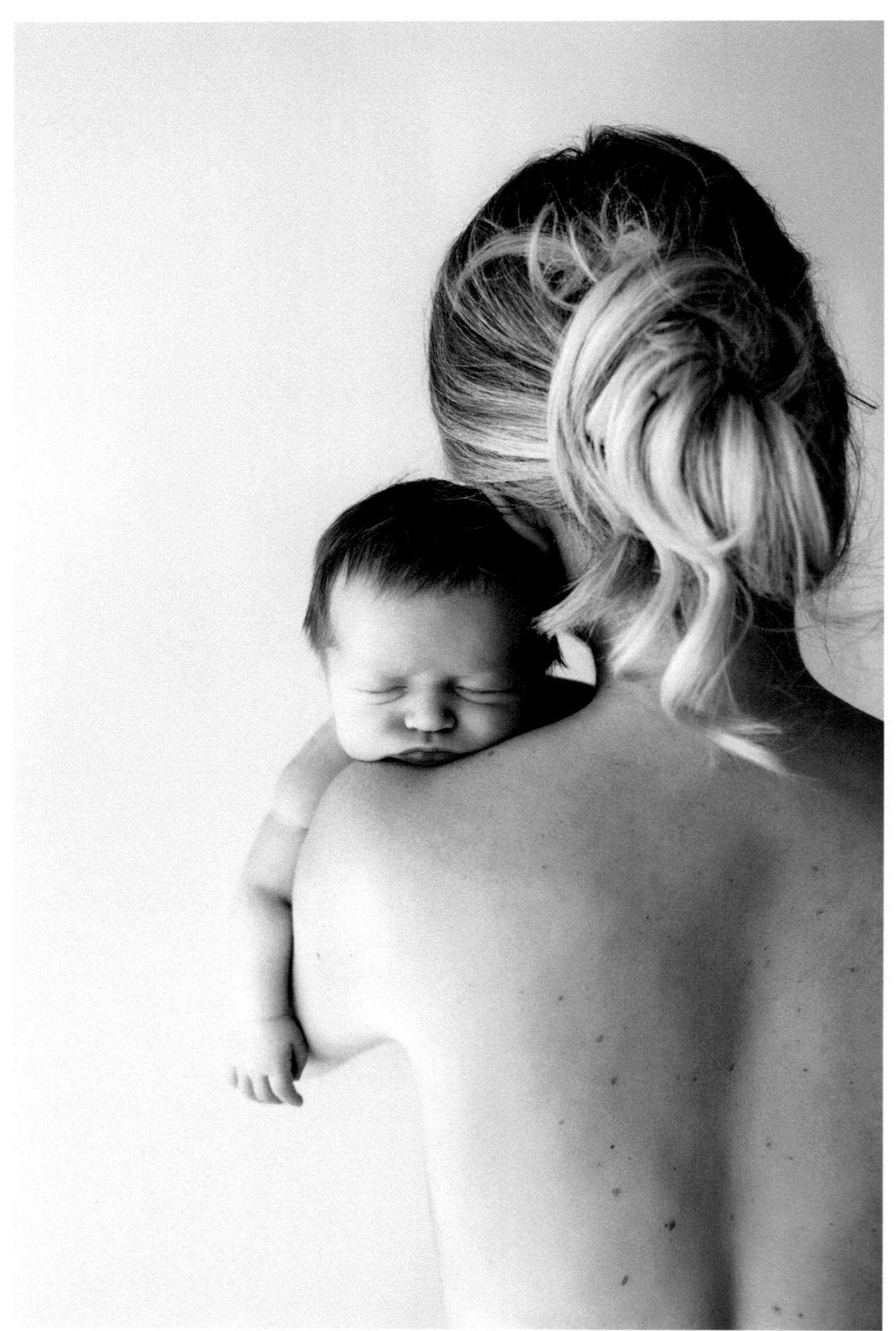

This is the end of the book, but hopefully, the start of a new chapter in your journey as a newborn and maternity photographer. I hope this book inspired you and that you learned a lot from it. The moment you decide to pursue photography as your career, the learning should never end.

Being a photographer means being an entrepreneur. You will need to wear a lot of hats, and to succeed will require a lot of skills – mastering lighting, styling, composition, posing, post-production, handling babies, mastering business and communication skills, to name just a few. Don't expect to become a master of all instantly. It will take time.

Focus on mastering a few skills first. I recommend starting with lighting, posing and learning how to handle babies. It will not be easy, and you will want to give up many times, but eventually it will become second nature. Once you are confident in your photography skills, focus on the business. Start from the beginning; remember, every house needs strong foundations and the same can be said for every business.

Newborn and maternity photography is not a career for those who want to work little and lead a leisurely lifestyle. Since starting my business, I have been working late nights, early mornings and weekends. This is my very own business, so I never think about it as a chore – but at the same time, it requires a lot of hard work, and even if I am on holiday, I never switch off. On the other hand, having my own business, which is also my passion, makes me truly happy. It allows me to be creative and also to have a career that I can drive in whichever direction I wish.

You need to get into this niche of photography for the right reasons. Your love and passion will get you through any hardship, and it will keep you from giving up after a hard session with an unsettled baby or the fact that your calendar is not as full with bookings as you wish it was. Nothing will happen overnight; don't give up if it's not going as well as you had wished, or if people around you are doubting your career choice. It will require a lot of work, so be consistent and keep putting in the effort. You can do it.

Keep this book close to you, take it with you to your photo shoots, scribble in it, write notes and highlight the most impactful parts. Refer back to the pages that are most relevant to wherever you are on your journey. Most importantly, never forget that knowledge is power, but if you don't implement that knowledge and keep driving forwards, you will stagnate, not just in business but also in your photography skills.

Lastly, be authentic and find your voice; experiment and create the work that makes your soul happy. Imagine if all the artists you love most came together to photograph a pregnant woman or a family with a newborn baby. What might they create? Go and create it. Your uniqueness, knowledge and the implementation of it will make you a master of your craft and an owner of a successful business.

I am rooting for you!

– Kristina, February 2024

LED 22
level 15, 18
meter 18, 78
mono 21–22
natural 13, 15–18, 21–24, 31, 78, 99, 155
portable 22
soft 17–18, 100,
source 16–18, 21–22, 24, 62, 99–100, 133
split 100–101
strobe/flash 16–17, 21–24, 78, 100
studio 78–79
Light Blue software 158, 175
Luminance 141

M

macro photography 14, 125
marketing 149, 151–152, 155–158, 162, 164–165, 173, 175, 178, 184
memory card 25, 178
mid-tone 24
mission statement 155
mode
auto 24
manual 13
money mindset 151
mood board 40–41
Moro reflex (*see also* startle reflex) 95
Moses basket 92
multiples 114–115

N

negative space 53–54, 102, 122
networking 170
nude 51, 59, 62, 71–72, 164

O

octabox 79
output
brightness 21
overexpose 21

P

pets 30, 132
Pinterest 48, 92
planning 82–87
policy 82, 161
portfolio 167, 184
portrait 15–16, 21, 35, 49, 127, 131–132, 139, 180, 182
posing 8, 12, 35, 48, 52–67, 76, 88, 90, 93, 98, 102–113, 128, 130–131, 178
baby-led 102

flow 102
post-processing 8, 48, 138, 160
post-production 21, 23–25, 71, 93, 95, 136–145
workflow 138
premature baby 84
pricing 82, 151–153, 156–157, 162, 176, 179, 181–184, 186
products 134, 151–153, 155–157, 161–162, 170, 173, 178, 180, 182–184, 186–187
props 12, 27, 33–35, 39, 43, 49, 51, 90–92, 102–103, 113, 115, 124, 151, 156, 160, 164, 178, 192

Q

questions (*see also* FAQs) 13, 40, 47–48, 66, 88, 90, 128, 130, 167

R

retouching 48, 138, 142–145, 160, 180, 182
routine 83–84, 114
rule of thirds 122

S

safety 90, 92–95, 102, 104, 109, 113, 126, 128, 130, 132
saturation 142
schedule 47, 82–85, 94–95, 98–99, 115, 162
search engine optimization (SEO) 166
set-up 16, 30, 49, 76, 78–79, 93, 100, 134
scale 125
shade 24, 48, 192
shadow 16, 18, 79, 99, 100, 104, 125, 126, 141
shutter speed 13, 15, 18
silhouette 16, 79
sleep 7, 83, 86–89, 95–97, 100, 103–104, 116, 133, 155
social media 40, 92, 156, 162, 165–166, 168–169, 173
softbox 17, 18, 21, 25, 79
soothing 86, 88, 94–98, 116, 133
startle reflex 92, 95, 96, 98, 115
storage 160
studio space 31
commercial 17, 21, 26, 31, 160
home 17, 26, 30, 160, 178
retail 26, 31, 178–179
style 36–39, 90–92
editorial 78
swaddling 35, 88, 90, 95, 97, 103, 116–118, 134

sync cord 25

T

target audience 152–153, 170
temperature
body 94, 96
colour 22, 24
light 24
slider 141, 143
ten-day rule 82–83
texture 17, 39, 40, 43, 90, 116, 125, 144
tool
Adjustment Brush 142–143
Clone Stamp 144
Healing Brush 144
Liquify 144
Targeted Adjustment 142
toys 35, 88, 90, 92, 131
tracking system 23
trends 40, 43, 49, 51, 138, 155
tungsten 24
twins 114–115

U

umbrella 21, 25, 79
underexpose 141
unposed 102

V

variable focal length 15
visual identity 40, 154–155

W

weather conditions 21, 23–24, 26
cloudy 17, 18, 24
sunlight 17
website 40, 92, 164–168, 173, 178, 183
white
balance 18, 23, 24, 141
noise 35, 89, 98
shirt 33, 51, 76
wind 27, 88, 96–97, 134
window
fake 22
witching hour 85
workflow 8, 128, 134–135, 138, 141, 145, 157, 158–163, 165, 180
workshop 151, 157, 178
wrapping 71, 95, 97, 116–121

Z

zoom (*see also* lens) 15

ACKNOWLEDGEMENTS

Words cannot express how thankful I am for this incredible moment in my life. Writing and photographing a book on maternity and newborn photography is a dream project that I never even dared to dream about! I have many incredible people to thank not only for the creation of this book but for the wonderful life and photography career that I have.

Having someone read what you write, consider your words, and attend to each paragraph is an honour that I'll never take for granted. Thank you for reading these pages and for trusting my knowledge.

Thank you, Mum and Dad, for fostering my creativity and giving me the freedom to become who I wanted to become. Mum, thank you for teaching me to draw and see colour and shades from a very young age and for letting me, even though not always willingly, fill the pages of your very special little orange book with my crazy drawings. Dad, thank you for not only letting me experiment with your camera, spoil endless rolls of film and boxes of photographic paper, but also for getting me my first digital SLR camera.

Thank you to my children for being my muses. You are the miraculous, amazing, gorgeous and most beautiful reason why I specialize in this photography niche.

Thank you to my husband for his support and for believing in me. Thank you for all the dinners you cooked while I was writing this book.

Thank you to my friends for always happily getting involved in every photography project I came up with and trusting me with your precious newborn babies when I had very little idea of what I was doing.

I would especially like to thank all the beautiful people that I have photographed over the years for their trust. Without you, neither this book nor my photography business would exist. You gave me the opportunity to grow as an artist and a business owner, and you enabled me to create photographs that will be cherished for generations to come.

Thank you, All Newborn Props, for creating custom blankets and props for my newborn sessions and for always listening and bringing my ideas to life.

Georgina Spearpoint, thank you for your support, energy and enthusiasm. I couldn't have done it without you.

Thank you to my make-up artists, stylists and retouchers.

As much as I'd just love to take all the credit for this book, there are a lot of people who had a hand in making this book come to life. A very special thanks goes to Richard Collins and Octopus Publishing Group team. Richard, from the bottom of my heart, thank you for giving me the opportunity and trusting me to write this book. Ben Gardiner, thank you for amazing design and vision, you made this book look far more beautiful than I ever could have imagined. Rachel Silverlight, thank you for editing this book and making sense of my words. You are the best.

Thank you to everyone at Octopus Publishing Group who worked on this book.

Lastly, thank you, my photography community, for inspiration and support.